Criticism in the University

Criticism in the University

Edited by Gerald Graff and Reginald Gibbons

TriQuarterly Series on Criticism and Culture, No. 1

Northwestern University Press, 1985

This volume was prepared and produced by members of the editorial staff of *TriQuarterly* magazine: Bob Perlongo, executive editor; Greg Meyerson, editorial assistant.

ISBN #0-8101-0670-1 (cloth)
ISBN #0-8101-0671-X (paper)
Library of Congress Catalog #85-60926

Printed in the United States of America

Contents

Cover design by Gini Kondziolka

Preface

> The acrimony of recent debate suggests . . . [that] the
> field of criticism is contentiously constituted by appar-
> ently incompatible activities. Even to attempt a list—
> structuralism, reader-response criticism, deconstruction,
> Marxist criticism, pluralism, feminist criticism, semiot-
> ics, psychoanalytic criticism, hermeneutics, antithetical
> criticism, Rezeptionasthetik . . . —is to flirt with an
> unsettling glimpse of the infinite that Kant calls "the
> mathematical sublime" . . .
>
> —Jonathan Culler, On Deconstruction:
> Theory and Criticism After Struc-
> turalism

As this statement suggests, literary-critical schools and *isms* have so proliferated lately that anyone hoping to make sense of the situation is easily beset by vertigo. Culler goes far toward alleviating this sensation by explaining, relating and contrasting the principles and methods of deconstruction and other schools. Yet Culler's book is also notable for what it takes for granted about the state of criticism and thus does not discuss. We spell out those unstated assumptions here, since they form the point of departure for the present collection of essays.

First of all, we note that criticism has come to be regarded as an academic "field," with all that this status may entail. As such, the domain of criticism is composed of schools which distinguish themselves from one another mostly by their interpretative methodologies—the kinds of textual readings they produce. Also, we note that the recent history of criticism is the story of the interrelations and conflicts between these academic schools.

In holding these assumptions about what "criticism" has become, Culler is in no way unusual—one finds the same assumptions in other recent histories. Others may tell a story different from Culler's, but they too take it for granted that the recent history of criticism is the history of academic criticism, and that this situation need occasion no comment, since it is appropriate and usual. Indeed, as Culler's list of schools suggests, the very word "criticism" has become synonymous with "academic criticism." To add the qualifier would presumably be redundant, since no other kind is considered, or perhaps even generally conceived as a possibility.

Culler knows perfectly well that this perception of the situation would

7

not have applied in the past and is not entirely accurate even now, after the expansion of literature departments and the drying up of the market for literary journalism has given universities a near monopoly on criticism. Yet so thoroughly has the university come to dominate criticism that the new situation feels unexceptional. To borrow Culler's deconstructionist idiom for a moment, the rhetorical trope by which the word "criticism" is narrowed to mean what is written and taught by professors involves the "forgetting" of something once thought important—that criticism was formerly part of a "literary culture" much broader than the university and, indeed, scarcely involving the university; that literary critics were once journalists and men (and too rarely women) of letters, usually outsiders to the university; that they wrote either for general readers or for the community of imaginative writers, rather than for a coterie of specialized professors and graduate students, and thus delivered their findings and opinions in an accessible style rather than in an esoteric jargon of methodological terms.

That historians and analysts fail even to mention this other conception of literary criticism, which until recently was the most familiar one, means not that they do not know of its existence but that they no longer regard it as important. The narrowing of "criticism" to "academic criticism" assumes that only the criticism written by academics within the prevailing academic methodologies and within academic intellectual society is worth talking about. Whether this judgment is fair or not, we think its pervasiveness marks a fundamental change in the cultural conception of literary criticism, a change that is at least as worthy of serious attention as are the intramural disputes and alliances within academic criticism. It is important to be able to differentiate between reader-response criticism, the older New Criticism, historicism, psychoanalytic criticism, structuralism, Marxism, deconstruction, the various schools of feminist criticism and so on, but it is also important to see that the differences among these competing academic schools are less wide than the difference which separates all of them taken together from the nonacademic forms of criticism they have displaced. To summarize the battles between New Critics, humanists, deconstructionists and feminists is not in any way to exhaust the central issues in criticism today, nor even to consider what is perhaps the fundamental issue, which is the relation between academic literary criticism and the writing and reading that go on outside the academy.

There are two very different ways of reacting to this new situation of criticism and unfortunately those who exemplify them rarely talk to each other, for their opposed reactions reflect the bitter polarization of the day. One typical reaction is a kind of superprofessional euphoria which views the triumph of the latest academic critical methodology as the culmination of a progressive struggle to free criticism from the amateurism and lack of methodological system of journalists and moralists.

This Whig view of the academicization of criticism has remained a fixture, whether the particular trend it was celebrating was the Germanic philology of the 1880's, the New Criticism of the 1940's or the post-structuralism and feminism of the 1980's. At the other extreme from the superprofessionals, however, are those who reject professionalism as such and long to return to a state of affairs in which critics were less preoccupied with methodology and theory and addressed themselves to a general audience. The most vocal of these have been journalists and disaffected professors who regard academic methodology as something which inevitably comes between literature and the student, the reader and the writer. Today the primary target of this group is theory, but yesterday it was New Criticism and before that it was historical research.

Neither professional complacency nor antiprofessional nostalgia seem to us to be useful attitudes: the one acquiesces to the present situation of criticism as a given, while the other refuses to see that some of its features are irreversible. As editors we accept and welcome Professor Culler's point that the self-consciousness that is the mark of "theory" is inevitable at a moment when once-accepted definitions, categories and disciplinary boundaries have become matters of debate and controversy. Indeed, "theory" is simply a name for the questions which necessarily arise when principles and concepts once taken for granted have become matters of controversy. We believe, however, that critical debates would be more productive if they included those who are not yet convinced that the whole of what matters in criticism is encompassed by the most advanced academic schools, and who doubt that the contraction of criticism to that compass is altogether a good thing. In other words, without falling prey to useless nostalgia, there may be something to be said for certain older conceptions of criticism that tend now to be generally ignored or, to use the deconstructive lingo once more, "marginalized" by the concerns of academic critics. The attempt to raise such questions and provide room for debate and discussion of them is the motive for the present collection of essays.

Since our contributors speak eloquently for themselves, we shall not use this preface to comment on their essays individually, but will restrict ourselves to noting some common themes. We have grouped the essays according to these, beginning with the most general and historical treatments of the state of academic criticism, then going on to essays that address specific aspects of the present situation, then to several that review the tradition and place of nonacademic literary journalism, and then to a more personal and polemical group. We conclude with a few responses and counter-responses—something in the nature of an abbreviated written debate.

Inevitably, the question of "theory" has aroused the most persistent comment, in a way that exemplifies the spectrum of pros and cons of our moment. Whether to theorize or not to theorize, and whether theory may have a legitimate place in the literature program of colleges and universities, are questions which have exercised several contributors, not always sympathetically. Others have taken the view that theoretical inquiry of some kind is inevitable in the development of literary criticism, and the only question is how and in what way theory will be integrated with older practices. Perhaps the most constructive suggestion that arises from the discussion is that the concept of theory needs to be expanded to include a Leavis, a Trilling or a Howe, as much as a Derrida or a Lacan. That is, it is not necessary to restrict theory to a sort of inquiry that is ahistorical and outside questions of evaluation and literary culture generally. "Theoretical" need not mean "isolated," "unhistorical," "self-referential," "technical" and so on. Nor need it denote a "system" which answers all questions, though system-making need not be a dishonorable activity either.

If anything ties our contributors together and transcends their local differences, it is the feeling that a revived "cultural criticism," based on general ideas and the largest sense of literary culture, and taking in contemporary imaginative writing (and other media), is what is most sorely needed .today to revitalize the humanistic study of literature. While it is not easy to say how this kind of cultural criticism can be translated into courses and programs, the desire for it seems widespread and cuts across the line that divides humanists and post-structuralists. That desire comes from a sense that, whatever its individual triumphs, contemporary academic criticism as a whole is lacking not only in its usefulness to the reader of an imaginative work, but also in its applicability both to the literary culture generally and to the largest pedagogical responsibilities of the university. To change this situation for the better, it may be a question not of getting academic critics to do different things from what they are doing now, and still less a question of getting them all to do some one common thing. We need rather to create a structure in which the sum of what academic critics do can add up to a dialectical whole instead of an inconsequential series of isolated activities. In other words, the point is not to rule out specialized study, but only to ask that it participate in the creation of a larger context of contemporary intellectual and social life.

The "traditional" study of literature has failed on its own terms to communicate tradition widely or to mediate between works and readers and has instead produced the enormous mass of exegetical and historical criticism with which only fellow-academics are familiar. It was the deterioration of traditional studies that enabled newer methods to establish themselves so quickly. But embracing these new methods is no answer in itself, for they too have been unable to create a usable cultural context for literary study. The close, concrete reading of literary works, which remains one of the primary tasks of criticism, is not likely to recover the sense of mission that once informed it as long as it takes place in a vacuum — separated from historical, philosophical and social contexts. Thus a fusing of cultural inquiry and the most scrupulous textual attention would begin to restore to criticism a constructive role in the literary culture.

It would appear that with semiotics, popular cultural studies, the new social history inspired by Continental thought, the best of traditional literary studies, and the great archival and investigative resources of the university, all the equipment needed for a literary criticism of a more generally useful kind is available. While it would be improper to urge on every individual critical work an overriding cultural concern, nonetheless it seems necessary that interpreters, researchers and theorists ask how their work contributes to an intellectual community. But this new culturally grounded criticism is not going to happen by a process of accretion. It can only arise out of focused debate that admits into academic criticism the presence of the cultural conflicts of the age. Interdisciplinary efforts, as we have had them so far, have not been enough, because they have been a mere addition to the curricular opportunities of students and professors, and not part of a concerted effort at rethinking literary and cultural criticism.

In contrast, the discussion we envision, and have attempted to represent in this volume, would lead to real and practical changes in university curriculum, the profession of teaching, the study of literature and the writing of criticism. By urging the largest concerns on all those who participate in literary culture, such discussion might ultimately influence imaginative writing itself, for, as represented by creative writing programs, this too is now intimately tied to the universities, yet in an undefined way which does not often permit the question to arise of how contemporary creativity is related to the study of the past and the critical scrutiny of the present. If anything fundamental is to change, we must recognize that these questions are part of literary study itself.

* * *

Seven Propositions on Teaching

1. The assumption underlying the organized teaching of literature has been that literature essentially teaches itself. A literary education, for any given student, is conceived as exposure to a certain number of authors, periods and masterworks of literature taught by "good teachers" representing a variety of periods, genres and approaches, and working in autonomous and isolated classrooms. Ideally, in the student's mind, the net result of this exposure is a coherent sense of the cultural tradition, an appreciation of the best that has been thought and said, etc.

2. But literature doesn't teach itself. Teaching it involves deciding what works to study and why, what questions to ask about them, what contexts to put them in. To teach the traditional canon assumes a theory of why it should be taught. By "theory" here we don't mean esoteric, technical concepts, necessarily, but the general ideas that give point and value to literary study.

3. Once, the social homogeneity of those who became students or professors made for tacitly shared theories about literature and teaching. Now that the university is—and should be—heterogeneous, theories are not shared, but their conflicts aren't brought under conscious and productive scrutiny either.

4. To understand and appreciate the literature treated in their classrooms, students need to understand the theoretical ideas that determine why it is being taught as it is.

5. Closely analyzing a series of literary works in chronological order doesn't add up to teaching literary history.

6. The university does not have a unified cultural tradition to impart but rather a set of cultural conflicts—including conflicts over what the cultural tradition is and has been thought to be. The organization of the university now prevents these conflicts from becoming visible and educationally functional. Professors' lives are consequently as much impoverished as students'.

7. The university is like a family in which the parents hide their disagreements from the children.

Gerald Graff
Reginald Gibbons
May 1985

The editors are grateful to Greg Meyerson for his thoughtful participation in the editing of this volume.

I. General Perspectives and Historical Insights

Academic Criticism and Contemporary Literature

Reginald Gibbons

What a writer of fiction or poetry misses in most contemporary literary criticism is an indication that the concerns of criticism are connected with those of imaginative writing. There seems to be neither a shared language among critics and writers, nor a sense of shared values. It is instructive to see that the closest affinities between the critics in vogue and imaginative writers are mostly in the arena of what is called variously metafiction, surfiction or postmodern fiction. These imaginative writers, like their critical counterparts, tend to be academic, ingenious and voluble; they tend, with a fairly gentle scorn, to dismiss other sorts of writing with the label "traditional," and say they speak for readers, or at least writers, who are dissatisfied with the illusionist pretensions of such narrative elements as plot, character, unity, consistency of point of view, reliability of narrative voice and so on. They tend to be interested in the play of ideas rather than in the exploration of existence.

It is much rarer to find a similar disenchantment with fiction among imaginative writers who are women, of racial minorities, or poets. It is rare, in fact, among any of these to find much critical writing of any kind, or much sense of a general literary endeavor shared with the critic—except for the case of the metafiction writers, who seem to produce a great deal of work tailored for the narrowed tasks of the classroom (such as abstracting the ideas and themes, noting the "subversive" formal disarrays and the ironies, etc.). Is it only the obvious affinity of classroom criticism for work from which ideas and themes can be abstracted that explains this current situation? What of the reader who would prefer a criticism that can capably discuss a wide range of contemporary writing? Is there a hint of this lopsidedness in the tendency of critics to mean only fiction when they speak of "literature" in a contemporary context? And is it a coincidence that the academic monopoly on criticism comes at a time when neither fiction writers nor poets have engaged in critical inquiry to a significant degree? Among English-language poets, at least, this has been a traditional and enormously valuable enterprise, till now.

Notable too, in our time, is the convergence of a number of current problems – the masses of undistinguished essays published for the sake of professional advancement or merely private pleasure; the lack of historical context in theoretical criticism; the abandonment of evaluative criticism by all camps; the virtual monopoly, by default, of the academy on general literary criticism, such as book reviewing – which it performs poorly; the possibility that the desire of students for creative writing programs may be partly to find a deeper engagement with literature – in their teachers, and for themselves – than what they find in the academic classroom; the declining enrollments and crush of applicants for teaching positions; the lack of consensus regarding courses of study (especially for B.A.'s and Ph.D.'s in English); and pedagogical crises over reading and writing skills, especially secondary school preparation for college courses. In what follows, I hope to address the interconnectedness of these separate problems.

1

The current state of literary criticism is characterized by a warring of opposites, and yet the warring seems false. Some advocates of theoretical criticism have said that the usefulness of "primary" criticism – by which is meant exegetical criticism that explores meaning and the interpretation of meaning – has ended, either because there has been so much written on works of Shakespeare, Faulkner and other writers that the spectacle of more, especially when the critic turns to authors whose merit is questionable, is embarrassing; or because the validity of any given response to a text is questionable anyway, because of the historical differences between author and critic and the impossibility of an "intentional" model of critical inquiry. The old sort of textual explication, which declines through generations of students and scholars until it merely hunts out the minor figure or the minor problem and then lavishes on it the detailed attention that Shakespeare deserves, seems a caricature of serious literary inquiry. Likewise the articles about newly discovered letters, minor texts, etc. Such efforts were brilliantly and hilariously parodied by Woody Allen years ago.

But all "primary" criticism cannot be dismissed by pointing to the worst primary criticism. Nor can such dismissal automatically confer privileged status on "secondary" criticism, which must properly be justified in turn. The most important mistake of condemning primary criticism is that the condemnation, and resulting neglect, is ahistorical and reactionary. It would leave the canon in a rigid state, not only by discouraging the resuscitation of lost authors from the past (such as the noted cases of American authors like Edward Taylor, Emily Dickinson, Melville, Whitman or Tuckerman), but by preventing the addition of new authors. Since our historical moment is not constant, how can an ahistorical approach to criticism guarantee that changed attitudes and new knowledge will not uncover a lost author, who deserves, or rather requires, exegetical criticism? How can such an approach provide for the necessity of examining work from the recent past as we gradually sift out the ephemeral and preserve the worthy for future readers? In other words, a wholesale rejection of primary criticism abdicates some of the essential functions of professional literary study.

By abandoning questions of canon formation in favor of more theoretical criticism, secondary criticism ignores the shifts in literary study and appreciation that alone can guarantee a reasonable, informed and sympathetic reader the chance to recover work from the past. Such a stance, while it may not be premeditatedly exclusionary, nonetheless has the effect of stopping the historical process of reevaluation, because so much criticism on a secondary level, like deconstruction, is itself ahistorical, and works against historical consciousness in the present. And such an effect, while not necessarily desired by those who achieve it, discriminates against those critics who wish to study what is not yet admitted by consensus to the canon. Worse, it excludes the writers who, whether past or present, have produced works that are still pleading for study. Several editions of the giant work on American literature edited by Spiller have left out all mention of the autobiography of Frederick Douglass; that is an historical example.[1] A contemporary one could be found in the stories and novels of William Goyen – translated into German by Curtius, into French by Coindreau, regarded in Europe as extremely valuable and fundamentally original, but not to be found, for example, in Frederick Karl's recent, huge, *American Fictions 1940–1980*.[2] How will secondary criticism redress these inequities?

Let me give an illustrative case of a critical theory distorting a literary reality, and the way in which this distortion feeds the specialist impulse in academic criticism. Eliot and Borges offered the idea that each *new* writer of importance alters the canon preceding him or her, shifting our perspective so that we see earlier work in a different way, and thus sometimes enormously enriching our appreciation of an earlier writer's prescience and modernity. In the bargain, a fair amount of exegetical criticism may be very useful, if what it is after is an element in the familiar work which only a new perspective has made visible. It's interesting to note in passing the apparent similarity of what Eliot and Borges have written to what Harold Bloom has said about the poet's links to his predecessors. For in fact, while Eliot and Borges note the way in which the historical procession of authors and texts is altered by each new great author, Bloom seems to say that the process is entirely psychological, not historical. Instead of altering contemporary perceptions of his

17

predecessors with his own accomplished work, Bloom's poet is always *striving* to outdo the predecessor. For the artistic intercourse between writers that Eliot and Borges see, Bloom substitutes an ahistorical, and somewhat petty, rivalry. He makes a fetish of destroying the poetic father, so that the poetic son can be entirely original, and even self-originating. (And making a fetish of the new is certainly tied to a modern and probably economic sense of competition, as well as to the artistic desire to "make it new.") But it is not certain that the impulse to destroy is primary in many poets, nor, if it were, that it is central. Eliot and Borges did not speak of the writer wanting or needing to *destroy* his predecessor, but of his *creating* his predecessor, in an important sense, by altering the historical, as well as the psychological, record.

The damage of such distortion as Bloom achieves is part of the enormous influence, by default, of academic specialists—rather than general readers—on the contemporary canon. Because academic criticism prizes especially those works which are the best fuel for the critical machinery, other works come to suffer a de facto devaluation, despite the absence of explicit and rational evaluative debate. It is particularly frustrating, for example, to see that the excellence and worthiness of the poetry of Wallace Stevens and Hart Crane is almost routinely designated as beyond question, while that of William Carlos Williams—while apparently canonized—remains less read, less esteemed, and perhaps less certain, in the secret thoughts of many, of surviving for future readers.

Not surprisingly, poets who follow the poetics of Williams versus Stevens must receive their attention from even narrower specialists in their "fields" (Olson, Creeley or, generally, "Black Mountain Poets," for example), rather than from the more catholic critics of contemporary literature. Specialist attention, in other words, seems sometimes a compensation for generalist indifference. But some poets who follow Stevens have already, and perhaps prematurely, been accorded a kind of canonical status, by those whose "field," "contemporary poetry" (not "contemporary literature"), seems to have the capacity to generate its own contemporary canon, as if without reference to the past. In the contemporary English department, the field tends to replace the larger history of literature; it offers its own, equally sizeable, history.

The reason for this is that since the contemporary is regarded by most academic critics as a specialist field of literature rather than the living center of literary culture, it is no longer a subject for debate, much less passionate adherence, but merely a field for professional disputes. I would not claim that Williams was a greater poet than Stevens; I would only note that for his works to receive some academic due they require specialists, whereas the canon has admitted Stevens and some of his epigones in such a way that they claim (but may not always receive) their due from everyone. What would be interesting would be a criticism in which the values inherent in the work of Williams and Stevens, say, could be passionately debated, rather than assigned to specialists who take no interest in each other's work, as if the works of Stevens and Williams had not even their status as poetry in common. No very strong consensus can ever be expected to range over the whole of literature; yet the most important consensus is the implicit one that the value of literary works *is* worth debate – is perhaps the *fundamental* subject of debate. And such a consensus of seriousness, if I may call it that, is what is presently lacking.

Hugh Kenner's genial and personal account of the formation of the modernist canon, recently published, is a rare example of the kind of criticism, however occasional, that everywhere implies the sense of the value of the works in that canon, not merely their interest, and nowhere in his account does one see any connection to the way of thinking about literature that characterizes current theoretical criticism.[3] But that current theoretical criticism, seemingly divorced on principle from value, even from the theoretical possibility of value, seems ill-qualified to aid in the formation of canons, while most traditional "field" criticism, unlike Kenner's, has also apparently abdicated responsibility for assessment and evaluation, in favor of expansion and specialization.

Insofar as contemporary academic criticism practices close reading, it tends to focus on *ideas* of form rather than material artistic effects, on semiphilosophical notions rather than thought or emotion. Such criticism and a good deal of what preceded it has often assumed that experiment is a primary literary value, but has defined and examined "experiment" in the narrowest way. Novels like those of García Márquez, Italo Calvino and Milan Kundera do not find their reason for being, for coming into existence, only in experiment with the *form*, but also in artistic assaults – and successful ones – on the rough ground of a contemporary reality, whether it is village life in a deprived and relatively primitive backwater, or the powerful influences on individual thought, feeling and behavior of the advanced industrial nations. "Contemporary reality," as the largest rubric, can *include* the history of the novel, formal and social; but the current history of the novel, especially as we get it from academic critics enamored of the postmodern writers, does not seem to include genuine, concrete, historical reality, so much as it makes a mere theme or novelistic trope out of the more disjunctive aspects of contemporary reality. Here both critics of contemporary fiction and Bloom, on poetry, feel an enthusiasm for the idea that literary reference and competition is the germ of imaginative writing. As Kundera shows, however, there's a logical flaw, at the very least, in assuming that it is primarily an insulated literary impulse that carries the writer toward a formal discovery.

When Milan Kundera considers the history of the novel, in "The Novel and Europe," he notes the way in which the novel *compensates*, or tries to, for the power of contemporary philosophy and science to abolish and forget "*die Lebenswelt*, the world of concrete living." The novel, as an art form, shares the modern "passion for knowing" (Husserl), but the object of its passion, Kundera says, is concrete existence, not theory. "A novel that does not uncover a hitherto unknown segment of existence is immoral," for the great novels are a "sequence of discoveries" of this sort:

> The novel discovered the different dimensions of existence one by one: with Cervantes and his contemporaries, it questioned the nature of adventure; with Richardson, it began to examine "what happens inside" and to unmask the secret life of feelings; with Balzac, it discovered man's rootedness in history; with Flaubert, it explored the *terra* previously *incognita* of the everyday; with Tolstoy, it focused on the role of the irrational in human behavior and decisions. It measured time: the evanescent past with Proust, the evanescent present with Joyce. With Thomas Mann, it queried the role of the myths that control our movements from the remote past of man. And so on, and so on.[4]

And whereas most *writers* would say, if asked, that novelistic form follows artistic, even spiritual, function—follows, that is, the expressive necessities of both the "subject" and the artist's desires—the current academic perspective (perhaps because it is inevitably critical and not creative?) more often assumes that first a formal experiment or formal play, arising out of a reaction to earlier works in the genre, dictates the ways in which a work will reshape the genre or remake some of its strategies.

Since criticism has for a long time occupied itself with *literary* history, perhaps this is only an expected failing, and an understandable one; the critic seeks connections between works, in order to understand each individual work better. And yet this entirely worthy search becomes distorted, even destructive, when the critic does not reach the point of asking other questions of a text, questions that extend into social as well as literary history, questions that implicitly recognize a living human being as the creator of the work and other living beings as the readers of it.

The case of deconstruction one might accurately call, after their fashion, a de(con)struction. The gleeful destructiveness of this criticism is very dispiriting. I quote, from the recent catalog of one of the most distinguished university publishers in America, the descriptions of two new books:

> . . . rigorously applies key motifs of deconstructive thought to four traditional philosophical and theological categories: God, self, history, and the book. Drawing out their implicit tensions and contradictions, he discloses the inherent instability of *the entire Western religious tradition* . . . What, he asks, are we to think . . . after the death of God, the disappearance of the self, the end of history, and the closure of the book?

And:

explication of the linguistic theories of Wittgenstein, Heidegger, and Saussure, with comments on the thought of Jacques Derrida, shows how their ideas have thrown representation, signification, and narrative unity into question. Contemporary writers . . . have taken the very stuff of language theory as their subject matter, often putting theory to experiential tests that *threaten* as much to *destroy* theory as to confirm it. [My italics]

One can only hope for the destruction with which this stupefyingly pretentious come-on concludes, if everything else is going to be destroyed as well. I think there are still a number of readers and critics who do not think that the self has disappeared, that history has ended or that the book is closed. As for throwing into question representation, signification and narrative unity—that was accomplished in *Don Quixote* and a thousand times since, but has never seemed to mean to writers and readers what it has come to mean to many critics—that there is no reliability at all in such human artistic strategies and that therefore they may never be trusted under any circumstance whatsoever. Nor does it appear that in the best works of the modern age authors have been at work first of all to put a theory, any theory, to a test, any test—unless it is in the two most notable formal experiments, poetic and novelistic, *Un Coup de Dès* and *Finnegans Wake*. And of all works of the modern period, these two are famed more for their intellectual riddles than for any accomplishment beyond the formal.

Inevitably, such theoretical study of literature comes to emphasize the ways in which all literary works resemble each other, rather than the ways in which a specific work of literature is structured and conveys its unique meaning. This is what technique, as opposed to history and sympathy, does. As a result, for such critics, there are no books, only The Book, and there is no writing, only Writing. And the nihilistic glee of post-structuralism is unmistakable, however muted it may be in these catalog sentences for the sake of academic decorum. Nothing could be more destructive pedagogically than the belief that the cluster of human values that has survived across millenia and cultures is an illusion—the cluster that includes the possibility of feeling, of reason, of meaningful human action and expression.

Instead of a proliferation of theoretical innovation, a plethora of new critical vocabularies, or a recidivist retreat into mere publication for its own sake, why is there not a criticism, of fiction at least, that addresses Kundera's issues? At a second level, of self-scrutiny this time, why is there not a greater attention—at least sheepish, if not repentant—to the sociological analyses, few as they are, that offer historical explanation for the current domination of both theory and, in opposition to theory, only too much stale exegesis? In celebrating unreason, or the recalcitrance, intractibility, and self-contradiction of all communications, however honestly attempted, theoretical criticism merely practices the philosophical reductionism that Kundera criticizes in science. It ignores existence in favor of intellectual conundrums (which certainly have their interest, but without a context provided by concrete being, become absurdly reductive and false). While exegetical criticism of the worst sort merely offers justification for theoretical excess, theoretical excess retaliates and drives the wagons of the exegetes into a circle.

Kundera notes:

> The time was past [at the moment Husserl gave his 1935 lectures on the crisis of European humanity] when man had only the monster of his own soul to grapple with—the peaceful time of Joyce and Proust. In the novels of Kafka, Hasek, Musil, Broch, the monster comes from outside and is called History, but it no longer has the aspect of the adventurer: it is inhuman, ungovernable, incalculable, unintelligible; and it is inescapable.[5]

If the highest goal of the novel is still to discover our existence to us, in our present historical conditions and in a way which is possible only for a work of art, then why should not the task of criticism be to discover the ways in which the novel does this? And why, parenthetically, does it seem very nearly impossible to imagine an essay like Kundera's written not about the novel but about poetry? I do not think it is for a lack of appropriate poetic texts of the twentieth century. It has to do partly with an absence of strong criticism by poets, as much as by critics, academic or of other sorts. And it raises the interesting and as yet relatively unexamined issue of the way translations make possible the study of something called the European novel, but not anything called European poetry.

Given such high and demanding tasks for the novel and for criticism (Kundera does not speak of criticism), it is no wonder that for one of the most original and powerful novelists, the notions of unintelligibility of language, or the end of literature, are absurd not for their implausibility, but for their being so often ascribed to the wrong, because "inside," causes. Kundera writes:

> Glibly pious obituaries of the novel seem frivolous to me—frivolous because I have seen and lived through the death of the novel, a violent death inflicted by bans, censorship, and ideological pressures in the world where I have spent much of my life and which is usually called totalitarian.[6]

University presses continue to manufacture books of exegesis and thematic readings of authors considerably over-examined already, they fail to issue books on works and authors needing attention and they publish—because they feel an obligation to intellectual fashion—a great many critical books whose aim and premise is to destroy the community of discoveries that still defines the possibilities and the value of imaginative writing. That too is an ideology, because it masks the merely professional functionality of so much published criticism.

If criticism is to regain value for readers outside the academy, it must address the issue of whether a poem or a novel, a story or a play, discovers our existence to us or whether, in Kundera's words, it "only confirm[s] what has already been said." Kundera says that the (authentic) novel cannot live at peace with the destroying, annihilating, murderous and perhaps merely floodingly loquacious spirit of our time (my characterization, not his). How is it, then, that criticism can live in peace with that spirit? Or better, how can it *counter* that spirit if it persists in merely adding to a deluge of unread or unreadable essays?

2

It was not original of Harold Bloom to speak of the poet's anxiety of influence. But however obvious the notion may be, and even incontrovertible at least in the lowest degree, this does not mean that it is a primary aspect of very many works. When Eliot and Borges suggested that the canon alters when a new work is added to it, they did so from the point of view of the reader who looks back at those earlier works rather less suspiciously than Bloom does, and from that of the writer, who may have seized some *enabling* possibility out of an earlier work—and not from the point of view, it seems to me, of the critic who looks first for a disabling and burdensome relationship.

Such a critical attitude is narrow and seems to want to imply that literature lives only in the realm of literature. And the academic prizing of postmodern fiction, like that fiction itself, is tied, it seems, to a preference for the belief that fiction, like poetry in Auden's famous words, makes nothing happen, can make only itself happen. The obvious corollary for the critic is that fiction itself will happen most often out of other fiction, *not* out of the broader reality of a writer's imagination—by which I mean only the real, historical, individual, expressive desires and needs of a given writer at a given moment, in a given room on a given day (which will include, of course, literary precedent, but will not be limited to it, nor even primarily dictated by it). By rejecting a traditional aim of art—in Edwin Muir's phrase for poetry, to create a true image of life—the postmoderns and their critical advocates make it seem as if it has been decided once and for all that such notions as a true image of life are themselves outdated and unsophisticated, and therefore unworthy of the contemporary artist or the contemporary critic. But this is a partisan position, one that goes against the very experience of reading a novel by Patrick White or Milan Kundera, or the poems of Seamus Heaney.

Thus one point where the language of criticism and that of imaginative writing separated with sad consequence is in speaking of the raison d'être of literary works. While criticism found this more and more in secondary aspects of writing—and whether minutely textual or abstractedly philosophical, these share the impulse to retreat from the literary work's first level of discourse—much imaginative writing has been going the other way. That is, when the critic's work calls into question the nature of the being of the literary work, it seems usually in order to deny the validity of expression; when the writer's work calls into question the nature of being of the literary work, it is to *seek* new possibilities of expression.

What we might call Kundera's paradox would hold that the more contradictory, implausible, brutal, horrible and absurd the world becomes, the greater the novelist's desire and need to discover to the reader the reality of our being in that world—*not* to answer that world with his own absurd contention that nothing means anything anyway, *nor* with lazy or complacent presentation of aspects of our being with which we are already too familiar. And yet most criticism seems to mimic these two failing and inadequate gestures of the bad novelist, either by questioning the ability of any text to move a reader or by performing without question accepted and not very useful critical tasks.

All this might not have come to seem calamitous—and need not have been calamitous—except for the concomitant changes in critical approaches, which simultaneously called into question all reliability of interpretation, indeed of language itself. And so the language of criticism veered away from the language of imaginative writing, even as it drew some of its speed from some imaginative works, like Beckett's (which is not at all to condemn those works, but rather some of the uses to which they have been put). In reaction to this direction of criticism—by implication prescriptive—many writers simply folded their tents without ceremony and stole away.

What writers heed, as opposed to critics, is a full range of expressive requirements that come from both inside—the writer's personal history, temperament and talents—and outside—the social and historical reality in which the writer, and his or her art, are situated. I wonder if many critics, using the terms "inside" and "outside," might not have reversed their significance, thus revealing the split once more—that is, using "inside" to mean the internal exigencies of the genre or form, as it has arrived from its use by other writers, and using "outside" to mean the writer!

Such a reversal might confirm the critical fashion of saying that all influences except those contained inside the work itself, that is, inside the work as an instance of the genre, are secondary—while the writer would feel the opposite. This fashion carries with it the implication that poetry and fiction not only make very little, if not nothing, happen, but *shouldn't* make anything happen, because to have that power of influence on human feeling and thought violates the current critical shibboleths of the purity and self-referentiality of art and the futility of language. Such mistaken notions gain ground because they have seeds of truth in them; however, they are seeds which grow into bizarre, dis-

24

torted plants without the proper context, like garden vegetables mistakenly sprayed with hormonal weed killer, that sprout mutant limbs and misshapen fruit because they too are a kind of glorious weed. Abetting this set of attitudes is a variety of contemporary poetry, more than fiction, that little threatens already-held critical opinions on the mildness and marginality of poetry, its lack of contemporary power or accomplishment. And a lack of accomplishments or power is much easier to accommodate in criticism than the opposite.

Flannery O'Connor said that the mere writing of a novel is a hopeful act, and thus put aside the philistine objection that too many contemporary works were about a depressing reality. The implication of her statement is that the language of novels does empower the imagination, if it does not precisely empower the reader to carry out some action arising from what he or she has read. (Unless sympathy and understanding may be considered actions, as I think they can.) When Richard Ohmann decried the way in which too often college composition courses make the student into a willing mimic of established attitudes and clichés, rather than empowering the student's intellect for critical thinking, he implied that he took for granted the vigor and effectiveness in language, if properly used. It would seem, then, that there ought to be some common ground for the writer, the reader and the critic.

3

Each aspect of the present crisis has its effect on what developments may follow. If the language of criticism has estranged it from the language of imaginative writing and thus from writers and general readers, then this estrangement can perhaps be laid at the door of academic critics, if only because in our time there is scarcely any other kind. While most readers—and writers—I believe, prefer a criticism that assesses works, the critic is too often practicing a criticism that either assesses prematurely or on the basis of extraneous standards, or entirely refrains from assessment in favor of new versions of taxonomy, but—in the case of the newest criticism—of classes rather than individuals, of theoretical possibilities rather than actual accomplishments, of varieties of impossibility rather than specific possibilities of real works.

Examples of this contradiction between the relative uselessness of criticism to the reader versus its professional usefulness to the critic can readily and frequently be seen. Donald Hall notes in an essay on Daniel Hoffman's 1980 *Harvard Guide to Contemporary Literature* that in the survey by A. Walton Litz on literary theory since 1945, "the subject of literary criticism is unconnected with the judgment or description of literature. One of this book's ironies is the discrepancy between the theology of literary criticism, as outlined by Litz, and the practical parish work which occupies the rest of the book. Litz regrets that he cannot spend time on criticism that serves texts—on Hugh Kenner, for instance—and that he must pass 'over the great achievements in literary biography, such as Richard Ellmann's *James Joyce* . . . and Leon Edel's *Henry James* . . . .'"[7]

A sociological explanation would perhaps be most useful, and some critics have ventured into this area, decrying the new professionalization, which has come to mean not a consensus of values and high standards, but the substitution of professional *activity* for professional excellence, a victory of quantity over quality, of pro forma institutional requirements (publication of criticism to gain promotion) over the intrinsic literary and philosophical questions and values of literary inquiry. Such professionalization is a part of something larger, the successive stages of decontextualizing literature that Gerald Graff has outlined in his essay, "The University and the Prevention of Culture" (in this volume). Professionalization is partly the result of the desire of professionals to have a technical language that is theirs alone, and which outmatches the language of the writer in its sophistication.

It seems that the revolutions in literary criticism over the last century have alternately tried to revitalize two aspects of the study of literature. The primacy of evaluative norms for literature was challenged by philology in favor of methodological rigor, and the same pattern prevailed in the challenge of theoretical criticism to established New Criticism. To put it the other way, New Criticism tried to restore to the study of literature the evaluative function that philology had condemned in the flawed normative impressionism that had preceded it. But as Graff shows, each revolution has decayed into a narrow practice of method, even the evaluative New Criticism, once its practice became divorced from its original social and institutional context.

The present situation, then, is yet another moment in a series of historical moments when old paradigms of literary study are replaced. Why, however, has it been the rule that this replacement has been characterized by extremism and by the complaint that the new paradigm, of whichever pole, has so far always been seen by opponents as removing criticism further from literature? The complainants are partly right, but if theoretical dispute removes itself from engagement with literary texts in favor of a more abstract disputation, exegetical and historical criticism has too often buried itself in minutiae and unreasonably speculative interpretation. What is it about criticism in the American university that has allowed such a confusion of purposes, such contradictions and oppositions? Beyond the obvious problem of professionalization, as defined negatively above, and the painful intersection of this drive with declining enrollments and fewer positions in university and college teaching, there are other causes for the present situation; or rather, there are other symptoms that point to causes beyond the merely academic or institutional.

Each critical revolution has arisen out of larger cultural concerns, yet each has ended up as an institutionalized method. The cliché of ivory tower seems never to have been more appropriate. Initiators of each revolution seem to have been engaged with the literary culture of their time, but followers have disengaged themselves from the larger questions, preferring to devote themselves to method. Eliot wrote essays for the general reader; Burke, Trilling, Winters, Leavis, Lévi-Strauss, Barthes—all wrote essays that addressed large cultural issues. The generation of European scholar-critics—Auerbach, Curtius, Spitzer—turned to contemporary writing as well as to the work of the past. Curtius translated a great range of contemporary work, from Eliot's poems to the fiction by William Goyen that I mentioned earlier.

In addition, the first writers to take a place in the academy, like Ransom, Tate, Warren, Jarrell—and a critic like Blackmur, with much writerly consciousness—often devoted themselves to a general exposition of critical issues, and even to polemics, and wrote not for professional journals but for literary magazines and the more sophisticated commercial magazines. The *New Yorker* ran not only Wilson's book reviews, but Louise Bogan's frequent reviews of contemporary poetry, as well. By comparison, Helen Vendler's in the same magazine are few and cannot pretend to the *general*, and *therefore* valuable, attention that Bogan gave to poetry. George Steiner, who must for the sake of analogy here fill Wilson's place at the *New Yorker*, offers reviews that do not seem to take the pulse of imaginative writing as Wilson's did; Updike has more curiosity, and may in fact display more brilliance as critic than as novelist, but he is resolutely individual, he speaks as one who browses among books, rather than as one who looks at each, as well, with larger questions in mind about imaginative writing and literary culture generally.

In any case, the context for such reviews seems to have changed over the years and they carry only enough weight, it seems, to influence sales, not thought. Does this enormous difference in critics now and then, academic and nonacademic, not suggest a cause for the crisis in criticism that lies outside the university as well as in? Would any theoretical critic today have the same influence, immediate or long-term, that Kenneth Burke seemed once to have? For that matter, do—for example—Yvor Winters, Randall Jarrell, F. R. Leavis, Edmund Wilson or Lionel Trilling have any effect now on the reading of books, or has their strong and humane criticism been dismissed as dated or naive?

4

It is a curious and perhaps melancholy fact that the proliferation of theoretical criticism and the avalanche of publication (already huge, and to which diluted methodological applications of new theory only add) has coincided with the founding of creative writing programs at many universities.

Is this mere coincidence? Isn't it more likely that the second generation of writers already in the employ of universities were not immune from the drive to professionalize—in the worse sense—the study of English? Their students, who in turn become teachers—although with an M.A. or M.F.A. rather than a Ph.D.—have been shaped in a professionalized atmosphere: that is, one in which professional success—advancement— is measured more by the number of publications than by their intrinsic merit. And there is the same lack of larger context despite the attempts by many creative writing instructors who are serious writers to offer an alternative to the readily discernible narrowness of the academic class-room at its worst. Too few poets of our time have made any substantial effort at criticism, and the English-language tradition of the influential poet-critic seems to be broken, for now. Instead, when recent poets have written criticism, it has tended to be either ephemeral or scanty. At times, it may even help define and promote yet another critical sub-field, that of creative writing. It has not often evinced the learning that distinguished Pound or Eliot, or the wide sympathies (which implied no undue generosity) that characterized Jarrell. In the academy, whether one speaks of critics or imaginative writers, the one thing that profes-sionalization has not meant has been a sharper sense of the need to *evaluate* work fairly and critically.

Professionalization has not meant that students now generally read poems or novels with greater sensitivity or clearer understanding or superior historical preparation. Professionalization has not, therefore, meant that a larger audience for serious writing—past or present—has come out of the universities, despite much higher enrollments over the last twenty years than in previous periods. And the decline in shared texts continues apace: recently I heard a poet of forty-five reminisce about the paperback books that had been available when he was in graduate school, little cheap influential editions of Blake, Lorca, Stevens, French poetry and so on, a *kind* of book that is not published now. Thus are the economic and industrial pressures inside, and against, publishing, also a lamentable influence on the literary culture that the university participates in.

Professionalization has not meant that more attention is paid to seri-ous books in the general magazines that have some cultural seriousness, or at least pretensions. It has not meant that the academic criticism of literature has had any great effect on the dissemination of important texts to new readers or the preservation of worthy new works that otherwise would have been lost. It has thus not meant a greater consensus regarding the importance of imaginative writing to the culture, but a smaller one, a fragmentation of purpose and values. "Interdisciplinary study" has not yielded great and useful insights into literary texts, the way it often does in such fields as paleontology or anthropology or art history.

Outside the academy, there is almost no criticism at all. Curiously, this reflects not only the disinclination of either traditional exegetes or deconstructionists to engage in work that is aimed at a general, sophisticated reader, but also a larger problem—so large, perhaps, that it has had great if unacknowledged influence on much of what has happened inside the academy as well: the hallmark of the age of information is not the production of information itself, but the specialized production of information. When criticism is ruled as well by fashion (or reaction against fashion, which is the same thing), then the quantity of information—not in itself good or bad—produces a degradation of the historical sense, because such an enormous quantity of energy is focused on the new, and the new has too little context. Criticism—like much else—runs amok with productivity. Together, fashion, specialization, and lack of historical sense destroy the context that is required for the interpretation and evaluation of literary works. Inevitably, these contemporary forces also begin to relegate new imaginative writing to a mere sub-category of information, as if on a par with the mass of critical writing. And in fact, theoretical justification is quickly sought for this development—it's pretty common now to hear that literary criticism is the equal of imaginative writing in importance, or that a literary work is merely an event in the history of interpretation, as Paul de Man said.

Too, the much-discussed "explosion" of information is not only a measure of the quantity of pages filled with type, but also of the way in which that information reaches people and is utilized by them, or *fails* to be utilized. The number of book titles published in the U.S. in recent years has climbed past 40,000 annually toward 50,000. Despite this, the major research libraries spend more than half of their acquisitions funds on periodicals, of which it is not uncommon to find 60,000 different titles in one large collection. A serious person who wishes to think carefully about matters of importance and make rational decisions cannot but be irritated by the lavish production and wide dissemination of consumer magazines as opposed to serious writing, fatigued by the sheer quantity of print, and dismayed by the continual stream of new information that seems to nag at every moment and every decision by holding up yet more possibilities. The flood of stimuli—printed and televised—is blamed for declining test scores of students, for the shattering of shared cultural values, for increasing crimes of sexual assault and abuse, for economic confusion, for a huge variety of problems. And merely because such accusations are numerous and do not often open the way to a solution, they are not without grounds. Thus in literary culture, the situation is also one of excessive supply that smothers the formation of real demand and creates in its stead an ersatz demand—for the new. What a disappointingly predictable demand in the age of incessant novelty!

It's no surprise that academic literary culture has reflected such influence. As well as pursuing specialization for reasons apparently intrinsic to professional and institutional life, it has pursued it in concert with proliferating specialization outside the academy. Many apparently discrete phenomena thus seem linked. The writer of the exegetical essay, the editor who founds a small publishing house for fiction and poetry, the short-story writer who publishes his book with that house, the critical theoretician who has broken interpretive ground—for these, specialization has been a needed refuge, and a further exacerbation of the problem as well, for the exegetical essay is read by only a few hundred persons, the publishing house is almost unknown outside its region, the book of short stories receives only two reviews, although somehow or other a thousand copies are sold, and the theoretician has several more graduate students interested in her work, but feels no larger effect has been realized.

The question is whether there is anything the academic students of literature can do to alter this course. And this question inevitably means, can literary study offer any critical thinking about the larger society of information around it? Can any motives or aims from the larger society have any constructive effect on the way literary criticism is practiced in the academy? Can the academic status of imaginative— "creative"—writing, bring in a livelier engagement that will enrich criticism? Or will the academic status of imaginative writing finally allow the larger society to write it off as marginal and specialized? That society has, after all, fulfilled the inherent utilitarianism and philistinism of the age by relegating literature to a mere category of information or "communication"—a branding all the more destructive because the general notion of communication includes various forms of manipulative lying, such as advertising, but the artist's idea of communication, while it might seem to share technical aspects with commercial lying (as Spitzer sought to show in his famous essay on the orange juice ad), participates in a spiritual, as opposed to a commercial, reality: imagination, empathy, thought, feeling and human actions explored in the most sensitive and enlightening way, not to make somebody buy something, literally or figuratively.

Literary study has not been immune from the pressures of this larger context and it cannot reform itself without running counter to them. This would be precisely the kind of engagement that is lacking in the watered-down versions of revolutionary critical paradigms. It is often the kind of engagement we ask of imaginative writers. When imaginative writers decry the present state of criticism, especially theoretical criticism, it is not only, I think, because they fear its strength, but also because they sense that the institution of criticism is very weak, given the complacency of traditional exegetical work and the lame defenses of the humanities against encroachment by science and technology. All would be better, if not well, if those who oppose deconstruction, say, were themselves engaged with large questions; if all critics sought to understand the ways in which the written work establishes its *value* for the reader, not just presents its aspects (see Kundera, mentioned earlier); if the more theoretical critics valued more energetically a literary study that respects the writer's engagement with the life around him rather than assuming falsely that he is primarily engaged with either an epistemological question or with other books; if literary-critical language bore some resemblance to the language of discourse by which men and women—writers among them—endeavor to understand their world, judge it and act to influence it; and if critics took up some of the general tasks of literary culture that too few are performing, so that the health of literary study did not seem a kind of entirely separate endeavor from the health of imaginative writing.

One might wish that the separation had remained greater in the case of the creative writing programs, for they may now be suffering from the same misplaced professionalism that afflicts the academic departments. But they offer an interesting perspective on the classroom, nevertheless. In a way, these programs suggest that the activity of reading has become debased because of the proliferation of trivial criticism and the inescapable consequence of the trivialization of literature, a consequence which naturally extends to the academic classroom. If the activity of reading is so devalued that it gives the student little sense of participating in an experience that is important for its value to life—and not only to courses and a profession—then the activity of writing enters the classroom to fill the gap.

Writing is more active, it requires a lively participation, it seems to be connected to the power to alter thought, alter feeling, even alter life. These are intellectual experiences that the student may never realize are potential in the experience of reading, if the academic classroom inevitably conveys some of the atmosphere of the profession at its worst—its most trivial, its least consequential.

That is to say, the proliferation of the writing programs is as much a negative reaction to the teaching of literature and the practice of criticism as it is a development in the situation of contemporary writing. (The extent to which this is true may vary with schools, but it seems generally proof enough of a crisis, as an indication of the pathology of present pedagogy.) The students wish to have an experience they are not finding in the academic classroom: some sense of the importance of imaginative writing in human life. Most worthwhile creative writing classes are reading courses as well as writing courses, and the texts with which students are engaged are intensively studied for their literary strategies, their accomplishments both large and small, their meaning. In such a class, there is rarely anything so abstracted as an investigation of the powers of signification generally; there is rather a faith in language, even if there is doubt about a particular poem's merits.

I have heard students say that the reading of a poem by Stevens or a story by Chekhov was far more thorough and illuminating in a creative writing class than it had been in an academic course. Poetry writing instructors may be the only teachers encountered by an English major who take the time to teach the history of meter in English and American poetry—that is, who teach a student how to read, historically. (If, in fact, even they do this.) The irony here is that while professors of English fear that the writing instructor who has his students write free verse is merely an apostle of formlessness and lack of substance, the truth is that students are meanwhile failing to learn in academic courses anything about the possibilities of formal verse. The reason is almost always the same, it seems to me—the academic classroom is scarcely ever a place in which the materiality, the sensuous substance, of verse, is discussed with understanding or passion. So a stanza of *Paradise Lost* discussed in a creative writing class may discover to the student the genius of that poem more readily, and more fully, than a semester-long class treating the ideas in the poem.

Conversely, it may be scrutiny in a creative writing class that reveals to the student for the first time that there *are* ideas—rather than merely themes and notions—in poems. Since the literary history in survey courses is not often historical, such courses being anthologies of great texts linked by themes, comparisons and contrasts, and other elementary relationships, it is a boon that some creative writing instructors spend as much time as they do studying poems and fiction of the past, and studying them carefully for their structure and literary technique, because such study can reveal to the student the way in which poems and fiction change historically as artistic techniques and strategies change. Perhaps in the creative writing classroom there will even be some investigation of *why* literary structures and strategies change with time—and *that* would be the literary history lacking elsewhere.

5

If there is a crisis in literary criticism as it is practiced in the academy, it is not the struggle between opposing theoretical camps, but the question of whether any kind of literary criticism is of great value now. Such a crisis cannot be ended by traditional humanists winning over deconstructionists, nor by both sides agreeing to peaceful coexistence as two great tribes of specialists. Neither side seems engaged with the larger literary culture which, historically, imaginative writing, more than criticism, has shaped.

The ostensibly robust health of literary criticism when judged by the number of publications is no indication of the health of literary culture, or even the preservation of or reverence for great work; it is rather a kind of forgetting (*vide* Kundera once more) of that work, a consignment of its lineaments as a human artifact—a living enactment of feeling and thought, a discovery of human existence—to the bins of categories and systems and theories and textual problems and the annual indices of critical journals. It is not an inquiry into the nature of literary meaning, but a denial—by sheer ineffectual quantity and by virtue of remoteness—that such meaning can have any effect on the living human being, beyond the momentary preoccupations posed by an intellectual problem.

Discovering the meaning of a literary work, and the way that specific meaning is made, remains the first task of literary criticism, followed by evaluating that work in comparison to other literary works, so as to account for its appeal or lack of it to generations of readers. As long as writers continue to write and we advance, however haltingly and with whatever trepidation, into the years, there will remain a great need for this work, not only in assessing new novels and poems, but in redressing the injustices of the past in forming the canon of works.

This is not a crisis unique to the United States. In *The Institution of Criticism*, a book about literary criticism in West Germany, Peter Uwe Hohendahl says that it is a mistake to think that literary criticism can be saved as a valuable institution if, in reaction to its apparent crisis, all that is done is to prefer a kind of criticism (theoretical) that substitutes an interest in the "conditions of meaning" of literary works, for an interest (more traditional) in "the meaning of an individual text."[8] While both these possibilities are at war in the university, and suffer from such narrow compass, it is also true that, given the present state of things, there may be no possibility of finding any common ground for the two larger wings of literary culture, imaginative writing and criticism, *except* in the university. If that is so—and I think it is—then it is mistaken to long for a past relationship that cannot be recovered, and which we may perhaps be inclined to idealize. There has always been an abyss, large or small, between imaginative writing and criticism. Otherwise, we would not have so many entertaining tales to tell of the blindness of critics who did not see the value of this poet's or that novelist's work. And yet the abysses in our time—and not only in literary culture—seem to have unprecedented width. If the university, in reintegrating its pedagogical and research activities in the humanities, could encourage a productive debate over values, issues and styles of discourse, it would thereby participate in the preservation of such literary culture as we have.

Outside the academy—where academic critics could exercise a more positive influence—some more effective means of attending seriously to contemporary imaginative writing, biography, textual criticism and literary history must extend the general reception of these endeavors. That is to say, something as basic as an appreciation of the art of reading needs to be cultivated in students at all educational levels. How this can be done I don't know, but I know it can't be done quickly. My own experience tells me that the highest ideals carried into the classroom can be subverted by forces as irrelevant as fatigue, bad weather, student party weekends and the rest. But surely some greater effort of conscience is required of us all.

Perhaps more urgently, the tasks of teaching and criticism must be integrated so that what is available to the student is not a kind of watered-down version of an intellectual activity practiced professionally with greater rigor, but the very heart of literary study, practiced with pleasure, keenness, even passion.

---

1. Robert Spiller et al., *Literary History of the United States*, 3rd edition, rev. (New York: Macmillan Co., 1963) contains no word of Douglass. Nor does the *Bibliography Supplement II*, published in 1972, contain an entry on him—only a single mention in a paragraph of names and titles.

2. Frederick Karl, *American Fictions 1940–1980* (New York: Harper & Row, 1983).

3. Hugh Kenner, "The Making of the Modernist Canon," *Chicago Review*, XXXIV:2 (Spring 1984), pp. 49–61.

4. Milan Kundera, "The Novel and Europe," trans. David Bellos, *New York Review of Books*, XXXI:12 (July 19, 1984), p. 15.

5. Ibid., p. 16.

6. Ibid., p. 17.

7. Donald Hall, "Hoffman's Slovenly Map," *The Weather for Poetry* (Ann Arbor, Mich.: University of Michigan Press, 1982), pp. 278–79.

8. Peter Uwe Hohendahl, *The Institution of Criticism* (Ithaca, N.Y.: Cornell University Press, 1982), p. 42.

Accidental Institution: On the Origin of Modern Language Study

Wallace Douglas

> *There is a very common feeling that the meetings are uninteresting, and after long attendance upon many conventions I have come to the conclusion that what is wanting is discussion and sociability.*
>
> —Daniel Coit Gilman, welcoming the annual meeting of the Modern Language Association, 1886.

I

In the earliest days of the Modern Language Association (MLA)—say for a decade after its founding in 1883—members were open to discussions of classroom methods and techniques in courses they were giving or hoping to give. Those who came to the annual meetings could have heard Francis Gummere, when he was principal of the Swain Free School in New Bedford, discussing the place of Old English philology in the elementary school (1885; he was president of the Association in 1905), A. H. Smyth, professor of English literature in Central High School in Philadelphia, explaining how American literature is to be used in classrooms (1897), and, at the same meeting, James MacAllister, the Superintendent of Schools in Philadelphia, fitting the study of modern literature into the general aims and objects of education.

According to the *Nation*, in a Note on the second meeting in 1886, such pedagogical discussions by members of this "union of the younger philological scholars and teachers of literature" were necessary because faculties had as yet given an "imperfect recognition" to study of the vernaculars and therefore to the question of "what constitutes a systematic course in the modern languages."[1] A dozen years later (1898), C. Alphonso Smith, then of the University of Louisiana, recalled that the organizers of the Association had

> found the modern language forces wholly unorganized; there was no centre, no cooperation; teachers in adjoining States or in the same State knew nothing of one another's methods except by the most casual intercourse. Able teachers were, of course, found here and there, but Modern Language instruction was not

receiving, nor seemed likely to receive, the academic reputation that it merited; and scientific research, with a few exceptions, was practically unknown.[2]

Smith seems to have thought that, in his day, the purpose of MLA was "by united effort to establish a centre of correct information for the settlement of questions relating to the Modern Languages and Literatures." Since he wanted this information for advanced students as well as teachers (p. 240), Smith was probably thinking of historical and grammatical material, not of speculation about classroom techniques. And indeed at the meeting which drew the comment from the *Nation*, H. E. Shepherd, of the College of Charleston, commenting on a paper by F. V. N. Painter, of Roanoke College, on recent educational movements and modern language study,[3] though admitting the paper's "intrinsic merit," dismissed it as having "no relation to any of the absorbing topics of modern philology."[4]

For Shepherd, that is, an association devoted to modern language study should construe its work quite narrowly as that of developing or discovering information about the modern languages and, possibly, their literatures. Probably he would have accepted Franklin Carter's phrasing of the contemporary conception of philology: the construction, etymology and history of the words in the modern lexicons, the study of each modern language—"its parentage, its modification of roots, its revolutions and complete evolution."[5] Only on such a firm developmental foundation, it was thought, could modern language studies be raised to the academic status of their classical forebears and rivals.

By the beginning of the nineties, the regard for teaching or talking about it among members of the Association had dwindled to such an extent that Edward S. Joynes, of the University of South Carolina, in a paper justifying reading knowledge as an object of foreign language study, felt obliged to acknowledge "the fitness of the reference of [his] paper to the Pedagogical Section," rather than to the general membership, and to express the hope that the Section "may more and more engage hereafter the attention and sympathy of the Association."[6]

Members must have become satisfied quite early (and perhaps easily) with the "systematic" courses they were putting together. Or, to follow the *Nation*, they came to feel secure enough in academic society and culture that they were able to put aside any questions about teaching that might from time to time catch their attention. Evidently the reputation of modern language study was on the way to being secured by 1891, when Landon Garland, the chancellor of Vanderbilt, announced, "The modern languages are now studied in [Vanderbilt] as Latin, Greek and mathematics are studied, for the purpose of mental discipline." They were even being "assigned an equal portion of [the students'] time."[7] No wonder, then, that in 1904 Alexander R. Hohlfeld, a professor of German at Wisconsin, who became president of the Association in 1913, could signal that the battle for "educational recognition" of modern language study (which had begun at Yale in 1828) was over.

Hohlfeld found part of his evidence in the "rapid, almost too rapid, decrease in the proportion of general or pedagogical papers" in the *Publications*. In the first volume, nine of seventeen papers had been devoted to pedagogy. After the first three volumes, the public interest of members in teaching and its problems was satisfied by one or two articles a volume. In the volumes from 1892 to 1896 there are no pedagogical articles; after that it seems to have become the duty or task of presidents of the Association to pay respect to teaching, though the *Proceedings* of the annual meetings record some discussions of teaching. Members, Hohlfeld said, were able to "see clearly to what extent the pedagogical ideal was then [in the early issues] over-shadowing the research ideal." Hohlfeld approved this triumph of "learning." But he was apprehensive too, because of the problems he saw would rise out of the "the frequent incompatibility of the claims of elementary instruction and advanced research," and he urged his colleagues to attend to "the wise and careful adjustment of the divergent interests of more or less elementary instruction and original research," which, he asserted, "constitutes the greatest problem now confronting the modern American university."[8]

In 1907 O. F. Emerson, also of Cornell, who was then president of the Central Division of the Association, and who would become president of the Association itself in 1923, commented on the shift in PMLA from pedagogical to scholarly articles. He echoed Hohlfeld by acknowledging the fact "that the college instructor lags behind [Whom? The high school teacher?] in methods of presentation." However much he may have been troubled by that perception, Emerson could only see that "exclusive devotion" to questions of pedagogy "would be manifestly improper" for members of an association such as he was addressing. "It is reason for congratulation," he added, "that the later volumes of the *Publications* have been given over largely to advancing our knowledge in hitherto unexplored fields."[9]

Of course "presentation" has become standard among the theoreticians of pedagogy as a synonym for "teaching," and perhaps especially among those who, for example, having worked out the topography of Tom Jones' journey from Bath to London, conceive it to be their duty (or privilege?) to impart that knowledge to young people. In O. F. Emerson's day, "methods" probably referred to nothing more complicated than, say, recitation, lecture, discussion, and seminar. And pedagogical questions would likely have been limited to matters of style in the classroom: how to phrase recitation questions to stimulate the full attention of students, or to antagonize them into alertness; how to emphasize the "points" of a lecture by gesture, intonation, variety in pace; how to arrange the material of a lecture so as to make note-taking easy, and take into account the inevitably early exhaustion of student concentration; how to "lead" a discussion, keep it going, make sure that no one shirks or becomes a monopolist.

Such questions suggest how wrong a direction was given the teaching-talk at the early meetings of MLA, or maybe they suggest how direction-less the discussion was to be. For of course there is a question that is—or ought to be—prior to those that have to do only with style or quality ("effectiveness") of performance. That question concerns the substance of what young people are expected to learn; or, at least, of what they are taught. Was it sensible to say, as Francis March did in 1892,

> This Anglo-Saxon study, delightful and important in itself to specialists, seems also to be necessary for a solid and learned support to the study of Modern English in college. The early professors [ca. 1875] had no recondite learning applicable to English, and did not know what to do in classes in it. They can now make English as hard as Greek.[10]

One of the happy hours in the early years of MLA occurred at the meeting of 1902, when James Wilson Bright, of Hopkins, declared that the Association had been freed of "the foreign fencing-master and dancing-master with the super-added 'arts' of the 'tongues' . . ." and congratulated his remaining colleagues because they had not yielded "to the allurements of becoming a Gild of Barbers." As the apparent refer-ence to the miracle at Pentecost (Acts 2.1–4) suggests, Bright enjoyed using a somewhat donnish wit; in this case, for his presidential address, he was retelling what he called the "unwritten history" of the Associa-tion.

Besides the foreigners, who merely taught their native tongues, there were two other groups that, Bright thought, were not properly members of MLA, or of the association it was trying to become. The first con-sisted of those who had been "concerned in founding or finding here a Teachers' Agency." The second group was "a known class of advocates of 'methods of teachings [sic].'" Bright admitted the need to know and follow "methods of imparting knowledge." But he had in mind "over-zealous teachers," who went further and "expostulated" that, if "method and knowledge" cannot both be had, then "one should at least have method."

That sounds like normal school doctrine; and if Bright heard it from any significant number of members, the fact simply confirms how ill-defined were the membership requirements, to say nothing of the job description, for the modern language guild. In any case, those who were taking control of the Association felt—in Bright's view correctly—that the "temperament of such systematicians" was "essentially incompatible with that of the scholar, and this conviction, in view of the cherished purpose of the organization, was happily sufficient to insure their gentle but unflinching suppression."[11]

When Bright spoke in 1902, "the cherished purpose of the organization," as given in the third clause of the original constitution, was merely "advancement of the study of the Modern Languages." It remained in that form through 1903. But in 1902 the secretary (C. H. Grandgent, Harvard) called "attention to the inadequacy of the present constitution of the Association," and the General Meeting "voted that the Executive Council be requested to report at the next meeting a plan for the revision of the constitution" (*PMLA*, 18, p. v). At the meeting of 1903, the Council presented the following clause:

> The object of this Association shall be the advancement of the study of the Modern Languages and their Literatures through the publication of the results of investigations by members, and through the presentation and discussion of papers at an annual meeting. (*PMLA*, 19, p. x)

From the floor W. H. Carruth, of Kansas, moved to insert after "Literatures" the words "through the promotion of friendly relations among scholars" (p. xii). The clause was passed as amended. It remained in effect through 1928, when the Executive Council was asked to simplify it to "The object of the Association shall be the advancement of the study of the modern languages and their literatures," but in fact presented the General Meeting with "The object of the Association shall be the advancement of research in the modern languages and their literatures" (*PMLA*, 43, p. xxxiii). The clause stood in that form until the end of the forties and W. R. Parker's term as executive secretary. But those later developments direct attention away from the formative controversies, which are the subject here. (The constitution is printed in the *Proceedings* of the Association, which are printed in the volumes of PMLA for the years after the ones when the business was done.)

Speaking in 1902, Bright had said of the original purpose clause ("advancement of the study of the Modern Languages"): "That is brief and to the point, if you please; or, if you prefer, it is comprehensive and points everywhere. . . ." Since revision was coming, he went on to suggest a text that would express "the simple yet lofty purpose of this Association." That purpose, Bright said, "was philological, and a concise and technically adequate modification of that third section of the constitution would therefore be 'the advancement of the philological study of modern life and culture,' or this, 'the advancement of philology in the departments of the modern languages.'"[12] Bright seems not to have noticed that his first version refers to educational policy, his second only to departmental politics.

Perhaps the comprehensiveness of early modern language study was best illustrated by an anecdote about James Russell Lowell told by Barrett Wendell in *A Literary History of America*. (I have also borrowed the subjunctive "were" in "were best illustrated" from Wendell; it is his persistent usage for Present English "would be.") According to Wendell, "not long ago" (i.e., around 1900) two former students of Lowell's met—in Harvard Square, I presume, since one of them, "an eminent philologist," was carrying a copy of the *Song of Roland*. Carried back twenty-five years to heaven knows what memories of Olivant winding away at Roncesvalles, the unprofessional exclaimed "rather enthusiastically: 'How Lowell used to give us the spirit of that!'—'Yes,' replied the other . . . and that was *all* he gave us.'" To which Wendell added, with clear disdain for the professional's values:

> In which emphatic little adjective [sic] is implied the place which the study of literature has now assumed. This range of human expression has been discovered, it has been enjoyed, an attempt has been made to understand its spirit, and now, if we are to keep pace with scholarship, we must pitilessly analyze its every detail.[13]

Lowell was president of MLA between 1887 and his death in 1891. He was a poet, an editor and a diplomat—a man or gentleman of letters, who, according to Wendell, saw himself above all as an interpreter of "the great modern masters" (p. 394), not as an investigator of their language forms. To many in MLA his urbane humanism must have seemed anachronistic, as indeed it was. Or at least the obituary speech, at the meeting of 1892, now seems designed as much to explain Lowell's understanding of the role of modern language teacher as to pay him tribute.

The speech was given by James Morgan Hart, of Cornell, who felt obliged as representative of "an organized body of instructors . . . to tell the world in general what Lowell was to us in especial."[14] Lowell was a scholar, Hart said, "a truly representative American scholar," in the old-fashioned sense of one who "read both widely and closely," and who directed his reading by a "vision" of the "eternal verities enshrined in the best books of the best men." To sum up Lowell's values, Hart turned to a couple of passages from his presidential address to MLA in 1890, in which he had expressed some feelings against a "tendency" of the time "to value literature and even poetry for their usefulness as courses of modern philosophy or metaphysics, or as exercises to put and keep the mental muscles in training." Lowell accepted that, to his audience, the "highest praise" for a book is that it makes readers think. But he offered them, as "next highest praise," the engaging idea that a book also "ransoms us from thought." Lowell must have sensed that some of his hearers would not have accepted the notion of escape through reading, even when it came in his graceful figure. For he added,

> Culture, which means the opening and refining of the faculties, is an excellent thing, perhaps the best, but there are other things to be had of the Muses, which are also good in their kind. Refined pleasure is refining pleasure too, and teaches something in her way, though she be no proper school-dame. (pp. 25–27)

More succinctly, but again in Hart's words, Lowell had two criticisms of the direction members of MLA were giving their work. The first was that they were emphasizing "the acquisition of a language" (chiefly information about it, the breaking of vowels in Old French, for example, or Grimm's and Verner's Laws for the Germanic languages) at the expense of "the enjoyment of the literary treasures locked up in that language." The second fear was that they "were making literature itself too much of a study and not enough of a pleasure" (p. 27).

The issue that Lowell was addressing was stated to MLA at the meeting of 1884, by Theodore W. Hunt, of Princeton. Since he was professor of Rhetoric and of the English Language—and a Ph.D. besides—Hunt would have had a mind that was both well disciplined and stocked with much proper furniture. If Lowell had three fears, Hunt saw three erroneous conceptions of English literature, which weakened its claim to be a fit subject for collegiate study.

First was the belief "that English literature is a subject for the desultory reader in his leisure hours rather than an intellectual study for serious workers." The second was "that it ranks as an accomplishment only." The third error was "that the terms literary and philosophic are mutually exclusive." These errors "have been strengthened," Hunt added, "by the superficial methods on which the subject has been taught in most of our institutions."[15] (I have omitted a comma after *philosophic*.)

For Hunt those "superficial methods" resulted from the undeveloped, unspecialized form that English had to take in a curriculum still dominated by what Eliot, welcoming MLA to Cambridge in 1889, called the "ancient subjects of academic study."[16] Hunt was looking forward to the day when the Classics, Mathematics, and Philosophy—Eliot's "ancient subjects"—would have to yield some space in the timetable for "enlargement of the collegiate course in English," which by itself, Hunt said, would "correct all this," that is, the errors he complained of (p. 126).

It is significant that Hunt spoke only of "enlargement." Like others in the period (for example, Charles F. Thwing in *American Colleges: Their Students and Their Work*, New York: G.P. Putnam's Sons, 1878, especially the chapter on Instruction), Hunt seems to have been willing to postpone consideration of the nature of the subject English as an instrument of education and to concentrate simply on getting it its fair share of the students' time. He and his like must have supposed that enlarging the numbers giving and taking English would somehow lead to a rational approach to the study of the language and literature of England. Or rather, as will be seen from what follows, they must have supposed they already had a rational approach, a deadly gift from the classicists, and simply wanted to be allowed to use it.

III

And of course time would prove Hunt right. "Enlargement" was to be enough. For in a few years after Hunt spoke (1884) eager "investigators" would have turned up enough "productive research" (Hohlfeld, pp. xxxi–xxxii), enough knowledge—or at least information—to fill any and all slots that could be imagined and budgeted. Meanwhile Hunt, at Princeton, evidently had to think of cramming the study of English literature into two hours a week for a single term. Hunt was struck by the inadequacy of such an allotment. Even just "the grand department of English Prose Authors" would require more time. And when Hunt considered the golden realm of English poetry, his mind teemed with subject matter, most of it quite justifying Lowell's fears. "What a host of topics," he cried,

> historical, linguistic, legendary, poetic and rhetorical—gather about such a poem as the Faerie Queen or Comus! What deep and broad-reaching questions of theology, metaphysics, social economy and [finally!] literature center in The Essay on Man! Who could study the Dunciad and not make himself familiar with a vast amount of English biography and history? The study of the great forms of poetry, of the principles of poetic art, of the leading causes of style as illustrated in English classics, of the influences of other literatures upon the English—the study of such germinal topics as these, now necessarily passed with discursive [i.e. "cursory"] comment, would by the readjustment of [the time given to] the course receive something like the attention they deserve. (p. 127; the titles are not italicized.)

Considering that array of topics—most of them having only a collateral relation to the nature and comprehension of literary works, it is easy to imagine how keenly Hunt must have felt what he called "the demand of the English in common with that of some other studies": "Give us a fair place in the general adjustment" (p. 122).

Touching language, Hunt said that, with time, students could be made

> substantially conversant with First English Philology in Cædmon, Bêowulf and Alfred; to study its characteristics and structure; to mark its transition through the middle English of Layamon and Langlande [sic] to Chaucer and Spenser; to mark the great historical periods of Modern English from the Elizabethan to the Victorian; to study it in its relation to other Teutonic tongues—in fine to take up for the first [time?] or more minutely a thousand questions on which the college student should be informed and in virtual ignorance of which he is, at present, compelled to graduate. (p. 127)

Hart also suggested that college courses in English would be improved if there could be developed and made available to students various reference works; for example, a handbook of English metres, some sort of discussion of the foreign relations of English, and a general history of England designed for the student of literature. What was needed, Hart said, was "a general essay upon those social, legal, political and religious movements which have engaged and affected the cultured classes, the school and university life of England during and since Chaucer's day."

He wanted the book to include material on the contrast between town and country, between small towns and London, between universities and grammar schools, between the aristocracy, including the gentry, and the bourgeoisie, between church and dissenters, including Catholics.[17]

Listening to Hunt and Hart, the Nation's "union of the younger philological scholars and teachers of literature" must have been pleasantly satisfied with their new organization, which, they could see, was already providing a base or forum from which, by making their case in public, they could get around the Maginot Line of "the ancient subjects of academic study" and assure themselves of what Hunt called "an equitable position among other important linguistic and literary studies" (p. 121). Hunt and Hart were asserting that English (and other modern languages) constituted a study with an intellectual and disciplinary value that entitled its practitioners to a place of power in curricular governance. "The question," Hunt said, "is, will the classics as taught in our colleges make any concessions of their amount of time to the modern languages appealing for such time?" (p. 121)

It took an administrator (William Pepper, M.D., the provost at Pennsylvania) to make explicit the role of MLA in the great controversy in academic politics and, if you will, educational theory that was going on at the time; indeed, had been going on since 1828, when some at Yale proposed shifting from the "dead" to the modern languages, so as to open the curriculum to "the interests of modern history, of social, political and natural sciences and of English" (Hunt, p. 121, citing Eliot's intentions).

In his welcome to the meeting of 1887, Pepper acknowledged that members came together—"in their publications and annual meetings"—"to confer as to the history and structure and literature of these languages, as to their true educational values and position, and as to the best methods to be used in teaching them." But Pepper seems to have been unwilling to leave MLA in so aseptic a role and went on to charge the Association with the revolutionary duty of redressing the balance of power in the old academic world. Pepper told members that they represented "a new and aggressive force in education; you are the leaders in the attack now being made on the stronghold of the classicists," an attack not made in any "ruthless or destructive spirit," but still an attack "to urge the claims of the great modern languages . . ."[18]

Pepper went on to assert, "Not only in the learned professions, but in every branch of our marvellously complicated commercial and industrial life, do we need men able to grasp instantly the new thoughts and facts which each day develop in whatever part of the world, and carefully trained to observe and think correctly and to express their opinions" (p. 6). Was it, then, that modern language teachers were to achieve their proper places in faculties, their proper share of student-time only to find themselves in the service of the world, not training governors for the *polis*, but only managers of factories in Youngstown, plantations in Hawaii? Many members must have asked themselves if they were to play Esau to the Jacob of the industrial-commercial system?

Today, the visions of Hunt and Hart may strike many with incredulity, but that is only because modern course-making may be even less principled than the original process—mitosis of the original one-celled "study," the transformation of Hunt's "topics" into courses—that went on in the last third of the nineteenth century. But as one who endured the English then developed, I can testify that Hunt and Hart were no waking dreamers, but authentic visionaries. They saw the future; and, ungainly though it was, it worked, and for a good many years.

I know it best as it developed at Harvard, and so I shall begin the next section by showing "enlargement" as it happened there.

IV

In 1869, the year of Eliot's election to the presidency, no English was offered among the required first year "studies" at Harvard. ("Studies" became numbered "courses" in 1870–71 and were attached to the various professors in 1872–73.) In the sophomore year Elocution and Themes were required; Child's Anglo-Saxon could be elected. Forensics (descended from Roman *controversiae*, I suppose) were required in the junior year.[19]

Five years later in 1874–75, there were still only three undergraduate courses, all given by Child. One of them was in the history of the language and elements of Anglo-Saxon; the second was called "Anglo-Saxon and Early English." *Beowulf* was studied in it, along with a book of Old English *Sprachproben* (*Language exercises*). But the course was bracketed in 1874–75. The third course covered Chaucer, Shakespeare, Bacon, Milton and Dryden.

After another five years, in 1879–80, there were seven advanced elective courses for undergraduates. Child was still giving the survey, if it may be called so. But he had split Shakespeare off for separate treatment. He was using Sweet's *Anglo-Saxon Reader* in a third course, and the *Sprachproben* in a fourth. Adams Sherman Hill, since 1876 the Boylston Professor of Rhetoric, in succession to Child, was giving "Principles of Literary Criticism," in connection with "English Literature of the Eighteenth and Nineteenth Centuries." He was also giving English 5 and 6, which had to do with rhetoric as practiced in themes and oral discussion.

By 1896–97 a dozen or so composition courses were on offer, including one for graduate students. The "study" of literature had undergone considerable subdivision into specialized courses. There was a "History and Development of English Literature," in which seven men had their hands. In addition there were half-courses in the periods of English Literature, the termini of which were generally marked by somebody's death; for example, "From the Death of Dryden to the Death of Pope (1700–1744)."

For graduate students primarily there were half-courses in the novel from Richardson to Eliot, and in the romantic poets, including Scott, both given by Hill. There were also half-courses in historical English grammar, in the history and principles of English versification, in "Anglo-Saxon.—Beowulf" and "Anglo-Saxon.—Caedmon, Cynewulf," in fifteenth- and sixteenth-century literature in relation to Italian and Spanish literature, in the English and Scottish popular ballads (for graduates only), in criticism since the sixteenth century, in drama from the miracle plays to the closing of the theaters, in Spenser, and in the works of Shakespeare. In an interesting early example of cross-departmental work, the economist F. W. Taussig, assisted by four members of the English Department, offered a half-course titled "Oral Discussion of Topics in History and Economics."[20]

There are hints of a chronological arrangement, which presupposes a theory of development. But the coverage is hardly worked out. Presumably completeness would come as men turned up who could deal with the missing periods. The precedence given the language in the titles of the two Anglo-Saxon courses probably reflects the philological interests of those who began "English." Some today may find periodization by deaths amusing. Others may wonder why one course was in "Spenser," while another was in "The Works of Shakespeare." Does the difference in titles reflect a difference in "approach"? It seems unlikely. On the whole, the list seems accidental, the product of shifting interests in the faculty; it leaves an impression of unreality in the whole enterprise. But plainly Hunt's great vision of 1884 (above, p. 42) was already on the way to being realized. By the end of the nineteenth century English at Harvard was well advanced in that enlargement which would see it go "from a humble handmaid of homiletics to one of the greatest departments— perhaps the very greatest—administered by the Faculty of Arts and Sciences."[21]

But that very development to greatness meant the final collapse, in practice, of the ancient value system that had informed education, or at any rate, educational thought, since classical times. Perhaps the school year 1883–84 is a good date for the end of classical liberal studies, except as referred to in decanal and presidential addresses. In that year Eliot was finally "able to announce the 'practical completion of a development which had begun sixty years ago'" (Morison, *Development*, p. 346). That is, the temporary subjugation of the curriculum at Harvard to the elective system, or to the whims and transient interests of immature students and specialist professors.

With more and more courses open to election, there was a corresponding weakening of the ancient notion that as a man's mind is properly disciplined and furnished by study of the classical poets, orators, philosophers and historians, along with some mathematics and natural science, it will gain the "power, richness, and openness to ideas" that constitute "a liberally educated man." Now the head of the nation's oldest university was insisting to all and sundry "that it did not really matter what you studied [so long as the subjects were "cultural" not vocational or technological], provided you were interested" (Morison, *Three Centuries*, p. 342).

This is by no means to say that there was not life in the old theory yet. Two years after Eliot's declaration of educational emancipation, James Russell Lowell, of the Class of 1838, devoted his speech at the ceremonies marking the 250th anniversary of the founding of Harvard College to a survey of modern language studies. Shaped as he would have been in "'knowledge, skills and habits of thought' that are 'of general and lasting intellectual significance,'"[22] Lowell can be expected to have felt some uncertainty about literary studies done in the fashion of German philologists. He did acknowledge that a debt was owed them, but wondered "is there no danger of their misleading us into pedantry?" Then he mentioned the editor (Henry Alfred Todd, an associate in Romance Languages at Hopkins) of an Old French romance (by Guillaume de Dole; it was printed in *PMLA*, 2), who had spent two and a half years with Gaston Paris, the great philologist, and had got through only the first three vowels of the Romance alphabet. Such a tale made Lowell think he could see "a tendency to train young men in the language as if they were all to be editors, and not lovers of polite literature."[23]

The opposition seems pretty complete, radical in the sense of involving fundamental differences. In Lowell it was between "letters" and "scholarship," between cultivation and pedantry, between knowing fully "what is truly literature"—limited by Professor Popkin, of the Class of 1792, to the Greeks (pp. 208–09)—and, in the words of H. C. G. Brandt, professor of French and German at Hamilton, "the historical scientific study of language, Beowulf and Chaucer."[24] To complicate matters, some in MLA were uneasy about the gradual specifying of "philology" from—in the words of H. C. G. von Jagemann, a Germanic philologist at Harvard—"the study of the whole range of human culture, of all the products of the human mind" to "the study of language" alone.[25] What they feared, of course, was the study of human speech alone—and of a demotic sort at that—unattended by any concern for the history of man, as revealed in the canonical books of the literary-historical tradition.

I want to return to Hunt's scheme for enlarged English, for it gives at least a hint of actual practices in the time, what was going on underneath all the great justificatory language. In the first place, Hunt wanted to "remand" the first year of college English to the schools, giving them

46

the history of the language, the etymology and structure of English, study of "the composite elements of the English vocabulary," and the study of English literature since Bacon, to furnish the minds of children with "the primary facts of historical English literature" (pp. 124–25). The facts having been gathered (or infused) in school, college study could advance "to something like the process of generalization. The inductive principle in literary study is as valuable as it is in other realms . . ." (pp. 125–26).

Nor would that be all. With elementary studies out of the way and generalizations about language and literature at hand, from lower division courses, English teachers of upper division courses could turn themselves to "a more advanced order of work." They could go beyond mere history and develop "philosophical and critical methods" that would let the study of English "rise from a somewhat formal examination of phraseology and structure to a real philosophical study of the tongue in its content and its great linguistic changes, its inner spirit, and its possibilities." As a consequence of that "rise," the study of literature "would become critical and comprehensive in distinction from being merely chronological" (p. 125).

But what a long rise it would have to be. From school-study of roots and stems (in the manner of "Root's roots" at Princeton, sixty years and more ago?), affixes, vowel mutation, and the rest to squirreling away "the primary facts of historical English literature," from which to derive, inductively (by simple enumeration, I suspect) the principles controlling the development of the language; then finally to philosophical questions about the meaning of it all.

V

The question to be asked, I suppose, is whether teachers and professors of modern languages have ever escaped the dead hand of the classical system, to ask, as Lowell did at Harvard in 1886:

> What and to what end should a university aim to teach now and here in this America of ours whose meaning no man can yet comprehend? And when we have settled what it is best to teach, comes the further question, How are we to teach it? (p. 216)

Lowell found alternative and conflicting ends. Should the university develop character? Mark Hopkins and a student on either end of a log. Or should it prepare students to make a living? Lowell, true to his classical heritage and training, said he would choose the former, if the two ends are necessarily incompatible (p. 217).

To put it another way, in all the discussion at the early meetings of MLA, did members ever develop a philosophy of modern language study that took into account the "modern" in the name? Remember that the original staples of modern language study were modern only in the sense that they were not classical, what Alphonso Smith called "fundamental courses," such as Old and Middle English, Old Norse, Old French, Old High German, and the like. In 1875, Smith reminded members of MLA, only twenty-three institutions were giving instruction in Old English. Michigan, Dartmouth, Princeton and Vanderbilt (founded in 1872) did not offer it. When he spoke (1899), however, Smith could say that a college that did not offer Old English and Chaucer was the exception (pp. 255, 264).

I think the record gives only the problems that were discussed or at least talked over. The first of these was to devise a formula that would allow members to surround themselves with whatever protection the teacher's role would give their privatized professional duties. The second question involved the reputation and, more or less accidentally, the nature of the subject and the ends for which it should be taught. I have touched on and perhaps disposed of the first problem in the opening section of this paper. But that was some pages ago, and it may be well to recall the solution worked out by A. R. Hohlfeld at the meeting of 1904.

Hohlfeld was speaking on the teaching of the history of a foreign literature. His subject, he said, perhaps in apology, was "primarily" related to members' "work as teachers and only indirectly to [their] interests in productive research." Though Hohlfeld thought his subject needed no justification, he proceeded by telling his audience that theirs was not an organization of "investigators" only, but rather, he offered ("I might say"), one "primarily of teachers." Then taking a line that was to become familiar, Hohlfeld defined a teacher as a specialist "in some one movement, or author or problem, which he tries to know thoroughly and in regard to which he endeavors to keep abreast of the latest theories and developments," looking perhaps "to sound scholarly production" (pp. xxxi–xxxii). Thus, by stipulation, was created the scholar-teacher.

The second question—about the reputation and, tangentially, the nature of modern language study—took the peculiar shape it did because, in the beginning at least, the study of English and the other modern and contemporary vernaculars was conceived as part of a single department of language and literature (Hunt, p. 122). The notion of specializing undergraduate instruction according to the scholarly interests of the faculty had not been invented, or at most was still aborning. Even an enterpriser like Theodore Hunt seems to have been able to think only of the large divisions of the curriculum (or possibly, of knowledge) that were being used "among the most advanced students of modern education"; namely, "Science, Philosophy, Language and Literature" (p. 118). Hunt knew that, within the language and literature "branch" of the students' time, English had no great place or esteem. Among "the educators and the educated public" of the day, it was at best an open question when and how English could be fitted into a still relatively unspecialized curriculum; at worst English was in a place of "decided inferiority," or even that of a "cipher" (p. 122). Yet Hunt could think only of "a more equitable regime" in that third of student-time that went to the study of language and literature. He proposed dividing it into fifths, one to each of the major languages (p. 131).

English was in so sorry a state, because as something new in the curriculum, it suffered the simple institutional disrepute that accompanies any intrusion into the known. It was open, Hunt complained, to the same kind of "invidious distinction" (p. 131) as the other modern languages. In the first place there had been all those fencing- and dancing-masters that Bright had been so pleased to see purged,[26] epitomized in Lowell's "stray Frenchman [who] was caught now and then, and kept as long as he could endure the baiting of his pupils." Failing as a teacher of his native tongue, such a man "commonly turned dancing-master, a calling which public opinion seems to have put on the same intellectual level as the other."[27]

For obvious reasons, the exotics who troubled Bright and, more mildly, Lowell were not found teaching English. But Hunt could still complain about men who were given jobs in English simply because they could speak grammatically and had "a general society knowledge of the literature" (p. 119). Some of them, "still experimenting as to what their life work is to be," took English jobs, he thought, only until something better—"a higher end"—turned up. Hence departments were in the hands of men who had "no experience in conducting" a department, nor any idea of the proper "scope" of English, or the "best methods" of teaching the material. Amateurs in "a day of specialties," to which English could be "no exception," they were in the work for "mainly personal ends" (pp. 119–20). Hunt meant that they had neither professional nor institutional interests, and therefore would not enter on any scheme of department building, such as he envisioned.

In Hunt's day, the men on the inside, in "the departments of philosophy and the ancient languages," were either indifferent to the claims of English, or took a "patronizing and cynical" attitude toward them, while the amateurs of English, accepting the inferiority of the subject, neglected to urge its development. Apparently Hunt thought that both groups were equally controlled by the "habit" of underrating the vernacular and its study.

> It is not one of the "substantial and necessary" departments . . . . Its philology, it is said, takes us back to the barbarous days of the Anglo-Saxons; its literature ranks among the self-acquired accomplishments of the student rather than among the difficult and "regular" studies, while its actual expression in composition and literary criticism must be left to natural methods. (p. 120)

Answering the criticisms of the classicists and the philologists should not have tried the intellectual capacities of those like Hunt, who were trying to establish English and modern language studies generally. But some of the defenses seem quite as lunatic as the criticisms. In 1898 Alphonso Smith argued that the elaborate paradigms and subtle concentrations of meaning in the inflections of the classical languages are useful merely for training the memory. In the modern languages, getting things right makes demands rather on reasoning (pp. 247, 249). Years before (1886) Edward S. Joynes, of South Carolina College, had asserted that in English the very absence of grammatical form, inflections, and sentence-structure gives English unexampled disciplinary value. This seems to be so because the thought of the English sentence is "revealed by the entire sentence only, as a unit of expression, since the whole is not known until the sentence is done." I think Joynes meant that, lacking the guidance of inflectional endings, the student must first take in the whole thought of the sentence, then decompose it (the sentence) into its parts, rather than, as he seems to have conceived the procedure in Latin and Greek, by working out the relations of the parts of the sentence. But I really can't be sure of anything about Joynes except his comment, "Of all the languages that I have studied, the English is the most difficult that I have yet tried to understand or to teach" (p. xxx).

That defense of English language study rested upon something like a demurrer. It granted the low, decayed state of English, then asserted that English language exercises and English composition can still be instruments of discipline because the inexactness or indeterminancy of the rules simply makes it harder to achieve Good English, Englishness, the equivalent of the classicists' *hellenismos* and *latinitas*. Another defense used by W. T. Hewitt, a professor of German language and literature at Cornell, in 1884, construed "discipline" first in a narrow sense, as found in classical studies, referring to "grammatical study, viz. the power to define at once and accurately any part of speech, the use of any mood or case, the etymology and history of any word, and its differentiation in meaning from its synonyms."[28] It's an odd assortment of notions that Hewitt gathered together under "grammatical study." Perhaps Hewitt expected his audience to make up the system from his reminders.

For Hewitt, however, such practice operations involved only "mental training"; or really, it seems to me, stocking the memory and strengthening recall. Hewitt felt that "discipline" should also be used more broadly to refer to translation and appreciation of literary works. He was arguing against those in the Association who would have emphasized the "language" in its name. He, therefore, asserted, "The study of language must be subordinate [to] the study of the thoughts of an author, and the intellectual enlargement and expansion which comes from it" (p. 34). "Intellectual enlargement and expansion" is not very precise; no doubt that very imprecision is the source of the power of the phrase, though the suggestion of muscles developing with use would of course contribute to the effect.

At the meeting of 1886, James M. Garnett, an M.A., who was a professor of English language and literature at Virginia, spoke on the disciplinary value of the English course, which he found in the study of English grammar. The pronouns, he said, "afford a wider field for linguistic training, especially the personal pronouns, which have preserved most inflections, and which become more interesting as the pupil learns more about them." Even better is the English verb system, especially the classification into weak and strong, or in school parlance regular and irregular. Garnett wanted "irregular" banished from school lingo, apparently thinking that working out the vowel series of the strong verbs would provide good mental discipline, a notion that is not without foundation.[29]

It is hard to believe that a professor of English language and literature at Virginia could have supposed that such exercises encouraged even mental, let alone intellectual, discipline, and that they should be kept on with, even though children might not be interested (p. 69). But the record is clear. And in the discussion following Garnett's paper, James W. Bright—who, it may be remembered, was to become president of the Association in 1902, and who taught at Hopkins—expressed agreement with Garnett's general point, "that English *does* furnish discipline" (Bright's emphasis). Indeed, for Bright, any subject, if it's studied correctly, will have a training effect. "Even if one were to take the dialect of the Fiji Islands and make a study of it, he would have in his hands a means of discipline." Then, perhaps becoming a bit aware of what he was doing to English, to say nothing of Garnett's argument, Bright added, "Much more evident would this be in the case of more cultivated languages."[30] I shall not comment on the naiveté of that "more cultivated."

Bright may have been poking a little fun at the disciplinarians. In 1902, discussing the "unwritten history" of MLA, he complained about those who, seeking a method and substance for English teachers, made "hard" a synonym for "disciplinary," and who therefore urged that English be taught as Greek and Latin were. The result, Bright said, was "the most foolish methods that ever brought ridicule upon any study" (p. lv). Of course Bright's speech came six years after he brought up the "dialect" of the Fiji Islands, and he may have had a chance to change his mind about discipline. Whatever the case with Bright, others accepted the idea of a relation between required effort and disciplinary value, irrespective of the significance of the instrument.

In 1890 E. H. Babbitt, of Columbia, instructing members on the object of modern language study, used the conventional definition of "mental discipline" as "the exercise of some faculty of the mind which results in increasing the power or readiness of that faculty." Then he noticed that modern language studies were supplanting classics because educators were beginning to accept "that a certain amount of work properly done by a certain faculty of the mind will give about the same increase in strength and readiness, whether the work be done in ancient or modern languages, or mathematics, or history, or science."[31]

Babbitt's figure, based on principles of industrial efficiency, is a neat example of the humanist habit of raiding a scientific—or in this case semi-scientific—system in search of conceptions sufficiently general in phrasing so as to be usable to shore up current teaching practices, or theoretical rationalizations thereof. I hesitate to call it a truth universally acknowledged that such maneuvers occur in periods of uncertainty or decline. But Babbitt does seem to have been seeking some "extramural" idea that would strengthen and preserve "mental discipline" as an object of education, while breaking its ancient ties to the classical languages and literatures.

The perdurability of "mental discipline" as an educational notion or—to be kind—principle is surely a wonder of history, at least of academic history. By the time MLA members took it up to help them create an academic reputation for themselves, it seems to have been on its way out. With the right sort of tinkering, however, members could still feel comfortable with it. Just as no academic ever asked how learning (and reciting) the paradigms of Greek and Latin might contribute to the development of Englishness, or how translating from or into Greek and Latin would develop control of the received forms and norms of style in English and other modern languages, so in this debate no one asked how study, abstracted from use and living purpose, of the grammar and standard forms of the native tongue (in the schooled dialect) could contribute to education. Indeed, in all the talk at these early meetings of MLA, I have been unable to find any questions about the nature of modern language study in its own terms. The discussants simply took the classical model for granted and devoted themselves to asserting their natural claim to the great inheritance.

Generally MLA members based their claim on the character-forming, cultural value of studying modern literary works, bearers, in F. V. N. Painter's words, of "what is best in human thought" and so a means for producing a present-day "perfect man" (p. 90). Horatio S. White, who though but an A.B., was still professor of German language and literature at Cornell, made the same point a year later (1887) in language of more splendor, though hardly of greater clarity. Teachers in modern languages, he said, cannot expect to spend their time preparing specialists, as is done in German universities. They must rather expect that their "labors must be consumed in helping large numbers of students to gain such a vantage ground of vision that their sympathies will be permanently enlarged, and their intellectual life possess a generous and catholic range whose influence will touch distant circles which we can never directly reach, but which ought to share whatever diversities of gifts a university may have at its command." White asked, "Is there any better method of advancing this aim than the careful and sympathetic study of the noblest expressions of modern literary thought?"[32]

What a lot of ideas, of varying degrees of compatibility, could then be brought together, in a simulacrum of argument, all to the end of finding for modern language study ends or objects which would clothe them in the respectability of the one systematic study of literature and language that the speakers all knew—because they had all been through it—classical philology. In his presidential address in 1897, A. S. Cook, of Yale,[33] claimed for the province of English philology "the forms in which the human spirit has, in various epochs, manifested itself, especially through the medium of literature." But since Cook asserted that philology must include the "phenomenal" as well as the "noumenal," I take it that he wanted to say that the human spirit expresses itself in the forms of language too, thus dignifying elementary language study. "The ideal philologist," Cook said, "is at once antiquary, palaeographer, grammarian, lexicologist, expounder critic, historian of literature, and, above all, lover of humanity" (pp. 195–96). What an "ascent" (p. 195) is there, in that wild collection of skills and competencies, all to be held together by loving humanity and taking the *logos* in "philology" in the largest sense (p. 202), as referring to learning and literature, not just to word or speech. The arguments used to defend modern language study were all derived from those used centuries before in discussions of the question that had riven Greek educational thought: in the words of A. S. Cook, are virtue and wisdom to be taught directly, or do they come as a secondary effect of the acquisition of knowledge, including knowledge of their natures (pp. 185–89)? Of course I don't mean that members of MLA were themselves dealing with that question, only that one of their defenses assumed that pretty direct moral and ethical effects follow upon the study of Great Books.

The result was that the defense of modern language study became spiritualized. As Morton Easton put it in 1888, undergraduate modern language study has to include a lexical and grammatical component, but only to assure competent translation. Easton worked at the University of Pennsylvania, which seems to have been sufficiently unspecialized—or understaffed—for him to have been both professor of comparative literature and instructor in French. Presumably it was as instructor that he encountered grammar and vocabulary work. Perhaps it was in his role as professor that he worked out the grand defense that made the drudge work tolerable, or at least fit for the course lists of colleges. Easton's line is clear: drill work is necessary to prepare students to do idiomatic translations into or from foreign languages, including standard schooled and literary English. The ability of students to produce idiomatic translations is, Easton thought, a necessary condition for conducting a modern language course "as an 'Arts' course, according to the older conception of the scope and purposes of the courses in the classical tongues."[34]

The capital and the quotation marks for "Arts" suggest that Easton wanted (in addition to borrowing the methods of the classics) to emphasize the word, so as to appropriate for modern studies all the value that remained in the belief, common among Greek aristocrats, rentiers, and philosophers, that certain lines of activity are appropriate to free men, others to slaves and artisans. Hence the division, systematized by Varro in Caesarian Rome, between *artes liberales* or *ingenuae*, which could be studied in leisure, by those who could support themselves in leisure (*scholé*), and *artes inliberales* or *sordidae*, which required expenditure of energy. Perhaps Easton had also already adopted that other ancient meaning of "art," which has been indispensable to the arguments teachers of first-year English composition have devised to bring respectability to their dubious enterprise. I refer to the notion that composing, even the composing of practice-writing in themes, can be thought of as an art, and its teaching viewed so too, because in both cases higher sorts of mentation are involved. The *locus classicus* is Barrett Wendell's *English Composition*.[35]

Evidently Easton felt that his ideas might be turning a little high for his more exacting colleagues. For he took some time to make clear that he did not intend to depreciate historical philology, especially that of the Romance and Germanic languages. At the same time, he wanted to call attention to the low state of the literary culture and to suggest—no doubt tentatively—that modern language teachers had too much aped the exact sciences, carrying on phonetic analysis without sufficient concern for meaning, describing institutions without teaching the values that clothed them. So he called upon the strict constructionists in his audience to remember, "Language is an art; it is not merely the product of certain historical factors, it is an art, and the study of its application as an art is worthy of our best energies as educators of undergraduates" (p. 21).

It is no surprise to find Easton in his peroration insisting that holders of graduate degrees must "in addition to showing a thorough knowledge of the historical development of a tongue," be able to "render a good account of the spirit of the documents involved and of their artistic or aesthetic value" (p. 23). Easton can hardly be blamed for the incongruity of his "the spirit of the documents," for of course he didn't have Panofsky's useful distinction between viewing a work of art as a "monument" and as a "document." Nor should we permit ourselves to be amused by what seems Easton's insensitivity to the nuances of the language he proposed to teach as an art. After all, it would be fifty years before Kant's *Zweckmässigkeit ohne Zweck* would get into collegiate literary studies in the United States.

Six years later (1895), J. M. Hart sturdily asserted that the study of English "should dominate everything else [in the curriculum] precisely because it is *not a study*, but the acquisition of a habit, of an art, of an indispensable gift."[36] For Hart the habit, art, gift consisted, first, of appreciating synonyms in English, a language "rich in shades of meaning, [but] singularly defective in the signs by which to recognize them"; second, of appreciating the function of word order in a largely uninflected language, which has "little or no syntax proper and in which word order counts for everything"; and third, of appreciating the importance of a "sense of form," or "saying a thing properly and effectively" (p. xv).

Since "form" is easily reduced to "forms," it would be in "sense of form" that most material for teaching and drill would be found. And Hart at once complained about students' "obtuseness to form in English expression"; somewhat harshly, he called it "unpardonable." He explained it as an American exaggeration of an Anglo-American trait, a "republican contempt of traditional etiquette—what we call the humbug of Old World ceremony." Like many after him, Hart saw himself as a more or less lone defender of standards surrounded by colleagues who "tolerate . . . if not actually encourage" students in their wayward misbehavior. Hart's situation must have been very grave indeed. He had "even known students to resent [his] correction of their misused words and uncouth sentences." Far worse, "They seemed to think that the blue-pencil or red-ink marks were a direct slur upon their statement of scientific fact" (p. xvi).

It is difficult to see a relation between red and blue correction marks and Hart's description of a study which is not a study. It is also difficult to see a relation between the defenses of modern language study that I have detailed and the enlargement of, for example, the Harvard English department that I have described (above, pp. 44–46). Did nobody notice the gap between the lofty defensive ideology and the degraded goings-on in the classroom or lecture hall, that seem to be revealed by the course titles?

There was notice but little else. In 1889 Lowell had reminded members of MLA that the time was not long, since the very languages they were teaching so "thoroughly and scientifically" had been "deemed not worthy to be taught at all except as a social accomplishment or as a commercial subsidiary" (*Study*, p. 69). But when he spoke, Lowell could note that at Harvard there were "nearly as many professors employed teaching [the modern languages] as there were students" in his day (p. 91). He could also call attention to the fact that Anglo-Saxon, Old and Middle High German, and Icelandic were being taught "in all our chief centres of learning." At Harvard Old French had a course to itself, whereas when Lowell had first become interested in its literature, the library texts appeared to him never to have been opened (p. 92). As a matter of fact, in 1886 five men were offering ten undergraduate courses in French language and literature; in addition there were four graduate courses in Provençal and Romance philology (Morison, *Three Centuries*, pp. 351–52).

In his welcome to the Association in 1901, Eliot sketched the development of the German department. In 1826, when Charles Follen was hired, he was charged with teaching the German language, ethics, and civil and ecclesiastical history. There was no other instructor in history. In 1901 the German department had three professors, eight instructors, two Austin teaching fellows, and an assistant. Follen had cost the University $500. The present bill was a little over $20,000. Eliot went on to note that in the modern language division courses were offered in English, French, German, Italian, Spanish, Celtic and Slavic.[37]

Lowell was, of course, bound to the notion that literary study was to turn out "lovers of polite literature," not editors (above, p. 46). But he seems to have been enough aware of the consequence of enlargement to feel able to hope

> that the day will come when a competent professor may lecture here also for three years [outdoing Gaston Paris by six months] on the first three vowels of the romance alphabet . . . .

Since he was speaking in Eliot's presence, he may have felt that such a hope was required of him. At least he finished the sentence with one of his antic put-downs: "and find fit audience, though few." Then more doughtily, he went on to his personal hope.

> I hope the day may never come when the weightier matter of a language, namely, such parts of its literature as have overcome death by reason of their wisdom and of the beauty in which it is incarnated, such parts as are universal by reason of their civilizing properties, their power to elevate and fortify the mind, — I hope the day may never come when these are not predominant in the teaching given here. (pp. 218–19)

The two passages are hardly consonant. The first speaks for the new specialisms of graduate training, the second for education in or by letters, which was intended to develop a cultivated citizenry. In accepting both, Lowell was reminding Eliot and the Governing Boards of the very opening of Eliot's Inaugural Address, delivered seventeen years earlier, on a "raw and cloudy afternoon" in mid-October. Before giving Eliot the insignia of office, the President of the Board of Overseers "took great pains to enter a caveat against certain kinds of 'science.'"[38] It must have seemed like a cue. For with his first words Eliot tossed aside the educational assumptions that grounded the warning. For a half-century, American colleges had been bedeviled by what Eliot called "the endless controversies whether language, philosophy, mathematics or science supply the best mental training, whether general education should be chiefly literary or chiefly scientific." Those controversies, he now proclaimed, "have no practical lesson for us."

> This University recognizes no real antagonism between literature and science, and consents to no such narrow alternatives as mathematics or science, science or metaphysics. We would have them all, and at their best.

Eliot meant to settle the controversies over the ends and means of education by the simple expedient of preserving at least the words for the ancient ends while finding money to pay for both old and new means. "The only conceivable aim of a college government in our day," he said, "is to broaden, deepen, and invigorate American teaching in all branches of learning."[39] So Eliot stepped into his role of *amplificator imperii*, as Morison called him, translating the phrase as "an enlarger of the intellectual empire" (*Three Centuries*, p. 344). Morison's "intellectual" may be somewhat generous and needs to be qualified by a couplet from Barrett Wendell's "De Praesede Magnifico," his Phi Beta Kappa poem for 1909, the year of Eliot's retirement. Of Eliot Wendell said,

> He loved statistics – never seemed to care,
> So we got freshmen, who they were.[40]

And of course it was those faceless, placeless, in Wendell's view, nearly nameless students who would make possible new subjects in an expanded course list. Eliot and the times brought them in increasing numbers. In the first decade of his presidency, enrollments in Harvard College increased by only 3.7 percent, much less than those of other comparable colleges. Presumably they were held back by public uneasiness over Eliot's reforms, especially the widening of elective options. By the eighties, though, the elective principle had become familiar, and enrollment increased 66.4 percent; in the nineties the increase was 88.8 percent. The year 1873 was the first in which more than 200 men entered the College. Not for fifteen years did more than 300 enter; but in only four more years the entering class numbered more than 400. Another four years and the intake was more than 500; then in only two years the entering class went beyond 600 (Morison, *Three Centuries*, pp. 365, 416).

Today Harvard supports eight language departments that can be listed in the MLA Directory (1983), along with Comparative Literature and (O battles long ago!) Linguistics and Classics. The last, by the way, is listed in the *Register* as "The Classics." Is the article an attempt to restore the old prestige? "The Classics" consists of Classics, Greek (nineteen courses), Latin (twenty-three courses), Medieval Greek, Medieval Latin, Classical Archaeology, Modern Greek (among "The Classics"!) and Classical Philology. Exclusive of English and American Literature and Language and "The Classics," the other departments offer courses in thirty-four different languages, some of them divided into historical dialects. Since the thirty-four include Korean, Vietnamese, Modern Arabic and Modern Hebrew, it seems possible to say that modern language studies at Harvard have followed the·flag and the needs of commerce and industry.

This is more or less what Eliot predicted, welcoming MLA to Cambridge in 1901, by congratulating members because their "study" (still in the singular!) was "beginning to connect itself intimately with the life of the nation." When the Association was founded, Eliot said, there had been only a slight connection between members' work and the "actual occupations of Americans." Now he could see "developing a real connection between Modern Language study and the actual national interests and aspirations."[41] In the light of the discussions I have been describing, Eliot's seems an odd notion.

What must members have thought, themselves so little removed from the Classical Tradition, of such an invitation to practicality and social obligation? Is it significant that it came from an outsider, and that such ends formed no part of the discussions at MLA meetings? Eliot expected that the study of modern languages would have to become more and more a part of the life of "the American people," and he congratulated members "on this relatively new prospect for the department of education" in which they worked. Indeed, with his imperial vision—which was often imperious too—Eliot could tell his audience that modern language study was "going to have a stronger hold [on the American people] in the next twenty years because in addition to [your] eternal interest in literature and learning you are to be supported by a vital connection with the industrial and commercial activities of the day" (PMLA, 17, 1902, p. v). How well Eliot knew faculty: the mundane concerns of industry and commerce here protected by eternal literature and learning, modern language teachers serving God and mammon both, by means of an expanded curriculum.

But who was listening to Eliot? On the evidence of the talk at MLA, plainly none of the speakers was. They were far more likely to be asking, as Easton did in 1888, "Where in all the vast mass of recent philological literature are we to look for any trace of the general study of HOMER as the divine poet?" Where, indeed, we might ask, and count ourselves lucky for the escape. But perhaps Easton's fault, if it can be called so, is more one of style than conception, for Easton was objecting because Greek and Latin philology had become "infected by the exclusive impulse to weigh, measure and count," to ape science, that is (Easton, 1888, pp. 20–21). (And, it may be added, to found journals to do just that: *Modern Philology, Philological Quarterly, Journal of English and Germanic Philology*. Note that last unspecified title.) But we should not be too harsh. What else could teachers of modern languages and literatures take for models than their classicist and philological rivals, in whose courses they had learned whatever they knew about literary study and teaching? Nor should there be any surprise if many of their questions and answers seem to emerge from the dark pages of the Yale Report of 1828. What else was there?

In any case, most of the argument at MLA had already become moot even as it was going on. For the shaping of modern language studies was to depend not on whatever theory, a skimpy one at best, might be derived from their borrowed justifications, but rather on changes in the material conditions that supported them. "It has been a period of specialization in scholarship," J. W. Bright proclaimed in his speech on the unwritten (and, I would say, largely unnoticed) history of MLA. He went on to predict "more specialization, much more, in the future" (Bright, 1903, p. lix). "Better things have come to pass," he said, "and they have come quickly." Bright meant the "funding of new departments, and of reinvigorating old departments of ideal pursuits [the classics?] in a practical world where 'alle thinges obeyen to moneye' . . ." (p. lvii).

Money meant new appointments, and with new appointments went opportunities to fill gaps in the course list. At Harvard, for example, at the end of the nineteenth century, there was a half-course (one semester) in the novel from Richardson to Eliot, which obviously cut too big a chunk out of the history of the novel. What of Elizabethan narratives: Nashe, for example and his Jack Wilton, or Deloney, the silk-weaver who celebrated the gentle craft of the cobbler? What of *Robinson Crusoe*, and what of Mrs. Aphra Behn's *Oroonoko, or The History of the Royal Slave?* They came along, sooner or later, as money became available, and as men who knew about them finished their studies.

Today at Harvard, there's a lecture course in the English novel before 1800, another in Defoe, Richardson, and Fielding. There's a course in the Augustan Age (Restoration to 1750), substituting for the old "From the Death of Dryden to the Death of Pope (1700–1744)," but why is 1660 better as a cutting place than 1744? Some time in that course is devoted to "Defoe, Fielding and the rise of the novel." There are "discussions" or "middle-group" courses (primarily for graduate students, but open to undergraduates) on "The Rogue Novel before 1800," on "The English Novel [of the second half of the nineteenth century] and Social Knowledge." The two period courses must go back a long way, to the very earliest days of the subject, when students of English literature were just beginning to accumulate (and transmit) the facts of their subject. But how explain their persistence, especially after the introduction of courses with more specialized topics?

It is hard to see that any real principles have controlled the divvying up of such "subjects" as the novel, except the random creation of whimsically specialized courses that are thought to fill in gaps in a chronicle of English literature. The result as we know — as we have known for fifty years and more—is a course list conspicuous for incoherence and intellectual vacuity, which was put together in the last quarter of the nineteenth century with the assistance of various educational enterprisers, like Eliot, Butler, White, Gilman and Angell (of Michigan), who needed activities to fill the time of the students they were getting in increasing numbers, and who were willing to find money and spend it on faculty. Fortunately, there were men here and there, like Child and Hill at Harvard, who were willing to go along with them, so they could get on with their own work. (It was an offer from Hopkins that finally forced Eliot to free Child from the Boylston Professorship, to finish the English and Scottish popular ballads.) And while all this building was going on, the *Nation*'s "union of younger philological scholars and teachers" was wrapping itself in self-justifications drawn from the most ancient of educational theories, thereby avoiding the crucial question of the nature of modern language studies in the world that was coming into existence around it.

---

1. *The Nation*, "Notes," 44 (January 20, 1877), p. 55.
2. C. Alphonso Smith, "The Work of the MLA," *PMLA*, 14 (1899), p. 254. Further references are in text.
3. F. V. N. Painter, "Recent Educational Movements in Their Relation to Language Study," *PMLA*, 2 (1887), pp. 83–91.
4. H. E. Sheperd, [Comment in "Proceedings," 1886], *PMLA*, 2 (1887), p. xxvi.
5. Franklin Carter, "Study of Modern Languages in Our Higher Institutions," *PMLA*, 2 (1887), p. xxvi.
6. Edward S. Joynes, "Reading in Modern Language Study," *PMLA*, 5 (1890), p. 34.
7. Landon C. Garland, Address of Welcome 1890, *PMLA*, 6 (1891), p. 4.
8. H. R. Hohlfeld, "The Teaching of Foreign Literature," *PMLA*, 20 (1905), pp. xxxvi, xxxvii, xxxv. Further references in text.
9. O. F. Emerson, "The American Scholar and the Modern Languages," *PMLA*, 24 (1909), pp. lxxxv–lxxxvi.
10. Francis A. March, "Recollections of Language Teaching," *PMLA*, 8 (1893), p. xxi.
11. James Wilson Bright, "Concerning the Unwritten History of the Modern Language Association of America," *PMLA*, 18 (1903), p. xlvii.
12. Bright, "Unwritten History," pp. xlvi, xlix.
13. Barrett Wendell, *A Literary History of the United States* (New York: Scribners, 1936), pp. 394–95. Further references in text.
14. J. M. Hart, "James Russell Lowell," *PMLA*, 7 (1892), p. 25. Further references in text.
15. Theodore W. Hunt, "The Place of English in the College Curriculum," *PMLA*, 1 (1884–85), p. 126. Further references in text.
16. C. W. Eliot, Address of Welcome 1889, *PMLA*, 5 (1890), p. 2.
17. J. M. Hart, "The College Course in English Literature, How It May be Improved," *PMLA*, 1 (1884–85), pp. 90–91.
18. William Pepper, Address of Welcome 1887, *PMLA*, 3 (1888), p. [3].
19. S. E. Morison, *Three Centuries of Harvard* (Cambridge, Mass.: Harvard University Press, 1936, 1942), pp. 345–46. Further references are in text.

20. [Harvard University], *Twenty Years of School and College English* (Cambridge, Mass.: Harvard University Press, 1896), pp. 59, 63.

21. S. E. Morison, *The Development of Harvard University* (Cambridge, Mass.: Harvard University Press: 1930), p. 98. Further references in text.

22. [Harvard University, Guidelines for Core Curriculum], in *Chronicle of Higher Education* (March 6, 1978), p. 15.

23. James Russell Lowell, "Harvard Anniversary," in *Democracy and Other Addresses* (Boston: Houghton Mifflin, 1887), p. 209. Further references in text.

24. H. C. E. Brandt, "How Far Should Our Teaching and Text-books Have a Scientific Basis?" *PMLA*, 1 (1884–85), p. 61.

25. H. C. G. von Jagemann, "Philology and Purism," *PMLA*, 15 (1900), p. 74.

26. James Wilson Bright, [Comment in "Proceedings" 1886] *PMLA*, 2 (1887), p. xlvii. Cf. p. 4 above.

27. James Russell Lowell, "The Study of Modern Languages," in *Democracy and Other Papers*, bound with *Books and Libraries and Other Papers* (Boston: Houghton Mifflin, 1871, 1898), pp. 68–69.

28. W. T. Hewitt, "The Aims and Methods of Collegiate Instruction in Modern Languages," *PMLA*, 1 (1884–85), p. 33. Further references in text.

29. J. M. Garnett, "The Course in English and Its Value as a Discipline," *PMLA*, 2 (1886), pp. 69–70.

30. Bright, Comment, p. xxviii. Bright's emphasis.

31. E. H. Babbitt, "How to Use Modern Languages as a Means of Mental Discipline," *PMLA*, 6 (1891), p. 53.

32. Horatio S. White, "The Teaching of a Foreign Literature in Connection with the Seminary System," *PMLA*, 3 (1887), p. 56.

33. A. S. Cook, "The Province of English Philology," *PMLA*, 13 (1898), pp. 185–205. Page references are in text.

34. Morton W. Easton, "The Rhetorical Tendency in Undergraduate Courses," *PMLA*, 4 (1888–89), p. 19. Further references are in text.

35. New York: Scribners, 1899, p. 40.

36. J. M. Hart, "English as a Living Language," *PMLA*, 11 (1896), p. 11. Hart's emphasis.

37. C. W. Eliot, Address of Welcome 1901, *PMLA*, 17 (1902), p. iv.

38. C. W. Eliot, Inaugural Address, in *A Turning Point in Higher Education. The Inaugural Address of Charles William Eliot as President of Harvard College, October 19, 1869*. With an Introduction by Nathan H. Pusey (Cambridge, Mass.: Harvard University Press, 1969), p. v.

39. C. W. Eliot, Inaugural Address, p. 1.

40. M. A. DeWolfe Howe, *Barrett Wendell and His Letters* (Boston: Atlantic Monthly Press, 1924), p. 201.

41. C. W. Eliot, Address of Welcome 1901, p. 4.

The University and the Prevention of Culture

Gerald Graff

Today one hears the complaint that literary theory has taken over the literature departments and is distracting students and professors from literature itself. It is said that the traditional study of literature as a humanistic enterprise is in jeopardy. Instead of advancing humanistic values, literature professors are cultivating opaque jargon and pseudoscientific systems. Hiding behind smoke screens of esoteric terminology, theorists turn their backs on outsiders, including most students, and carry on endless private conversations with other theorists. Literary works have been demoted to secondary importance, serving as mere occasions for displays of theoretical agility. If only we could get back to "traditional literary study," all would be well—or at least better than it is now.

Yet in the polemical dust thrown up by recent debates, it has tended to go unnoticed that the sins for which theorists are blamed today are the same ones for which "traditional literary study" was attacked when *it* was thought to be an assault on tradition. When literature departments were formed in the 1880's and imported the scientific methods of Germanic philology and literary history, this change was bitterly resisted by the traditionalists of that day, the genteel moralists of the old nineteenth-century college. When Irving Babbitt subtitled his *Literature and the American College* (1908) "*Essays in Defense of the Humanities*," he was defending the humanities *against* the university and its research scholars. As late as 1931, the Renaissance scholar Edwin Greenlaw still felt it necessary to defend literary-historical research against what he called "incompetent but vociferous exponents of the good old times," who objected that research "apes scientific methods, that it is against ancient standards, that it is immersed in subjects of no possible use, that it destroys the ability to teach. It is neglectful of culture. It stifles creative art. It looks at facts rather than at the soul."[1] Substitute "theories" for facts and "the experience of literature" for "soul" in the last sentence and the attack on research described by Greenlaw would pass for one of the current attacks on literary theory.

At the same time, the scorn of scientific historians like Greenlaw toward earlier moralistic critics resembles the contempt expressed by current avant-garde critics for anything smacking of "naive" attitudes. In 1931, it was still possible to regard the resistance to historical research as an expression of nostalgia. Literary history was still in its heroic phase, presenting itself as the vanguard of enlightenment, progress and sophistication, opposed only by a motley rearguard of provincials and gentlemen amateurs whose most coherent expression was the New Humanism of Irving Babbitt and Paul Elmer More. But if Greenlaw had looked more closely he could have perceived that the opposition also included the elements of a new vanguard, one which would soon make historical scholars like Greenlaw look as if *they* were the ones blindly clinging to the good old times and resisting change. The partisans of "criticism" who were challenging the dominance of the literary historians included not only New Humanists but "New Critics," as John Crowe Ransom would term them in his 1941 book of that title, and the New Criticism had a high-powered technical methodology which could compete on equal terms with that of the literary historians as the New Humanism could not.

When "criticism" triumphed after the war, the charges of subverting tradition which had been hurled against research scholars when they had been upstarts began to be redirected at upstart critics. In his bitter 1948 Presidential Address to the Modern Language Association, Douglas Bush attacked the New Criticism for its "aloof intellectuality," its "avoidance of moral values," its reduction of literary commentary to "a circumscribed end in itself," and its rejection of the common reader, who still thinks that "poetry deals with life." Bush added that "though the critics have censured scholarship for aping science, their own aims and methods seem much more deserving of the charge."[2] The old resentments against literature's dehumanization at the hands of "science" still persisted, but now that critics occupied a prominent role in the department they could be made the target of these resentments while "scholarship" took on the mantle of the humanistic and traditional.

When this hostility began to die out in the late fifties, the words "scholarship" and "criticism" no longer denoted incompatible or even necessarily separable activities. The new generation of instructors who entered the literature department in the great expansion of the sixties and seventies had only a dim sense of the old conflict. Thus critical explication in its turn rather quickly became one of the "traditional" methods, even though only a few decades earlier it had been considered as much a threat to tradition as literary theory is felt to be today. When opponents of literary theory like Helen Vendler urge us to get back to studying and teaching literature itself, their program sounds curiously reminiscent of the one which scholars like Bush in the forties denounced as an antihumanistic innovation.[3]

It is as if charges of antihumanism, cerebralism, elitism, and coming between literature and students are a kind of initiation rite through which each new professional mode has had to pass before it becomes accepted as part of "traditional humanism." The terms by which traditionalists have defined treason don't change, even though the activities the terms denote change every generation. In an amnesiac culture, today's tradition tends to be only yesterday's revolutionary innovation, and those who oppose it without awareness of the fact only hasten the next innovation.[4]

The point is not that innovation at first offends tradition and then later becomes tradition in some eternal cycle, which would be a platitude, but rather that the tendency to organize our thinking about the humanities around oppositions like Innovation vs. Tradition obscures those factors which have persisted through successive changes. The noisiness of conflicts between old scholars and New Critics, old-style readers and newfangled deconstructionists, distracts attention from the professional attitudes which characterize all these academic schools and separate them more sharply from the journalistic man-of-letters tradition of criticism than from one another. Insofar as academic critical battles are seen as conflicts between tradition and innovation (or old fogeys and avant-garde), problems inherent in academic literary studies as such are either ignored or blamed on some scapegoat group.

It is perfectly true that recent literary theory has become a private enclave, that many theorists write in a private jargon designed for other theorists, that theory deflects attention away from literature and towards itself. But then, these things have been only marginally less true of all the literary "fields" for the last hundred years. To the average outsider, literary theory may be more impenetrable to read but it is not substantially more inward-looking than most research scholarship on Blake or Wordsworth, most explication of Emily Dickinson, or, for that matter, most serious contemporary poetry and fiction or most serious contemporary cost accounting and stockbrokerage. Academic commentary on Faulkner addresses a lay public about as much or as little as commentary on Derrida. It chiefly addresses "Faulkner studies," which predetermines independent of any lay audience what constitutes a problem worth taking up and what evaluations are orthodox and heretical.

The goal of Faulkner studies is to "cover" the as yet undiscussed "areas" in the field, like so many stains in a rug, and, when the old areas have been covered, to create new ones. Naturally, Faulkner studies, like all the other academic fields, formally pretends that, in covering its terrain, it is contributing to a larger national and international "literary culture," but this is obviously little more than a polite fiction. Indeed, what makes literary theory seem so outrageously different from standard research and explication is that by flaunting its difficulty and esotericism it shows it has simply abandoned the sentimental pretense that it has an audience outside the field, that outsiders still care what academic literary commentators have to say.

Granted, individual professors frequently transcend the boundaries of the field and some of them do reach a wider journalistic audience. But this is as true of the occasional theorist — a Roland Barthes, say — as it is of the orthodox scholar or critic. In any case, generality of scope tends to be an individual achievement rather than something which has informed the institution as a whole, and the institution as a whole speaks more eloquently of itself to outsiders than do all but the most charismatic individual teachers. What René Wellek says of the old philological scholarship has proved equally true of New Criticism and newer theory, that gestures towards synthesis have "remained mostly the private virtues of an individual who was unable to make his ideas effective institutionally."[5]

If all the academic critical methods are to a greater or lesser degree in the same boat, then it becomes tempting to blame the problems of academic literary studies on specialization. Since specialization is obviously here to stay, however, and since it is hard to imagine valuable professional work being done without it, such a diagnosis only makes the problem seem all the more hopeless. It becomes rather like those diagnoses which blame the problems of modern culture on industrialism, technology, capitalism, or consumerism, each of which is eminently blamable but is not likely to disappear very soon without a cataclysm that might be more disastrous than benign. It would be less pessimistic to begin by assuming that, in the university realm at least, it is not specialization itself that occasions problems so much as the failure to bring specializations into relation with one another in any planned way. Specialization becomes self-enclosure only when there is no institutionalized correlation of specialties — which means not only no integration but not even any conflict of specialties. It is not inability to *agree* that is intellectually stultifying, as many analysts argue, but inability to *disagree*, for a dispersed set of independent fields can't even add up to an instructive set of antagonisms.

There is an argument, then, for turning our attention away from the inside disputes between critical methodologies and the problems of overspecialization and looking at the larger institutional setting in which these things function. We need to look particularly at the proliferation of fields, which has happened in a way that paralyzes conflict and community and terminates accountability to outsiders. As Wallace Douglas points out in his contribution to this volume, the literature department since the 1880's has evolved not according to any educational or cultural philosophy but as an "accidental" product of the opportunism of scholars and departmental administrators.[6] This is another way of describing that process of miscellaneous random "accretion" mentioned in the contribution of Wendell Berry.[7]

Here once again, the current battle over the institutional status of literary theory provides a useful illustration. Literary theory today seems clearly to be recapitulating the institutional fate of Germanic philology, positivistic literary history, modern and contemporary literature, New Criticism, linguistics, American studies, black studies and women's studies. In the classic pattern, the first appearance of innovation initiates a period of resistance and acrimony. Soon, however, ambitious departments recognize that if they hope to continue to be thought up-to-date — a condition of attracting graduate students, top appointments, money from the dean, etc. — they will need to "cover" the new areas. The history of professionalism shows that once any trend captures the aura of the "new," the "advanced" and the "sophisticated," the battle is essentially over and further resistance will be futile. At that point a "search committee" is formed, over the helpless protests of the retrograde minority, which however can take consolation in the assurance that its own interests won't be interfered with by the insurgents. What might have produced an instructive conflict of old and new ideas is institutionalized instead as an armed truce.

As all this is taking place, the proponents of the innovation will have invoked the underdog rhetoric of suppression and discrimination, and in the early stages of the conflict, before it has become obvious that the innovation is going to have to be assimilated, their complaints will be well-grounded. The crustier minority among the old guard will be openly willing to oppose professional progress, but most will see the handwriting on the wall and will accede to the innovation on the condition that it occupy a marginal place in the department, or at least no less marginal a place than everything else. Gradually, a few of the once-resistant scholars, or their heirs in the following generation, start assimilating the new subject or method; after a while the conflict and acrimony are forgotten, and, to the next generation, seem hardly to have ever existed.

The once-radical innovation — philology, positivistic literary history, New Critical explication — eventually begins to be considered a "traditional" practice, and the professors who embrace it have no trouble thinking of themselves as "traditional humanists." Alternatively — and this is a recent development — "radicalism," with its rhetoric of persecution, itself becomes a field with permanent standing, thus occasioning the now-familiar paradox of the institutionalized revolutionary, whose rejection of the System was so uncompromising that there was no choice but to award him a tenured chair and make him head of his own program. This paradox tends to be overlooked or minimized by the revolutionaries, since it ill accords with the theory of establishment repression that constitutes their field.

If institutional history continues to run to form, we can expect literary theory to be defused not by being repressed but by being accepted and relegated to the margin where it will cease to be a bother. This indeed has already happened. Instead of being used to create a context of general ideas that might bring the different viewpoints and methods of the literature department into fruitful debate, literary theory becomes yet another field, a fact which encourages it to be just the sort of self-promoting and exclusionary activity that its enemies denounce it for being. Forward-looking departments rush to their theorists, who form a new ghetto alongside those occupied by the black studies person hired several years ago and the women's studies person hired yesterday. Once literary theory has been thus "covered" in the department's table of "areas," the rest of the faculty is free to ignore the issues theorists raise.

By blocking or muffling any cross-factional communication that threatens to erupt, the university absorbs potentially disruptive innovation without the pain of open conflict, which would risk exposing to outsiders the embarrassing possibility that a common cultural tradition no longer exists. To avoid such conflict, the university merely *adds* another unit to an aggregate which remains otherwise unchanged. The pressure is thus relaxed all around: the outsiders who had proposed the innovation are appeased, having now become insiders with their own positions or programs. The university, on its side, gets to congratulate itself for its up-to-dateness and tolerance without anyone's having had to change his behavior in any way.

This dynamics of divide-and-evade plays a large role in the routinization of scholarly, critical and theoretical methods. Consider again the fate of the New Criticism, which on its entry into the university aspired to overcome the alienation from literature and from cultural and evaluative concerns to which the old literary history had been prone. When we think of the New Criticism now, we usually think of its method of textual explication popularized in textbooks like Cleanth Brooks and Robert Penn Warren's *Understanding Poetry*. But the first generation of New Critics, as Morris Dickstein notes in this volume, were not mere explicators but engaged critics of culture, part of the generation of Orwell, Auden and Caudwell.[8] The New Criticism arose during conditions of international political crisis between the wars, when it was difficult to keep literary matters completely separate from politics even when one wanted to. Though it defended the autonomy of literature against the incursion of politics and society, this very ambition was a self-consciously political and social one, and did not hide its animus against what F. R. Leavis called "technologico-Benthamite civilization."[9]

Neither T. S. Eliot nor I. A. Richards was ever an exhaustive explicator. Eliot, with his longing for a culture in which poetry would be instinctively and unconsciously understood instead of requiring elaborate explanations, always distrusted what he later would call "the lemon-squeezer school of criticism." After the late twenties the tendency of his prose writing is increasingly political, cultural and religious. Richards' early program of practical criticism was not a pure technique of analysis but a therapeutic for ideological conflict and misunderstanding, aimed at neutralizing the destructive potential of science and nationalism. Yvor Winters' moral rationalism and the early political and social commitments of Kenneth Burke are too well recognized to need pointing out, as are those of Ransom, Allen Tate, Robert Penn Warren, Cleanth Brooks and the other Southerners who contributed to the agrarian manifesto, I'll Take My Stand (1930).

Nor were these social and political interests merely "extrinsic" to these writers' literary criticism, however much some of them claimed. The preference of Eliot and the Southern New Critics for organically complex over didactically "Platonic" poetry accorded with their admiration for organic, hierarchical societies over the abstractions of mechanistic industrialism. The very concentration on the poem as poem "and not another thing," in Eliot's famous phrase, with its conception of the disinterested nature of aesthetic experience, was an implicit rejection of commercial-utilitarian values and was thus itself a powerfully "utilitarian" gesture. Even when they overstressed the purely literary element of literature, the New Critics were reacting against the ingrained philistinism of the American lay public and of many of the old scholars, who thought modern literature immoral and embraced a Victorian oratorical view of literature as "great thoughts" clothed in elevated language. In this sense, the suspension of "extrinsic" criteria that made the text's internal dynamics into the criterion for evaluating it was a revolt against the provincialism into which traditional folk and craft standards had degenerated. Even at its most "formalistic," the New Critical program had a cultural rationale.

It was this cultural rationale which was left behind when the New Criticism became an academic methodology. Tailored to the needs of the fifteen-page article or the fifty-minute class session, the cultural context of first-generation New Criticism fell away. To have preserved it would have meant tying literature to history and society, and in the new mass-education conditions after the war neither students nor faculty could be depended on to presuppose a common history or a language in which historical differences could be compared. Furthermore, increased numbers and pressures reduced the amount of informal contact which had in the past helped overcome the disparities. The expedient thing in these circumstances was to isolate and mass-produce the New Critical technique of reading, which did sharpen a student's powers of critical attention as the older pedagogy did not.

There was also the pressure of intramural disciplinary competition, which put a premium on methods which looked rigorous and could be applied virtually anywhere. During the quarrels of the twenties and thirties, literary historians had dismissed criticism as a subjective and impressionistic technique which could never achieve the scientific rigor of philology. As one historian put it in 1929, "our literary critics are a cheerless lot. Either. . . they are still groping for a principle of order, or they have an axe to grind that is sociological or journalese rather than literary."[10] Such a comment ominously signaled the conditions which criticism would have to meet in order to qualify for academic acceptance: it would have to have a principle of order and no axe to grind that might incur suspicions of sociology or journalism. After the war, partisans of criticism in the university were all too eager to meet these conditions. In 1953, René Wellek called for criticism to develop a "technique and methodology that would be teachable and transmissible and applicable to any and all works of literature."[11] Wellek seemed not to notice that in defining the program for criticism in this way he was letting the enemy dictate the terms.

In its "teachable and transmissible" form, stripped-down and decontextualized, the New Critical method was even more susceptible to routinization than the most arid of the old factual scholarship had been. For in order to ape the old scholarship one had had at least to find out some information, whereas to do a fair impersonation of a New Critic one required no prior knowledge of any kind. Concentrating on "the poem itself" immeasurably eased the task of the instructor who faced students with no common stock of cultural and historical experience. And as long as the poem itself dictated how it was to be taught, the department still did not need to come together and try to thrash out problems of context. Each instructor could still go his or her own way, the faith being as before that individual initiatives would somehow add up to a coherent enterprise.

Earlier, the partisans of criticism had complained that the scholars merely "accumulated facts without regard for any purpose beyond them."[12] Now, in the wake of the critical revolution, critics could accumulate interpretations without regard for any purpose behind them. As Randall Jarrell noted in his famous 1952 essay, "The Age of Criticism":

> New critic is but old scholar writ large, as a general thing: the same gifts which used to go into proving that the Wife of Bath was really an aunt of Chaucer's named Alys Perse now go into proving that all of Henry James's work is really a Swedenborgian allegory. Criticism will soon have reached the state of scholarship, and the most obviously absurd theory—if it is maintained intensively, exhaustively, and professionally—will do the theorist no harm in the eyes of his colleagues.[13]

Why did this happen? One can blame the blindness of individual critics, so overtaken by a gold-rush mania for interpretive breakthroughs that they failed to see how the critical currency was consequently being cheapened as one "absurd theory" topped the last. I think a more satisfying explanation has to take into account the institutional setting in which critics operated, one which separated literature professors not only from lay audiences but from one another.

The very function of a university department, one might say, is to keep professors isolated and thus incapable of coming into conflict. This in any case is the effect, for departments are so arranged that latent intellectual conflicts within the faculty never become part of the educational process. Each of the existing disciplines originally came into being through a history of cultural conflict—as "English" was formed by wresting power from classical Greek, "creative writing" by breaking from scholarship, etc.—but this history of conflict forms no part of the context for teaching the discipline. The cultural struggle which led, for example, to the teaching of modern and American literature is not part of the context in which students study that literature, which tends to be taught as a series of masterpieces.

Thus, though the university at any moment embodies the central cultural conflicts of its time, it fails to make these conflicts visible to its public, or even to its own faculty. These conflicts end up as the business of those who specialize in them and quarrel over them in the professional journals devoted to those issues. No longer representing a unified culture as the old college did, yet having no way to dramatize its disunities, the university ceases to provide a usable cultural context for any of its subjects. The harm is not so obvious in the sciences, which presuppose widely understood practical applications, but the sciences are not unaffected, since they, as much as the humanities, are products of cultural conflicts that cannot be ignored without loss. It is noteworthy that, despite its recognized importance in the shaping of modern culture, the conflict between the sciences and humanities is not part of the regular subject-matter of either. The conflict is not studied because it is nobody's specialty—or else it is studied (by a few) because it *is* somebody's specialty.

Having no way of making visible the conflicts that make up its history, literary studies becomes a set of fields geared to advancing methodology for its own sake and generating "productivity." Humanists have long complained of this routinization of literary studies, noting that the production of literary interpretations has come to resemble the industrial assembly line. But humanists tend to blame this routinization on the displacement of tradition by specialization or on the inevitable effects of bureaucratic institutionalization. It might be argued that, on the contrary, routinized criticism results not from specialization or institutionalization as such but from a type of institutionalization which isolates specialties and prevents exemplary conflict. Relieved of having to engage in intellectual confrontation with their colleagues, professors naturally cultivate the techniques of running literature through the various available interpretive grids, holding themselves accountable only to others who use the same procedures. Routinization is the child of disconnection and isolation.[14]

It was a great encouragement to routinization that New Critical technique was conceived as "applicable," following Wellek's prescription, "to any and all works of literature." Eliot in his early criticism had promoted the poetic values of irony, paradox and indirection, but he usually made clear that he was defending a partisan idea of poetry, not defining "poetry" and "literature" in general. Eliot's attacks on Milton, Keats and Shelley, and his denigration of eighteenth-century and Victorian poetry, at least conceded that there were kinds of poetry that lacked the admired New Critical characteristics, even if they were thereby relegated to the second-class status of which historical scholars complained. By 1947, however, Cleanth Brooks was conciliating these scholars by showing in *The Well Wrought Urn* that Milton, Keats and Wordsworth (if not Shelley) and Pope and Tennyson were really just as paradoxical in their poetry as Donne and Yeats. What Brooks called "the language of paradox" was no longer a quality recommended by a partisan sect but the nature of poetry as such. If this was so, then all past literature could now be reinterpreted accordingly.

The argument of *The Well Wrought Urn* reflected a subtle shift in the emphasis of the New Criticism from embattled reevaluation to inoffensive reinterpretation. Again, for the new generation of instructors who came in after the war, the old battles which had pitted Milton against Donne and Tennyson against Yeats had lost their meaning and even seemed professionally counterproductive. Why force a false choice between Milton and Yeats when so much remained to be done to consolidate Milton studies and Yeats studies? As for the even more crotchety challenges to so many major reputations made by mavericks like Winters and Leavis, there was certainly no point in arguing with them, for the accumulated weight of Whitman and Conrad studies made argument superfluous. Not only had the political context of first-generation New Criticism dropped away, but so had the literary context as well.

New Critical reformers had hoped to revitalize the neglected practice of evaluation and to combat that unthinking guild mentality whereby the scholarly specialist in a writer or period is assumed to be a *promoter* of that writer or period. But in its decontextualized form, critical explication proved to be even more prone to the uncritical promotion of literature than the old scholarship had been. While accumulations of sources, influences and other scholarly information had functioned as a silent endorsement of a work or a writer's value, explication presented itself as an even more authentic endorsement, purporting as it did to lay bare the innermost structure of the work. Then too, the very stockpiling of competing explications eventually came to seem a *prima facie* proof of a work's admirable complexity. Actually it was a valid proof in many cases, but the unintended effect might be to intimidate potentially dissenting students and teachers into passivity.

None of this might have had damaging consequences had not the American cultural climate been loosening up during the period in which New Critical interpretive tactics were being standardized, making the attack on philistinism less necessary than it had been earlier. Rationalizing strategies may be a necessary way of combatting aggressive philistinism in some colleges or communities, but where strong literary prejudices have never been acquired in the first place such strategies will only be duly recorded in notebooks and delivered back on the examination. Demonstrating that a literary work justifies itself through its own internal organization makes sense when addressed to an audience accustomed to judging literature by the correctness or elegance of its sentiments, but outside such a context the demonstration loses its purpose and becomes a kind of declaration of literary infallibility.

In this fashion the New Criticism was transformed after the war into a technique by which literature is actually protected from criticism. It was this period which saw the perfection of the now-familiar conventions by which explicators could prove and teachers could teach that any literary feature which looks like a defect is actually a virtue, being organically in harmony with the internal demands of the work. That previous commentators regarded a feature of a work as a flaw was only a stimulus to the ambitious explicator to demonstrate that the work was in fact intended to have that feature, or at least that it is all the better for having it. In the classic pattern, enterprising Explicator E starts by observing that all previous critics have taken a certain feature of a text — failure to achieve a satisfactory resolution of theme or plot, say — as an artistic defect. The occasion is set for Professor E to "demonstrate," with copious marshalling of detail, that the alleged "failure" is in fact an aesthetic triumph, since the irresolution in question is wonderfully consistent with the internal structure of the work. The premise underlying this practice is always that since the canonized work must make sense, the only problem is to discover that sense.

Another convention that works to similar effect has been wittily described by Richard Levin in *New Readings vs. Old Plays*, who calls it the "my-theme-can-lick-your-theme gambit." The gambit consists of justifying one's "'new reading' by proving that the central theme he has found in the play is superior to those proposed in earlier readings."[15] The standard assertion is that while previous commentators on a given work have found it to be based on Themes A, B, C, D and E, all of them have "curiously overlooked" Theme F, which the present writer will proceed to show to be "the fundamental underlying theme" that either replaces or subsumes the others. A heartbreaking number of critics and term-paper and dissertation writers clearly feel they must make this competitive claim if they hope to be published or passed, and they may be right. Again, the literary work is assumed infallible and the only question for the critic is how that infallibility is best described. A contributor to the *James Joyce Quarterly* states the principle with unusual candor:

> As with the Mass, Joyce requires faith and insight, both inside and out, and the rewards are proportionate to the fervor of the believer. He offers us the sacrament, the creative process, and . . . by participating in it we are able to become, in our own small way, counterparts to Joyce himself.[16]

Such poetolatry is perhaps too easy to ridicule; suspending critical judgment may be methodologically necessary for certain purposes, permitting an entry into Joyce's world that a more reserved attitude would forbid. The problem arises only when the technical understanding of literary works on their own terms is not counteracted by other models.

Hershel Parker, in *Flawed Texts and Verbal Icons*, adduces an impressive amount of evidence to show that the impulse to make coherent "verbal icons," at all costs, of canonized works has led interpreters of American fiction to attribute ingenious thematic unities to textual botches resulting from careless authorial revision or insensitive editorial tampering. "Confident that their aesthetic goosebumps are authorially planned," or indifferent to whether they are authorially planned or not, "critics are lured into seeing authority where the passage they are reading contains nonsense."[17]

Parker's most striking case in point is Mark Twain's *Pudd'nhead Wilson*, a text so spectacularly botched by Twain's carelessness in revising that it is "patently unreadable" as a thematically coherent whole. The novel's interpreters, however, "approach the text as the most trusting of New Critics, and what they find is unity. They find the book 'a far more unified, more balanced novel than many of its critics have been willing to grant,' they find 'a unity of theme and general organization,' unity from themes and images, unity from the 'concern with property,' 'artistic and philosophical unity' and 'unity from metaphors.'"[18] To be specific, critics see "the slavery theme" and "the heredity vs. training" theme as informing "brief passages or longer units of the book which were written before Mark Twain introduced these themes into the manuscript and which were not later revised to contain those themes. . . ." They talk about characterization "throughout" the novel in which "chapters survive from stages when a character was white and a stage when he was part black," and in which some chapters "date from a stage when that character had not been invented." They see a "major structural device" in the cynical "affyisms" which Twain composed independently and later "placed at the chapter heads more or less casually. . . ."[19]

It is, of course, not impossible for genuine order to come about fortuitously, or for a writer, in revising, to perceive some previously unplanned order and deliberately let it stand. But Parker's point is that Twain's critics do not recognize the burden of proof for the unity of the text as resting with them. Since Twain is a canonized author, his works can be assumed *a priori* to possess structural unity, and the only question is what that unity consists in. The critics, Parker says, "define their role as bringing order out of a chaos which they insist is only apparent, not real. The order *must* be there, awaiting the sufficiently attentive and unbiased reading which the present critic is always the first to supply."[20]

Of course deconstruction has recently exploded this cult of the unified text, in ways more various and challenging than can be explored here. Yet as deconstructionists themselves have begun to complain, deconstruction has in some cases become just the newest gimmick for producing explications. The text's claim to stand as an autonomous icon or a realistic representation is shown to be a tropological strategy which masks its own rhetorical nature and represses the desire or power which enables it. The text is shown to "undo" the "logics of signification" on which it is predicated, etc. What is not so widely noted is how such deconstructive gestures can serve obliquely to patronize literature and keep it on its cultural pedestal. The critic worships literature not for its timeless, static perfection, but for its terroristic, defamiliarizing otherness, or what Paul de Man calls its "vertiginous possibilities of referential aberration."[21] Deconstructive readings formally challenge interpretations which attribute organic unity to texts, but this doesn't stop them from serving just as organicist readings do to normalize texts and render them immune to criticism. The reason this can be so is obvious: the vertigo in the "vertiginous possibilities of referential aberration" long ago became a respected cultural value. In replacing the New Critical fetish of textual unity with a fetish of textual disunity and "aporias," deconstructionists continue to "valorize" that complexity in excess of rational or logical reformulation which has been an honored critical criterion since the forties.

Indeed, on the complexity scoreboard, an ostensible unity that unravels into a self-undoing "heterogeneity" and "puts its own discourse into question" earns more points and sets off more rockets than the most complex unity. Deconstructive readings are superficially iconoclastic because they take texts previously thought to be under the sovereign control of the author and reveal them as allegedly undoing themselves. But a post-Freudian culture tends to find a rich state of decontrol more interesting than any narrow, puritanical control.

I recently taught a course in American literature which included the short story by Nathaniel Hawthorne, "The Artist of the Beautiful." The hero of this tale, Owen Warland, is an artisan in watches and other fine mechanisms who cares so much more about the aesthetic qualities of his creations than about their utility that he is ostracized by his community. Condemned to loneliness and failure, Owen nevertheless perseveres in his art. Finally, after years of discouragement, Owen produces a masterpiece, an animated mechanical butterfly, only to see it shattered to bits, with perhaps obvious but still moving symbolism, in the infant grip of the town blacksmith's boy.

Up to the final catastrophe, Hawthorne seems to be clearly presenting his artist-hero's isolation as a pitiable condition. But the last three sentences of the story introduce a curious reversal. Hawthorne describes Owen as oddly serene in the face of the sudden destruction of what it has taken him so many years to create. "As for Owen Warland," we're told, "he looked placidly at what seemed the ruin of his life's labor, and which was yet no ruin. He had caught a far other butterfly than this. When the artist rose high enough to achieve the Beautiful, the symbol by which he made it perceptible to mortal senses became of little value in his eyes while his spirit possessed itself in the enjoyment of the Reality."[22]

This hopeful conclusion, which the narrator seems to endorse, appears flatly at odds with what has gone before: all along, Owen has been presented as desperately *desiring* acceptance from the community. More than that, it has seemed to be one of the author's givens that it is *bad* for art to be so "spiritualized" that it loses any link with the "material" life associated with marriage, family and occupation. The assertion in the last sentence that the creation of art is finally its own sufficient reward — even with the destruction of the physical product — upsets the earlier glorification of the "spiritualization of matter." The social neglect that has been so convincingly treated as a serious problem is too abruptly dismissed as if it were only a small price to pay for the transcendence of art. These, in any case, were the problems I wanted my students to think about when I assigned them to write a paper discussing the apparent contradictions of the ending.

On reading the papers, I was struck by a pattern that had troubled me in the past but without any clear sense of why. Many students went to great lengths in order to avoid dealing with these contradictions as such, devoting their ingenuity to constructing accounts of the ending that made it cohere with the story as a whole. Several writers accomplished this end by means of an ironic interpretation, according to which, when Hawthorne pictures his artist at the end as beatific in the face of the destruction of his art, he wants us to see him as self-deceived. If Hawthorne means for us to see Owen as deluded in cherishing "the Beautiful" over the human community, then we don't have to take seriously the implication at the end that belonging to a community doesn't matter. Then there will be no contradiction with the earlier implication that it matters a great deal.

After querying several of the students, I began to see what had happened and why. The students had grasped the contradictions of the tale, but when they came to write their papers they had no terms for talking about contradictions except as things to be resolved. Their interpretations had been predetermined by an assumption drilled into them since high-school English, namely, that when you encounter an apparent anomaly in a literary work—especially if it is a canonized one—it's not a real anomaly. The students who read the ending as ironic did so because that is the only plausible way to make it cohere with the rest of the story. That there are occasions when the elements of a literary work *don't* cohere was a possibility they either hadn't been led to consider or had no terms to express, at least not in formal writing. Not surprisingly, it was the *better* students in the class who were least able to treat the story's contradictions *as* contradictions. This makes depressing sense: it's the students who have best mastered a particular interpretive strategy who figure to be most its captive.

Only later did the extent of my own unwitting complicity in this episode dawn on me. I had asked the students to "discuss the apparent contradictions of the ending." Given their experience, what else could this have seemed but a familiar pedagogical gimmick, the setting of a "critical problem" posed by a text which cries out to be removed by explication? In my students' experience, "problems" posed in literature classes exist chiefly for the purpose of enabling explicators to dispose of them. Literature, as these students had encountered it, was like Owen Warland's mechanical butterfly—a fragile object which might shatter if its flaws and contradiction were exposed.

In a way, my students were instinctive followers of Stanley Fish. They psyched out my "interpretive community," or what they took it to be, and thus "created" exactly the kind of text which they had every reason to think I wanted. They behaved with the same aggressive docility which Fish describes in his own students' transformation of a group of names on his classroom blackboard into allegorical poems, supposedly proving Fish's contention that "theories always work, and they will always produce exactly the results that they predict. . . ."[23] One need only read closely Fish's own book, *Is There a Text in This Class?*, to find reference to cases in which theories (or "interpretive strategies") were disconfirmed by textual evidence not predetermined by them,[24] but of course reading *can* be a mere recycling of what the reader expects or thinks he is supposed to expect. Students tend to accept the "interpretive strategies" which win approval, with attitudes ranging from bright enthusiasm to passive cynicism.

There was, however, one difference between my class and the suspiciously pliant one described by Fish. None of Fish's students seems to have lacked facility in imputing clever allegorical meanings to anything presented to them, whereas in my class a number of students hadn't mastered this technique. Far from applying an overly powerful interpretive strategy that glibly resolved the story's contradictions, these students lacked the interpretive strategies needed in order to grasp the contradictions in the first place. A few of these didn't try to hide their opinion of the discussion as a precious bore, though most swallowed their C-minuses and went on struggling to sound just as glibly mechanical as the good students did.

Much of the current malaise of literary education is summed up in the opposition between these two kinds of students—the one who hasn't learned how to locate thematic coherence and the one who hasn't learned how *not* to locate it. Which type poses the more serious problem varies with the school, college, university or locale, but both are creations of the professional interpretive community, the one unable to imitate it successfully, the other producing an unintended parody of it. Both types are symptoms of pedagogical pathology, but the source of the pathology goes deeper than matters of pedagogical method; it lies in the academic model of the critic as an explicator in a vacuum.

If you need further proof, consider the way the conventions of textual rationalization are packaged for use in the many available handbooks which have been designed to show students how to write themes about literature. Like the *Cliffs Notes* study guides (a much-neglected subject for sociologists of criticism), and the glossaries of literary and critical terms, these handbooks are easy to deplore as a prostitution, but such guidebooks arise from a realistic assessment of the classroom situation. They are based on the recognition that most students don't see the point of the kind of literary discussion which they are endlessly goaded to carry on in classes and papers. The good students can master the standard formulas without needing to know why they are doing it, but those who don't master them so easily feel a desperate need for ready-made examples.

These are the students who, if they don't plagiarize from a fellow student or *Cliffs Notes*, turn to a handbook with a good down-to-business title like *Writing Themes About Literature*, which may be part of the course's required or supplementary reading. There they pick up advice like this: "what might appear to be a problem [in a literary work] can often be treated as a normal characteristic, given the particular work you are studying." For example, "you may find a problem about an 'unreal' occurence in a work. But if you can show that the work is laid out as a fantasy or a dream, and not as a faithful representation of everyday reality, then you can also show that the 'unreal' occurence is normal *for that work*."[25]

Now this is eminently sensible advice as far as it goes, and it would be absolutely necessary advice for the frequent type of student who objects to "an unreal occurrence" on the grounds that good literature is always realistic. What our author fails to mention, however, are those occasions when a student's naive skepticism is actually justified: an unreal occurence which fails to harmonize with the purpose of a work, say, or one which harmonizes with purposes which are puerile. Avant-garde art and criticism have tried to alter the convention that coherence is necessarily something to be expected in a work of art, but readers are still safe in provisionally assuming an intention of coherence in a text until they have evidence of a contrary intention. There is nevertheless something patronizing about assuming *a priori* that coherence is necessarily achieved, or—as in the case of deconstruction—necessarily undone.

If my classroom story suggests what is wrong with the theory that interpreters create rather than construe texts, it also points up why the program of getting back to literature itself will only deepen the problem. The reason for this is not, as Fish would have it, that there are no prior literary "texts in themselves" to get back to, but that access to those texts requires hermeneutical reconstruction, particularly when the codes and tacit assumptions informing the text are not already shared by a reading community. A literary education that operationally boils down to a series of blunt confrontations with texts "in themselves" will leave students at a loss as to what they are to say about literature. For the problem is that literary texts in themselves go only so far in telling us what we are supposed to *say* about them.

Speech-act theory, pragmatics and various forms of current reader-response criticism agree in emphasizing that interpreting the meaning of any text involves making inferences about the kind of situation to which it refers or which it presupposes. Interpreting "the text itself" means inferring a vast number of tacit assumptions which may not be explicitly "in" the text at all and have to be reconstructed by the competent reader. As Ross Chambers has recently put it, "meaning is not inherent in discourse and its structures, but contextual, a function of the pragmatic situation in which the discourse occurs."[26]

A structuralist like Chambers is actually more "traditional" than the kind of traditionalists who oppose literature itself to its theoretical contexts. He is only trying to give a reasoned account of something which the best of the old literary historians knew in their bones but did not know how to formulate adequately: that the historical circumstances which must be inferred in order to understand any text are not a mere "extrinsic background," as positivist historians and New Critics both supposed, but something presupposed by the work and thus necessary to line-by-line comprehension of it. If, as Chambers argues, a text's "indication" of "the narrative situation appropriate to it" depends on the reader's ability to recognize the relevant "situational phenomena," then this establishes "the social fact that narrative mediates human relationships and derives its 'meaning' from them; that, consequently, it depends on social agreements, implicit pacts or contracts, that themselves are a function of desires, purposes, and constraints."[27] The point is of crucial importance for teaching, explaining why students will inevitably have difficulty when they haven't inherited the requisite "social agreements" and "implicit pacts or contracts" which the text takes for granted.

Hawthorne's preoccupation with "the Beautiful," the artistic transcendence of local and material circumstances, presupposes an acquaintance with a certain line of aesthetic speculation; his setting of the problem of art in utilitarian, practical-minded America presupposes a rough sense of American cultural history. Such thematic tags, aesthetic transcendence and American philistinism, constitute what Chambers calls "the pragmatic situation in which the discourse occurs." The narrative can't be comprehended "as literature" apart from these historical contexts because it is essentially a response *to* them. One could always argue that these historical givens are merely a scaffolding which make the literary experience possible and which have no aesthetic importance themselves, but even then one is conceding that the reader cannot dispense with them.

Little in my students' previous background prepared them to recognize either of these aspects of Hawthorne's "pragmatic situation," and certainly nothing prepared them to connect that situation with their own as Americans. Those who were able to recognize the contradictions of the tale could therefore only see them as structural motifs in a literary work, not as real historical conflicts that might illuminate still-present conflicts in American culture. Reading the work as "literature itself," divorced from the cultural situations to which it had responded, they had no problem resolving its thematic contradictions, which were now merely pretexts for exercising explicative facility. The poorer students, not having even that context, were unable to go beyond the level of the kind of plot summary that they are always being told to avoid.

What exact structural reforms might significantly rectify the problems I have been analyzing is difficult to say, but I would suggest that no proposal for reform will go far unless it sets its sights on abridging the structural isolation of individuals, groups and departments that now prevents the possibility of an intellectual community of debate. When all units are isolated, autonomous experiences—literary periods, critical approaches, departments, ideologies—teachers are spared the risk of unseemly confrontations, but with the loss of the experience of *contrast* they and their students need to give definition to their subjects. Proposals on the right or left—for core curricula founded on "basics" on the one hand, or for interdisciplinary departments based on "discourse analysis" on the other—seem to me limited at the outset precisely because they reflect only one point of view within a divided cultural scene and make no provision for dramatizing contrasting views.

Core curricula suffer from the perennial weakness of the general education programs which arose after World War II: even if the choice of the "core" subjects does not seem arbitrary, as it often does, there is no context for relating these subjects, which means that at best incoherence is reproduced at a more distinguished level.[28] As for discourse analysis and semiotics, when separated from history these methods become arbitrary in a different way, and they leave no apparent place within their structure for those groups in the university that don't happen to agree that the most important goal of education should be to deconstruct the text of social behavior.

The "cultural studies" conceived and practiced by Raymond Williams and the cultural history programs now in effect or under development at various universities seem to me to offer a more inclusive model, one in which we could imagine conservatives, liberals, apoliticals and others besides Marxists like Williams being able to work—while still retaining enough definition to avoid being simply a catchall. For Williams, cultural studies includes "the works which have been the normal material of literary courses, but it offers to read them in relation to a much wider cultural history and in conscious collaboration with elements of linguistics and sociology,"[29] to which should be added philosophy, anthropology, economics, the other arts and the history of science and technology. The starting point should be the recognition that the broad consensus which underlay traditional liberal education no longer exists, and that reestablishing coherence is now necessarily a matter of dramatizing exemplary conflicts and controversies rather than expounding the received great books, ideas and traditions.

Those who fear that such a program would sacrifice literature to sociology, politics, philosophy, etc., seem to me to underestimate the tremendous variety of viewpoints on these subjects, which would work powerfully against any one kind of reduction at least. They also ignore the fact that a certain degree of useful reduction is a prerequisite of any learning whatsoever, if not a prerequisite of the intellectual life itself, which—let's face it—is largely transacted in competing reductions. Professors who shudder fastidiously at the prospect of their students being contaminated by clichés might reflect that a cliché is better than nothing at all. Even a student who has been taught to reduce literature in the crudest fashion to ideas, politics or linguistics has at least a starting point on which to refine and eventually to discard for something better. He or she is to that extent in a better position than that of most students now, who have been so protected from reductionist dogmas that they have no way of sorting the particularities with which they are confronted—and who thus have to embrace even deadlier clichés than the ones some reductionist school of critics might have taught them.

But the very controversy over "reduction" is one of those which can't be decided by fiat, one which needs itself to be made part of what literary education is about rather than remaining a topic of esoteric behind-the-scenes wrangling in journals which students don't read or of casually organized after-hours discussions which few have the time or patience to go to. The controversy between those who would keep literature departments "literary" and those who would historicize or politicize them is itself just the kind of central cultural debate which, at present, the university has no way of making visible to outsiders or even most insiders.

The problems discussed in this essay all began a century ago when literature ceased to be a part of a received cultural tradition within a closed class culture and became an academic subject to be taught to masses of students. The literature departments then failed to adjust to the new situation, something which was understandable enough given the extraordinary complexity of the new situation and the rapidity of the changes which had brought it about. What is less easy to forgive is the complacent lack of interest in making major institutional readjustments which marked literature departments (and not only literature departments) then and still by and large marks them now, despite the general agreement that a crisis is at hand.

In the absence of intellectual community, there ceases to be a context for literary criticism, which has little choice but to become – when homogenized for institutional use as it inevitably must be – one or another form of technical manipulation. Studying literature and learning to become a critic become largely an affair of learning how to "create" texts the way the slickest professors do. Eventually, it becomes hard to remember why the professors wanted to create those texts in the first place, but by that time nobody needs a reason.

---

1. Edwin Greenlaw, *The Province of Literary History* (Baltimore: Johns Hopkins University Press, 1931), p. 4.

2. Douglas Bush, "The New Criticism: Some Old-Fashioned Queries," *PMLA*, 64, supplement, part 2 (March 1949), p. 20.

3. Helen Vendler, "Presidential Address 1980," *PMLA*, 96, No. 3 (May 1981), pp. 344–50.

4. As Hazard Adams has said, "to fall back and rally 'round in this way is to harden into dogma the results of the violent revolutions of a previous generation of scholars and surely to lay the groundwork unknowingly for a new revolution, as violent as the preceding one, now forgotten." "How Departments Commit Suicide," *Profession 83: Selected Articles from the Bulletins of the Association of Departments of English and the Association of Departments of Foreign Languages* (1983), p. 30.

5. René Wellek, "American Literary Scholarship," *Concepts of Criticism* (New Haven: Yale University Press, 1963), p. 300; first published as "Literary Scholarship," in *American Scholarship in the Twentieth Century*, Merle Curti, ed. (Cambridge, Mass.: Harvard University Press, 1953).

6. Wallace Douglas, "Accidental Institution: On the Origin of Modern Language Study," this volume, pp. 35–61.

7. Wendell Berry, "The Loss of the University," this volume, p. 207.

8. Morris Dickstein, "Journalism and Criticism," this volume, p. 152.

9. On the utilitarianism of anti-utilitarian aesthetic theory, see my *Literature Against Itself: Literary Ideas in Modern Society* (Chicago and London: University of Chicago Press, 1979), 164 ff.

10. William A. Nitze, "Horizons" (MLA Presidential Address), *PMLA*, 44 (1930), p. v.

11. "American Literary Scholarship," p. 311.

12. Norman Foerster, "The Study of Letters," in Foerster, John C. McGalliard, René Wellek, Austin Warren, Wilbur L. Schramm, *Literary Scholarship: its Aims and Methods* (Chapel Hill, N. C.: University of North Carolina Press, 1941), p. 15.

13. Randall Jarrell, "The Age of Criticism," *Poetry and the Age* (New York: Vintage Books, 1959), p. 75. Jarrell's example could have been better chosen. Quentin Anderson's *The American Henry James* (1957), to which he here alludes, is (a) as much a work of "scholarship" as of "criticism," and (b) debatable in its contentions, but by no means "absurd."

14. These generalizations are developed more fully in a forthcoming book on the history of American literary studies.

15. Richard Levin, *New Readings vs. Old Plays: Recent Trends in the Reinterpretation of English Renaissance Drama* (Chicago and London: University of Chicago Press, 1979), p. 30.

16. R. Bruce Kibodeaux, "Counterparts—*Dubliners* without End," *James Joyce Quarterly* (Fall 1976), pp. 91–2; as Harold Fromm notes a propos of this statement, "the tone of this is exactly right for a modern 'Imitation of Christ,' even down to the 'modesty' of the priest advising that we can become like the Lord in our own "small way."" ("Literature as Religion," *Chronicle of Higher Education*, XIV:4 (March 21, 1977), p. 40.

17. Hershel Parker, *Flawed Texts and Verbal Icons: Literary Authority in American Fiction* (Evanston, Ill.: Northwestern University Press, 1984), p. 11.

18. Ibid., p. 139.

19. Ibid., p. 143.

20. Ibid., p. 142.

21. Paul de Man, "Semiology and Rhetoric," *Textual Strategies: Perspectives in Post-Structuralist Criticism*, Josue V. Harari, ed. (Ithaca, N. Y.: Cornell University Press, 1979), p. 129.

22. Nathaniel Hawthorne, "The Artist of the Beautiful," *The Centenary Edition of the Works of Nathaniel Hawthorne*, Fredson Bowers, ed. (Columbus, Ohio: Ohio State University Press, 1974), p. 475.

23. Stanley Fish, *Is There a Text in This Class? The Authority of Interpretive Communities* (Cambridge, Mass.: Harvard University Press, 1980), p. 68.

24. See my forthcoming essay on Fish in *New Literary History*, Fall 1985.

25. Edgar V. Roberts, *Writing Themes about Literature* (Englewood Cliffs, N. J.: Prentice Hall, 1982), pp. 89–90.

26. Ross Chambers, *Story and Situation: Narrative Seduction and the Power of Fiction* (Minneapolis: University of Minnesota Press, 1984), p. 3.

27. Chambers, p. 4.

28. A good example of the unfortunate way "traditional" humanities education tends to be conceived is the recent report by NEH Chairman William Bennett, "To Reclaim a Legacy," published in the *Chronicle of Higher Education*, XXIX:11 (November 28, 1984), pp. 16–21. Bennett wants to restore the cultural heritage as a "body of knowledge," as if what that heritage is had not been seriously contested by many of the thinkers he includes in his list of accredited masters. Bennett seems to me right to demand coherence in humanities education, but the kind of core program he recommends has failed to produce coherence in the past and seems no more likely to succeed now.

29. Raymond Williams, "Beyond Specialization," *Times Literary Supplement*, No. 4158 (December 10, 1982), p. 1362.

II. Marxism, Feminism, Theory

English in America Reconsidered: Theory, Criticism, Marxism, and Social Change

William E. Cain

> *But let's be serious.*
> –Jacques Derrida

> *The conditions we live among we tend to take for granted, especially if we have no such acquaintance with different conditions as can be a challenge to judgment and give us a standard.*
> –F. R. Leavis

When Richard Ohmann's *English in America: A Radical View of the Profession* appeared in 1976, it received many reviews, nearly all of which reached the same conclusion.[1] Reviewers generally agreed, first, that Ohmann addresses urgent problems in English studies, and second, that his Marxist sympathies distort and confuse his analyses.[2] Since the reviewers conceded that serious problems do exist and need to be remedied, and did acknowledge that the state of literacy and culture, the commerce between knowledge and politics, and the degree of complicity between literary study and the social order deserve serious scrutiny, one might have expected that theorists and critics would quickly come forward to correct, qualify, and extend Ohmann's account. Where does Ohmann go wrong? Why does his Marxist angle of approach skew his interpretation of "English in America"? Is Marxism so irrelevant to the American scene that we need a very different set of analytical tools to make sense of "English" as a discipline? Or does the fault lie instead—as Ohmann himself would observe—with "liberal" and "humanistic" academics who cannot bear to recognize and act upon the truths that Marxism teaches, truths that jar against comfortable, privileged habits? These would appear to be obvious questions for members of the profession to investigate and answer.

But, strangely, no one has sought to revise Ohmann and give a more focused and persuasive critique of "English" as a discipline, method of study, academic field, and haven for humane values. Critics have failed to engage the issues that Ohmann confronts, and this is particularly striking during a period when many lament the condition of English studies and feel hard-pressed to justify their labor.[3] Literary theory is thriving, intensive commentary on interpretive procedures abounds, and an astonishing number of sub-industries have emerged which take as their rationale and resource the writings of Jacques Derrida, Michel Foucault, Harold Bloom, Stanley Fish, or some other prominent figure. Yet Ohmann's book remains the first and last of its kind, its concerns judged to be important but apparently not compelling enough to merit further study. Why, one wonders, has this happened?

In part this failure is Ohmann's own fault. In his effort to prosecute his case powerfully, he sometimes lapses into overzealous phrasing and caricatures—rather than characterizes—the problems he treats. But this failure is also due to the inability of academics to take their discipline as an object of study and reflection. Most of us profess that English studies are in trouble, even in "crisis," yet we instinctively recoil from any sustained attempt to evaluate the discipline, probe its methods, review and assess its history, explore its rituals and statements of purpose. Literary theory continues to prosper, and to an extent it does sponsor work on the aims of interpretation and teaching. But theory has not caused members of the profession to reexamine their enterprise in fundamental ways. In certain respects it actually hinders and deflects the type of critique of English studies we need, and ensures that Ohmann's book—and the issues it raises—will stay distant from the center of critical attention.

I

Ohmann argues that we should inspect "the folkways of teachers" and practices of the profession. He provides good discussion of the Modern Language Association, departmental structure and ideology, the rise of New Criticism and its effect on the teaching of literature, and he is particularly astute in his polemical attack on the Advanced Placement Program and freshman composition texts. He contends that the AP exams reveal a marked "formalist" bias, abstracting the literary work from history and obliging the student to trace intrinsic patterns and themes. "The work of literature that emerges," Ohmann states,

> has almost no intellectual content: the same process of distillation and attenuation that turns people into characters and feelings into attitudes turns ideas into *themes*: A theme is an idea, with the verb and the direct object taken away: age, time, innocence, human fallibility, and the like. The Advanced Placement work of literature contains themes, and it may even contain issues, but there is no suggestion that it may actually contain an idea or press a claim. It is intellectually bloodless. (p. 60)

A similar "impersonal" quality and absence of historical grounding are evident, Ohmann contends, in the freshman composition manuals and handbooks. These texts, in his view, teach the student to write mechanical prose in response to banal, numbing assignments. "Textbook writing," says Ohmann,

> begins in the nowhere of the assignment, moves into the unbordered regions of the student's accumulated experiences, settles on one region – the topic – and *then* looks around for feelings and beliefs to affix to that topic, with supporting details to be added afterward. (p. 153)

Ohmann saves his most severe appraisal, however, for the "professional" ethos that encourages bad pedagogical practices and allows them to survive. Our "professionalism" is basically just another name for self-interest, he declares. We tell ourselves that we uphold noble values and traditions, and that the discipline of "English" has its own unique methods and goals. But the truth of the matter is that "English" as it now stands is pretty much an assemblage of unexamined customs and self-serving routines:

> There is no common core of knowledge, no "discipline," no theoretical framework, no central pragmatic problem to be solved. As in most academic fields, the profession of MLA members is simply whatever activities have grown up round certain subjects and have somehow become respectable. There are very few techniques that must be specially mastered and very few intellectual abilities that differ from the completely general ability to frame hypotheses and weigh evidence – that is, to be an intelligent human being. So "professional standards" means simply the standards of those who have achieved prominence in the profession. (p. 39)

Ohmann's statement is excessive and overdrawn, but his general diagnosis is accurate, at least to the extent that it highlights the manner in which "professional" ethics override – and even substitute for – intellectual rigor and coherence. It is hard not to react defensively to the sting of Ohmann's words, and many readers have protested against his blunt assessment. But these same readers have not been able, it seems, to muster forceful arguments on behalf of the discipline and thus counter Ohmann's charges. They have been able to note quite easily where Ohmann exaggerates or permits his tone to be more contemptuous than analytical, but they have generally avoided the task of defending and justifying English studies in positive terms, as though to do so would be to convict oneself of bad faith or to perform a job that has been done before and does not bear repetition.

Throughout *English in America*, Ohmann calls attention to issues that every teacher and critic should feel required to consider – the relation between the skills taught in English and the personnel needs of the economic system, the influence of "class" and "governing interests" on the structure (and values) of the discipline, and, above all, the social and political contexts for "knowledge." "There is just no sense," Ohmann maintains, in pondering the function of literature without relating it to the actual society that uses it, to the centers of power within that society, and to the institutions that mediate between literature and people. . . . The function of literature and the role of English teachers cannot be understood except within the context of a given society and politics. (p. 303)

This seems to me to be indisputable, and it indicates a line of inquiry and debate that theorists, critics, and teachers should want very much at the present time to pursue. As we know all too well, English studies is now afflicted with declining enrollments, a painfully contracted job market for new Ph.D.'s, and undergraduates who are dubious about the rewards of the humanities in an era of economic scarcity. It would appear essential for us to survey the discipline and articulate both what *is* and *should be* its function in the college and university, its social role, its slant on political and economic questions. But despite the proliferation of conferences, symposia, new journals, MLA special sessions, summer schools in literary theory, and programs in criticism and interpretation, there has been only minimal interest in exploring the discipline itself—its history, techniques, structure, curriculum, social and political cast. "Theory" is vital and exciting, yet it is also becoming self-contained, a showy preserve for specialists where few seem able or willing to address practical matters in straightforward speech.

II

The boom in literary theory is indeed remarkable, and it produces texts and commentaries at an amazing rate. But even as this theoretical work prospers, it oddly comes to feel less significant, divorced from the issues that Ohmann highlights. "Theory" today is rapidly developing its own domain, compartmentalizing itself and making only the barest contact with pedagogy, where much of the real work of "English" occurs. The plain fact is that the surge of theory has exerted only a marginal influence on the academic discipline of English studies, and, as Tony Davies has remarked with admirable candor, it has proven almost wholly irrelevant to teaching. "Whatever I may write or think," Davies confesses,

however pure, rigorous, and systematic my discourse may be on such occasions, when once again I sit down to a tutorial or seminar, with "Lycidas" or *Middlemarch* open in front of me, and turn, in that expectant pause, to the surrounding faces, what comes out of my mouth then is likely to sound, by the highest standards of discursive rigor, decidedly limp: 'Well, what do you think of this, then?'[4]

True, the face of academic publishing has altered, as new models and authorities have appeared—Derrida, Lacan, Foucault, and others—to help shape and buttress critical arguments. But even this change has been minor; most publishing—the kind that secures promotion and tenure—remains geared to "close reading" the great tradition. About all that "theory" has accomplished is to provide new ways of explicating classic texts, texts that might otherwise have seemed exhausted, "used up," unable to grant still more "readings."

To say this is to risk overstatement, to be sure. At its best, theory has usefully exposed the shortcomings of the New Criticism—its rigidity, overemphasis on purely literary categories, and abstraction from history. And theory—most notably in feminist criticism and its offshoots—has also delved into (and unsettled) old and untenable distinctions between canonical and noncanonical texts. But it nevertheless remains the case that theory has won its widest support when it has aided in the job of explication. When theory supplies new forms of textual exegesis—and thereby dramatizes the richness and inexhaustibility of the great books—then it often gains even the acclaim of those who are *opposed* to theory. And this accounts, I think, for the speed with which one theory after another arrives on the scene, causes a commotion (as both its advocates and foes overrate its impact) and then gets incorporated into the standard ways of conducting interpretive business.

Nowhere is this more evident than in the case of "deconstruction," which was once fearful and terrifying but which has now been transformed into yet another object of study and tool for devising explications. As recently as six years ago, many in the profession voiced concern that Derrida and his American disciples were destroying the foundations of literary study. M. H. Abrams, for instance, in a critique of J. Hillis Miller, noted that "if one takes seriously Miller's deconstructionist principles of interpretation, any history which relies on written texts becomes an impossibility."[5] And E. D. Hirsch, in the Introduction to *The Aims of Interpretation*, cited Derrida as exemplifying the "antirationalism, faddism, and extreme relativism" that were bringing about the downfall of humanistic values and the literary tradition.[6] But while the controversy lingers, it has certainly diminished in intensity. English studies has survived, disordered but not destroyed, and no one worries that deconstruction is on the verge of overthrowing the discipline.

Why has this occurred, and why so quickly? Why has deconstruction made so little impact? In part the hostilities ceased because it soon became evident that both the deconstructionists (at least in America) and their antagonists shared much common ground. On the surface, Hillis Miller might seem to be proposing radical views of "meaning" and questioning our usual devices for interpreting texts. But whatever his deconstructionist tenets, Miller accepts the uniqueness of "literary language" (which is self-deconstructing, self-dismantling); he adheres to the traditional canon; and he proclaims that the strength of the deconstructive method lies in its ability to generate "readings." "The ultimate justification of this mode of criticism," Miller states, "as of any conceivable mode, is that it works. It reveals hitherto unidentified meanings and ways of having meaning in major literary texts."[7] Deconstructive "readings" are often subtle and cogent, but they depart only modestly from the academic procedures to which we are accustomed. These "readings" were of course originally touted as a marked advance beyond the New Critical variety, but, as Miller's own theory and practice demonstrate, the current academic version of deconstruction basically updates the New Criticism, is not so much an innovation as a mesmerizing "option" added to the familiar make-and-model. "My instincts," Miller admits,

> are strongly preservative or conservative. I believe in the established canon of English and American literature and in the validity of the concept of privileged texts. I think it is more important to read Spenser, Shakespeare, or Milton than to read Borges in translation, or even, to say the truth, to read Virginia Woolf.[8]

"I'm still true to my primary interest in the New Criticism," Miller elsewhere observes, "in that ultimately my real interest is in accounting for literary texts."[9] What this radical theorist might once have denied — that deconstruction resembles New Critical formalism — he now openly acknowledges and gladly affirms.

But deconstruction has grown less menacing for other reasons besides its affinities with the New Criticism. One of these involves the stylistic obscurity of Derrida's work during the past ten years, an obscurity that makes his earlier books such as *Of Grammatology* (1967; trans. 1976) and *Writing and Difference* (1967; trans. 1978) now seem lucid. Even in translation, Derrida's recent texts — *Dissemination* (1972; trans. 1981) is an obvious case in point — are extraordinarily dense and difficult, and very resistant to appropriation; critics in search of new methods for explicating texts cannot extract anything "useful" from them. Because these texts are so daunting, they exist primarily for Derrida's most devoted followers — the explicators and celebrants who take his writing as their special field and subject matter. A great deal of Derrida has appeared in translation during the late 1970's and into the 1980's, but one wonders how much of it is read — or could be read — outside the circle of experts.

Increasingly, too, Derrida has become a figure whose work is summarized, reported on, interpreted. To grasp deconstruction, it is not necessary to expose oneself to his intimidating texts. Instead, one can pick up a handbook or guide to Derrida and receive a sturdy paraphrase of what he practices, what deconstruction is, and how it might be employed in textual analysis. This is the form through which most people learn about deconstruction; they read Jonathan Culler, Barbara Johnson, Christopher Norris, or Hillis Miller, all of whom (some more than others) seek to be faithful to Derrida's complexity but who inevitably domesticate his work, untangle the gnarled, tortuous prose, and give us access to new interpretive schemes.[10]

But in one important respect, deconstruction is still controversial. The traditionalists, including Hirsch and Abrams, are no longer anxious about it, but curiously enough, many vanguard theorists *are*. They perceive deconstruction as a conservative, even reactionary, force, in league with the scholarly establishment that it initially seemed to threaten. Terry Eagleton, for example, sees the "new Yale School" to be practicing deft criticism but evading ideology. These deconstructionists, he avers, fetishize literature, making it "the last place to play, the sole surviving antechamber of liberal hesitancy."[11] Frank Lentricchia, in an essay on Foucault, indicts the Yale School and their clientele even more harshly. Paul de Man, he asserts, "has no desire to employ the literary in the redemptive work of social change" and communicates "no sense of his work's place within social and political crisis—his talk of 'critical crisis' is academic in the most debilitated sense of the word: it can only interest professors of literary theory."[12]

Up to a point, I share Eagleton's and Lentricchia's discontent. Deconstruction is now—and is likely to remain—an instrument for literary critics, and in its isolation from the thick texture of history, it does minister to political withdrawal and quietism and distances itself from the crucial academic, disciplinary, and institutional matters that Ohmann underlines in *English in America*. Deconstruction promotes ongoing inquiry, radical skepticism, and analysis of the linguistic "ground" upon which authority rests—all of this is important and any ideological critique will benefit from the illuminations that Derrida, de Man, and the others offer. But obsessed with "difference" and "demystification," deconstruction has never managed to halt its swirling patterns of negation; it is a formidable weapon for undermining other methods, positions and beliefs, yet seems unable to furnish positive terms of its own. It is in the very nature of deconstruction to turn upon and undercut its moments of apparent stability, and thus it cannot substantiate or solidify the reasons for political choice or even justify an act of choice in the first place. Politics involves resistance and opposition, but it also implies work *for* something, *on behalf of* something, and a serious concern for the reality—which is not figurative, linguistic, or textual—of cruelty, suffering, and exploitation. Because deconstruction boldly claims to revise our notion of the "text" and subvert the basis for criticism, it appeals to many academics as a thrilling exercise. But it goes nowhere; as Eagleton concludes, deconstruction "provides you with all the risks of a radical politics while cancelling the subject who might be summoned to become an agent of them."[13]

A striking instance of the political flaws in deconstruction occurs in Norris' recent book, *Deconstruction: Theory and Practice*. In his chapter titled "Marx and Nietzsche: The Politics of Deconstruction," Norris states that Derrida teaches us to discern the "figurative" or "metaphorical" ground upon which Marxism and all other political theories rest. "To deconstruct a text in Nietzschean/Derridean terms is," he affirms, "to arrive at the limit point or deadlocked *aporia* of meaning which offers no hold for Marxist-historical understanding."[14] Norris is right to be critical of any "politics" that claims to lie wholly "beyond" or "outside" language, and he scores good points against post-structuralist forms of Marxism now being advanced in the academy. But in a perverse twist of argument, Norris closes his discussion by endorsing (if joyously) defeatism and despair. "Once criticism enters the labyrinth of deconstruction," he insists,

> it is committed to a skeptical epistemology that leads back to Nietzsche, rather than Marx, as the end-point of its quest for method. Nietzschean "method" is no more perhaps than a lesson in perpetual self-defeat, but a lesson more rigorous and searching than the compromise assurances of post-structuralist Marxism.[15]

Norris believes that his political vision is sharp and vigilant, yet it is queerly self-satisfied, sophisticated in its procedures but smug in its conclusions. The deconstructionist spins in "perpetual self-defeat," soothed by the knowledge that his or her methods, though directing us always to a "dead end," are at least "rigorous and searching" and hence the sign of superior insight.

But I am suspicious of the political judgments on deconstruction, even though these seem apt and accurate. Literary theory right now is immersed in political talk, and the most current means for detecting the bankruptcy of a certain theory or method is to uncover its political blindness, its irrelevance to any program for "radical social change." Political awareness is surely preferable to being apolitical, but one wonders whether the "politicizing" of literary theory signals a new awareness or is, instead, the latest attempt by academic critics to find "something" that will finally disprove our fears of marginality and make clear just how important we are—it's as though we have discovered ourselves, much to our surprise, on the front lines of ideological warfare after all.

Attacking deconstruction for its "political" naivete may prove bracing to the person who launches the charge, and who can thus announce his or her own political right-mindedness. But if political change is going to occur, it will not occur because we have suddenly recognized that deconstruction is the last place for the liberal conscience to assuage itself. Political change, if it comes at all, will come through specific acts of work. As teachers and critics, we do indeed have roles to play, but we ought not to expect the world to be remade because we have decided that deconstruction is trivial and that the truth lies somewhere else, in some other global theory, philosophy, or political platform. The proponents of the new, politicized criticism do not see that their desire for immediate fulfillment, for the heady pleasure that results from labeling heroes and villains, merely duplicates the desire for the quick thrill and easy gratification so common in contemporary culture. "Politics" must be part of our discourse in the academy, but it threatens at the present time to become yet another route to marginality and isolation, another opportunity for indulging in high-powered rhetoric and avoiding problems in methods of instruction, teaching and research, departmental structure and curricula. And it also threatens, even in the case of a critic as shrewd as Lentricchia, to edge into a kind of intolerance for merely "academic" labor, for work that does not light up the path to "radical social change" in an acceptable fashion.

I am not arguing against politics, but urging that we make our politics more local, tactical, situational, pragmatic. Like F. R. Leavis, I believe that "the tendency of our civilization" is *away* from intellectual rigor, high standards, and shared values, and that this predicament

> must be of the utmost concern to everyone who thinks literature really matters. That anyone seriously preoccupied with the problems of education, and of literary criticism as a function that can enlist the powers of a responsible mind, can *not* see the given tendency as a major fact, exacting attention every day, seems to me impossible.[16]

Critics and teachers must, in my view, acknowledge and accent the social, cultural, and political bearings of their enterprise. To fail or refuse to do so is to blind oneself to the worldly contexts for knowledge and to disable, right from the start, any serious claims for the critical, inquiring spirit that English studies should display and encourage. As Leavis elsewhere observes, it is "an urgently necessary work" for those in English studies "to explore the means of bringing the various kinds of specialist knowledge and training into effective relation with informed general intelligence, humane culture, social conscience, and political will."[17] But also like Leavis, I would want to insist that "one does not take one's social and political responsibilities the less seriously because one is not quick to see salvation in a formula or in any simple creed."[18] The danger of a "politics of interpretation," a danger that many theorists seem unable to avoid, is that it distracts us from the actual work we can undertake and prevents us from instituting significant reforms in the discipline that might eventually create political differences.

Leavis' words do not always satisfy me, and they may seem elusive and evasive. But they have the advantage of turning our attention away from a certain bad kind of political argument now prevalent in the academy—a kind of argument that welcomes political discussion but only on a grand scale safely removed from the details of pedagogy and practice. Rather than focus on either deconstruction or politics "in the large," I judge it to be more profitable to examine the sorry state of English studies and advocate particular changes there. The discipline lacks system and coherence, and in fact its degree of disorder regularly proves shocking to people who teach in other fields. On the undergraduate level and in most graduate courses as well, we persist in explicating the classic literary texts and lining them up in very familiar periods and groupings, and we do so at the expense of other, more imaginative and historically enterprising arrangements that could provide students with a different (and less narrow) set of skills. Despite the sophistication of literary theory and many appeals for radical "political" change, we still abide by humdrum routines in organizing the discipline. We still allow students, for example, to jump from Romantic poetry to American realism to Jacobean drama and then to other areas equally disconnected from one another, deluding ourselves that we have thereby enabled the students to "structure" their major. With so much concrete work to be done within the discipline, it is no wonder that many theorists prefer to envision loftier tasks, rushing to embrace deconstruction and preach the end of metaphysics or else anxiously declaring their political conversion and disdain for deconstruction and the timid souls who have adopted it.

The jobs that demand attention are not very glamorous. We need a much more systematic curriculum, new techniques in pedagogy, clearer statements of the relation between work in composition and the study of literature, and a recovery of the texts and traditions—what Foucault terms the "subjugated knowledge"—that the canon as we know it conceals. We should also be willing to ponder the fundamental questions that now make us edgy and uncomfortable and that we would rather not address: What should be the collective "work" of the department? What kinds of knowledge does such a division of labor foreclose? How do the department and discipline "structure" knowledge? What is our relation to traditional literary culture—the texts of the great tradition? Do we have a responsibility to preserve this culture or should we aim instead to destabilize, reorient, and revivify it? Deconstruction has taught us valuable things about textuality, and the new "politics of interpretation" has made us alert to the limitations of Derrida's, de Man's, and others' methods. But to get entangled in either deconstruction or political assaults upon it is to misdirect our energy and avoid confronting the disarray of English studies. It is to refuse, once again, to analyze and evaluate the discipline we "tend to take for granted" and to guarantee that Ohmann's book is never improved upon.

III

I have stressed the need to study the discipline and argued that neither literary theory nor the academic brand of political theory is taking this direction. But it may seem that I have not done justice to Marxism, which provides the underpinning for *English in America* and is now winning a number of zealous converts in English studies and departments of foreign languages. Marxism, some have suggested, is the analytical method and philosophy that will make visible and articulate the workings of the academic institution and its place in late-capitalist society. But is Marxism the project and vision that we should embrace? Is Marxism likely to revise our understanding of English studies, its function, aims, values? I am not convinced, and I fear that Marxism is once again, as in the 1960's, tantalizing academics with impossible dreams and disfiguring the process of critical thought. Much of the Marxist writing in the academy strikes me as obscure and jargon-ridden, generated by and for a coterie and detached from the interests and comprehension of the profession as a whole.[19] But the inadequacy of Marxism has less to do with the alienating language of its devotees than with its inapplicability to the disciplinary practices and problems that teachers and critics worry about. Here I think it is instructive to return to *English in America*, the only full-scale Marxist treatment of the academy, in order to scrutinize the manner in which Ohmann's politics impairs (and impedes) his critique. Ohmann, as I have pointed out, does a fine job of setting out a range of disciplinary, professional, and institutional issues, issues that contemporary theorists and critics have failed to engage. But Ohmann continually violates and simplifies these issues by his dogged adherence to a Marxist approach that leads him into oddly naive statements and warped judgments, and that prohibits him from interpreting issues and relationships keenly. Compared to the general run of academic Marxists, Ohmann's writing is lucid, and the explicit cast of his polemic means that his assumptions and judgments are easy for us to apprehend. But while this is a reason for praise, it also means that his errors are equally easy to detect, and these help to demonstrate, I think, why Marxism fails—so far, at any rate—as an interpretive model for the critique of English studies and reform of "English in America."

Ohmann contends that "the ruling classes want a culture, including a literature and a criticism, that supports the social order and discourages rebellion, while it sanctions all kinds of nonthreatening nonconformity" (p. 25). He paints his picture with very broad strokes and leans on phrasing that seems unduly ominous and conspiratorial; as always, one wants to know just who are "the ruling classes." There is undoubtedly a kernel of authenticity to Ohmann's words, but this results from the generality of his assertion: it is hard to imagine any social system that would encourage its own overthrow, that would actively promote "a literature and criticism" of rebellion.[20] Yet while Ohmann's point is too general in one respect, it is too narrow and one-sided in another. Ohmann sees the work of English studies in terms of limitation and constraint; he does not consider in detail whether English studies has done or can do productive labor that fosters (and provides tools for) criticism and social protest. I am not certain whether English studies could or should spark open "rebellion"; in any event, if we hope to win assent for this course of action, we are going to have to wait an extremely long time. But in teaching and critical writing, we can exemplify a socially engaged "critical spirit"—what Leavis once described as a general "co-ordinating consciousness"—that is not meekly submissive to the guidelines issued by "the ruling classes," one that testifies instead to the *general* function of the analysis and judgment that literary training promotes.

Ohmann, however, has a darker view of our "function":

> I used to wonder why it is that society pays English teachers so much money to do what by and large is fun: teaching fine literature. I now think that our function is extremely valuable: namely, to ensure the harmlessness of all culture: to make it serve and preserve the status quo. (p. 63)

Ohmann may be partially correct to say that "society" intends for us to "serve and preserve the status quo." But once again he accentuates the negative in his appraisal and excludes the positive. His account is not attuned to the paradoxical fact that English studies unsettles and resists "the status quo" as well as preserves it, is both in alliance with and in opposition to vested social and cultural interests. Ohmann offers evidence for this himself, but it is evidence that he does not truly reflect upon. Near the end of his chapter on the New Criticism, he notes that the "denial of politics" in the academy "could not continue forever" (p. 90). The events of the 1960's—the war in Vietnam, the destruction of the environment, revolution and uprising on the international scene—disrupted the pieties of English studies, making us at last attentive to politics. But there was still another factor, Ohmann admits in his final paragraph: "the very humanism we learned and taught was capable, finally, of turning its moral and critical powers on itself." What we witnessed, he concedes, was the emergence—however indirectly—of a critical consciousness that "English" helped to form. It is striking that Ohmann does not develop this insight; with the aid of a melodramatic quotation from Christopher Caudwell, he brings his chapter to a halt and then proceeds to his next section on "English 101 and the Military-Industrial Complex." Ohmann's failure here to treat the *enabling* power of English studies signals a flaw in his Marxist thinking throughout his book and exposes his restricted, deformed estimate of the critical powers he seeks to redirect. Ohmann knows on some level that the relations between English and the social order, education and advanced capitalism, are much more complex than his polemic suggests. But he buries his own insights, underrepresenting the impact of criticism and playing up its role as handmaiden to "the ruling classes."

The same imbalance occurs in Ohmann's anatomy of academic "professionalism." He identifies certain self-regarding, anti-intellectual tendencies in the profession, but he then fails to ask whether teachers and critics, whatever their shortcomings, have at times indeed accomplished something worthwhile and capitalized upon literary study as a source (and training ground) for critical awareness, recognition, and understanding. Admittedly he does observe that English, while curtailing freedom in some ways, ratifies and extends it in others. But again his presentation suffers from his inability or unwillingness to take these observations seriously. "Better the MLA than the FBI," he remarks. "Partly for this reason the university is one of the institutions that occasionally turns progressive" (p. 252). This is an insight that Ohmann should examine further, yet he exiles it to a footnote and thereby does not allow it really to inform, modify, and deepen his critique. He fastens himself to the severe evaluations that Marxism propounds and is not able to perceive the force of the adversarial role that criticism *has* played – as he grants himself – and can continue to play.

"Recall from earlier chapters," Ohmann says late in his book,

> some of the things we have traditionally attempted to teach: organizing informa-
> tion, drawing conclusions from it, making reports, using Standard English (i. e.,
> the language of the bourgeois elites), solving problems (assignments), keeping one's
> audience in mind, seeking objectivity and detachment, conducting persuasive
> arguments, reading either quickly or closely, as circumstances demand, producing
> work on request and under pressure, valuing the intellect and its achievements.
> These are all abilities that are clearly useful to the new industrial state, and, to the
> extent that English departments nourish them – even if only through the agency
> of graduate assistants – they are giving value for society's money. (pp. 301–02)

Ohmann assumes that because we teach these skills, we place our-selves (and enroll students) in the service of the State. He does not inquire whether these same skills might be invoked to criticize the State, nor does he make any effort to measure each in its own right. Is it a bad thing to know how to "organize information"? Are we in fact sadly mistaken when we value "the intellect and its achievements"?

Ohmann invites his readers to "teach politically with revolution as our end" (see p. 335), but he does not envision the type of "revolutionary" work that should occur in the classroom. Nor does he sketch the rele-vant procedures and methods, outline the standards for judgment and assessment, or, most important of all, tell us where the impetus for "revolution" is going to come from and how it will thrive in an American context. At times he hints at explanations, yet he invariably fails to elaborate them. In his chapter on the MLA, for instance, where he once again intimates that English studies and "literary culture" possess a real "critical" force, he refers admiringly to several major figures in the canon. "The literature we are to preserve," he reports,

> includes works by Milton, Voltaire, Rousseau, Swift, Goethe, Byron, Blake, Shel-
> ley, Carlyle, Shaw, and others of that rebellious ilk. Beyond that, I think it is
> accurate to say that every good poem, play, or novel, properly read, is revolution-
> ary, in that it strikes through well-grooved habits of seeing and understanding,
> thus modifying some part of consciousness. (pp. 48–49)

Ohmann does not specify how teaching "works" by these "rebellious writers" is connected to the goal of Marxist revolution. It is one thing to state that we should emphasize – as, it should be noted, Stanley Fish, J. A. Wittreich, Christopher Hill and many others have already emphasized – the iconoclastic power of Milton, and another to define how this relates to and charts a particular Marxist path and nourishes political reversal in the society-at-large. Ohmann also appears to introduce a literary category here—the "good" poem, play, or novel—that seems apolitical, or, at best, political only in the most capacious sense. Is a text "good" because it is "revolutionary" or "revolutionary" because it is "good"? Do we value a text for its "rebellious" political message or do we instead—and much more generally—value it for its unsettling of familiar "habits of seeing and understanding"? I feel my criticisms may seem untidy, but this is the result of the muddled nature of Ohmann's writing here, its terminological slippage and begged questions. What does Ohmann mean by "properly read?" Is this a literary or political designation? How is "proper reading" taught and measured? Is it encouraged or enforced? How much sympathy (if any) should the teacher show for "improper" reading among students?

IV

I respect Ohmann's courage and determination to tackle vexing problems, but I think that there is a basic unreality to his Marxist angle of approach. "Marxism" comprises a potent and complex body of texts—no one denies its importance and interest. But it is not going to offer much more than a partial diagnosis of the ills of English studies, and it almost certainly is not going to win the endorsement and affirmation of the students and public constituencies that Ohmann desires to reach. Though *English in America* claims a historical orientation for itself, it is an oddly unhistorical book in certain key places, and these gaps prevent Ohmann from grasping the quixotic nature of his proposals. In closing his discussion of the New Criticism, Ohmann concedes that a different course for English studies in the forties and fifties is difficult to imagine, but he adds that Marxism would have supplied us with a more integrated view of literary study and politics:

> Where else we might have gone, under different historical circumstances, it is profitless to guess. Marxism did, of course, offer a logical alternative: criticism written as part of a world revolutionary movement. Marxism could connect literature and goals for action, thus rebuilding somewhat the whole person. It could bridge the seeming gulf between high culture and the lives of ordinary people. And it could use literature as an agent of liberation, rather than of bourgeois freedom, which depends on exploitation. But that is another story. Given how American academic intellectuals were functioning in the forties and fifties, Marxian criticism was bound to be excluded from among the possibilities for respectable discourse about literature. (p. 89)

The other "story," however, is precisely the one that Ohmann should narrate; his glancing allusions to McCarthyism and the Cold War (pp. 79–80) do not furnish an adequate historical context to explain the academic "flight from politics" he denounces. What Ohmann is saying about the apolitical thrust of the New Criticism may well be true—though it is worth remembering that the New Critics, in their agrarian phase, assailed capitalism in severe terms and always assigned a real, if somewhat hazy, redemptive social mission to criticism.[21] But he requires much more detail and should press his point further. In Ohmann's scheme of things, Marxism appears to be the "logical alternative," but this "logic" ignores the persistent marginality of Marxist politics in America; as Edmund Wilson once remarked, the problem with Marxism is that it is incisive as a theory but irrelevant to the facts of "real life" in America. Ohmann might wish it were otherwise, but the truth is that a Marxist rendering of "English in America," like other, more general, Marxist prescriptions, seems destined to fall on deaf ears. Marred by internal confusions and obscurities, and unable to make contact with a sympathetic public, Marxism is primarily a refuge for academics who seek reassurance about their social conscience and commitment. This judgment may seem unduly harsh, but I think that Marxism, as discussed in the academy, is as out-of-phase with American political realities as is the deconstructionist party that the Marxists regularly condemn.

From time to time in American literary and cultural history, intellectuals have rediscovered Marxism, and they have invariably done so in a heightened manner that shows their eagerness for conversion, for an instantaneous movement from critical questioning and doubt to certainty. During the years of the Great Depression in particular, Marxism secured the allegiance of a relatively small but vigorous and vocal group of intellectuals. Marxism seemed, first of all, to offer an alternative to the skepticism and despair preached in the great modernist texts. And it also appeared to testify to the *power* of literature, as a means of explanation and instrument for reform. Marxism affirmed the connections between literature and society, writing and revolution, and thus beckoned to intellectuals as a kind of vitalizing true religion.

As soon as one uses the term "intellectuals," however, one begins to perceive the reasons for the failure of Marxism to enter significantly into English studies. Marxism did have its members in the academy, but their activities were veiled in secrecy and were often laughably irrelevant to the day-to-day business of teaching and research.[22] Marxism never managed to secure itself in college and university life; administrators and politicians resisted it, and made abundantly clear—the situation is somewhat better today—that the academic Marxist would find his or her job in jeopardy. Intellectuals and social activists—Granville Hicks, Michael Gold, Joseph Freeman, and others—fought hard for Marxism at conferences and congresses and in books and journals, as Daniel Aaron and others have noted in their studies of the period. But through the National Industrial Recovery Act (1933), the Wagner Labor Bill (1935), the Social Security Act (1935), and other legislation, the Roosevelt administration was able to turn many liberal and left-leaning men and women away from Marxism and towards the New Deal.[23]

Marxism further lost supporters as a result of its endless polemics and factional rivalries among Communists, Socialists, and those who drew upon Marxist terminology but resisted membership in either party. And the horrors of Soviet policy eventually rent asunder the last vestiges of a united front. Once the truth of the purge trials of 1936–38 came to light, and once Stalin signed his pact with Hitler in 1939, it was impossible to remain a Marxist with a clean conscience. Though it kindled heated exchanges, Marxism never threatened to control or even influence the academic study of literature. As Alfred Kazin concludes, Marxism in the 1930's was "a phenomenon, rather than a body of critical thought."[24]

Marxism proved alluring to intellectuals during the 1930's; it reemerged, in highly uncritical ways, as a result of the social conflict and upheaval of the 1960's, and it is now appearing once again, as the nation's economy lags and as academics, like other groups, seek to affirm the centrality of their labor and criticize injustices. These injustices are real and angering, but what is crucial to recognize here is the limited audience to which Marxism appeals and the self-defeating (because self-isolating) nature of a specifically Marxist commitment. For the most part, the audience for Marxism consists of a few intellectuals, academics, and graduate students. Even in the 1930's, Marxism did not win many converts in the labor force as a whole, at least not converts who kept faith for very long; and Michael Gold's and others' advocacy of a "proletarian realism" now seems feeble at best. Today Marxist academics generally do not even seem intent upon making connections to the proletariat or linking theory and criticism to new forms of art: there is a marked disproportion between their vigorous rhetoric and its actual relation to the American scene. As Milton Cantor aptly states about the Depression years—and his judgment applies to the present as well—"one thing appears indisputable. Economic deprivation did not rouse the exploited and revolutionize consciousness."[25] The high degree of social mobility in America, the absence of a true "class consciousness" in the work force, the system's capacity for adjustment and accomodation—these facts of American life are extremely hard to dislodge and overcome. Marxism can aid us in understanding them, but we would be naive to take Marxism as the road to a reformed academy or new America. By tossing off a single-sentence alternative to the entanglement of private industry and research—"what we need, for a starter, is public industry" (p. 329)—even Ohmann seems to acknowledge the hopelessness of his Marxist remedies.

Let me be clear about what I am saying. I am not discounting the value of Marxism, nor am I claiming that the failure of Marxism to secure itself in America is an argument for its falsity. I am instead suggesting that Marxism is not likely to provide more than a partial (and very limited) means to renovate English studies and renew the critical powers that the college and university should ideally display. We might prefer to believe that Marxism can secure itself at last and guide us to a better future. But to affirm a Marxist position can be no more than a futile gesture, one that sparkles with moral certainty and a seeming unity of thought and action, but that will end in enclosure and alienation and that will cripple the function of criticism.[26]

It might seem that my judgment is extreme, and that among other things I badly underestimate the risks involved in professing Marxism in academic work. But while I agree that Marxists do not always enjoy an easy time, I suspect that they are less endangered than they believe and that this is an index to their marginality. In literary-theory circles, Marxism has acquired a special status and is now the predominant subject and system of belief in debates about the politics of interpretation. No one dares to utter liberal doctrine, and any attempt to voice a "left-conservative" position—one that strives for social-democratic courses of action yet retains certain traditional views of criticism and education—is guaranteed to provoke the ire of those anxious to bear witness to more "radical" visions and eager to triumph at the game of political one-upmanship. There has long been a serious need for political awareness and analysis in academic discourse, and Marxism is at present (at least in criticism and theory) the most visible and vocal means of satisfying it. But the relative success of Marxism in vanguard circles is less the proof of its essential rightness and relevance than the sign of its failings. Marxists in the academy should ask themselves why their path has not been more difficult, why they are without serious opposition. Marxism lays claim to and touts its potent explanatory power, but it has no vital connection to the real political scene and hence is destined to remain a marginal enterprise. And this perhaps suggests the reason for its privileged place in current debates about "English in America." It is often easiest to accept what we know we will not be required to act upon, and to endorse a doctrine whose consequences and implications for our lives we know we will never face.

What, then, must we do? We need, I think, to recognize that the most realistic political course of action for us at the present time is liberal, reformist, and progressive, and is a course of action that an American, not a Marxist, social-democratic vision impels and guides. Marxists will, I know, object to the language I am using here, and will quarrel with my esteem for American democratic ideals. But I would say in reply that this is the language (and the politics) that we must embrace if we hope to work constructively today to meet the immediate challenges of the American political scene and to counter the conservative right's assault on the poor, the helpless, the underprivileged. The problems of the present are simply too urgent for us to indulge in yet another invocation of Marxism and its "revolutionary" rhetoric. We cannot afford to deceive ourselves once again about the irrelevance and inapplicability of Marxism to American politics, culture, institutions.

How does the political alternative that I have sketched – all too briefly – figure in academic practice, in the field of English studies where the daily labor of the literary critic and teacher occurs? Such a politics implies, in a word, an oppositional relationship to vested interests and customary practices in scholarship and pedagogy. It means, more precisely, that we should move beyond the usual categories of "the literary," extending the canon to include texts by women and minorities; that we should reorient the curriculum *away* from courses that highlight "close reading" the masterpieces and *towards* courses that reflect an "opening up" of the canon and foreground historical, cultural, and political issues; that we should view "theory" as inescapable – and inescapably in need of being geared towards practice; that we should actively encourage judgment and discrimination among students – and other academics – who tend to lapse into relativism and indifference to intellectual rigor; that we should stress the continuities between the "criticism" we perform on literature and the critical thinking we ought to apply to the more general concerns of social, cultural, and political life.

Many members of literature departments resist these kinds of changes, and their resistance often shows an anger and intensity that they never devote to Marxism. They know that *these* are the changes that are truly significant, radical, and disruptive. And they also know – and fear the fact – that it is indeed possible to gain, if with difficulty, a sympathetic hearing among at least some teachers, critics, and students for the kind of oppositional work on behalf of change I have described. This work may not seem very glamorous, as I indicated earlier. But it can make a real alteration and adjustment in the "politics of interpretation" and, more importantly, can assist us in instituting essential differences in the politics and educational policy of contemporary America. Here is where our current task lies, and it is one that will demand as much energy, resourcefuless, and determination as we can summon.

---

1. Richard Ohmann, *English in America: A Radical View of the Profession* (New York: Oxford University Press, 1976).

2. Important reviews of Ohmann's book include Steven Marcus, "A Syllabus for Radicals," *Times Literary Supplement* (August 27, 1976), pp. 1042-43; C. L. Barber, "Is There Hope for English?," *New York Review of Books* (May 2, 1976), pp. 29-32; William Kerrigan, "English in the Death House," *Virginia Quarterly Review*, 53 (Winter 1977), pp. 180-92; and Patricia Meyer Spacks, "English in America: A Commentary on Ohmann," *The Yearbook of English Studies*, 8 (1978), pp. 197-207. See also Gerald Graff's discussion in *Literature Against Itself: Literary Ideas in Modern Society* (Chicago and London: University of Chicago Press, 1979), pp. 103-27. I discussed Ohmann briefly (and inadequately)

in "Making Judgments: Criticism Past, Present, and Future," *College English*, 42, No. 1 (September 1980), pp. 25–30.

3. I say this even though I am aware of the recent formation of "The Group for Research into the Institutionalization and Professionalization of Literary Studies" (GRIP) by the Society for Critical Exchange. This is an encouraging sign, and we should be grateful to GRIP's founders. But it is much too early to tell whether GRIP will manage to establish itself, secure a broad base of support, and reach a general audience.

4. Tony Davies, "Common Sense and Critical Practice: Teaching Literature," in *Re-Reading English*, ed. Peter Widdowson (London and New York: Methuen, 1982), p. 34.

5. M. H. Abrams, "Rationality and Imagination in Cultural History: A Reply to Wayne Booth," *Critical Inquiry*, 2 (Spring 1976), p. 458.

6. E. D. Hirsch, *The Aims of Interpretation* (Chicago and London: University of Chicago Press, 1976), p. 13.

7. J. Hillis Miller, "The Critic as Host," in *Deconstruction and Criticism* (New York: The Seabury Press, 1979), p. 252.

8. J. Hillis Miller, "The Function of Rhetorical Study at the Present Time," *ADE Bulletin*, 62 (September–November 1979), p. 12.

9. J. Hillis Miller, "Interview," conducted by Robert Moynihan, *Criticism*, 24 (Spring 1982), p. 111.

10. Jonathan Culler is the best of these commentators on deconstruction, and like other readers, I have profited from his authoritative analysis of Derrida's and de Man's writings. But there is a tension in his work that he has not yet entirely resolved. In his important essay "Beyond Interpretation," first published in 1976 and reprinted in *The Pursuit of Signs: Semiotics, Literature, Deconstruction* (Ithaca, N.Y.: Cornell University Press, 1981), he argued against "the widespread and unquestioning acceptance of the notion," fostered by the New Criticism, that "the critic's job is to interpret literary works" (p. 5). But one of the consequences of his books and essays on literary theory—and on deconstruction in particular—has been to increase the speed with which critics deploy new theories "to interpret literary works." Against his own inclinations, he is strengthening (and thereby helping to perpetuate) the New Critical legacy of "interpretation."

11. Terry Eagleton, *Walter Benjamin, or Towards a Revolutionary Criticism* (London: New Left Books, 1981), p. 109. If there is a problem with Eagleton's formulation, it is that he overestimates the "risks" involved in practicing deconstruction. To equate the "risks" of deconstruction and radical politics is to assign this literary theory more credit than it deserves.

12. Frank Lentricchia, "Reading Foucault," Part 2, *Raritan*, 2 (Summer 1982), p. 57.

13. Eagleton, p. 139.

14. Christopher Norris, *Deconstruction: Theory and Practice* (London and New York: Methuen, 1982), p. 80.

15. Ibid., pp. 84–85.

16. F. R. Leavis, "Reply to Martin Jarrett-Kerr," *Essays in Criticism*, 3 (July 1953), p. 365.

17. F. R. Leavis, *Education and the University: A Sketch for an "English" School* (1943; rpt. London: Chatto & Windus, 1972), p. 24.

18. F. R. Leavis, *For Continuity* (Cambridge, England: The Minority Press, 1933), p. 161. I deal briefly here with issues that I examine in more detail in *The Crisis in Criticism: Theory, Literature, and Reform in English Studies* (Baltimore: Johns Hopkins University Press, 1984). Leavis' criticism, especially that which he wrote later in his career, is defective in certain key respects. But it would be a mistake not to see the kinds of radical changes in criticism and pedagogy that Leavis, whatever his shortcomings, can help us to inaugurate.

19. Marxists should show more concern than they do about the obscurity that afflicts their style. No doubt they would argue that their style is rigorous, even scientific, in its

precision and is intended to disrupt the comfortable clarities of liberal styles of writing and thought. But it is nevertheless queerly ironic that Marxists present their revolutionary program, one with a general working-class orientation, in a style that few readers can grasp. This fault has increasingly come to mar the work of Fredric Jameson, who is among the most sophisticated and wide-ranging of academic Marxists. His recent books, *Fables of Aggression: Wyndham Lewis, the Modernist as Fascist* (Berkeley: University of California Press, 1979) and *The Political Unconscious: Narrative as a Socially Symbolic Act* (Ithaca, N.Y.: Cornell University Press, 1981), are often provocative, but too frequently the contorted style prevents Jameson from capitalizing upon his best discoveries.

20. In *Literature Against Itself*, Graff makes the additional point that Ohmann presents a monolithic—and outmoded—account of high culture: "A high culture which includes both Arnold and Artaud, Samuel Johnson and Samuel Beckett, has no ideological unity. As for those who rule, it is self-flattering but mistaken to think that these flexible pragmatists require high culture as a means of justifying or consolidating their power" (p. 117).

21. See *I'll Take My Stand: The South and the Agrarian Tradition*, by Twelve Southerners (1930; rpt. Baton Rouge: Louisiana State University Press, 1980).

22. See, as a representative pairing, Stuart Browne, "A Professor Quits the Communist Party," *Harper's Monthly Magazine*, 175 (July 1937), pp. 133–42, and anonymous, "A Professor Joins the Communist Party," *New Masses*, (October 5, 1937), pp. 2–7. In *The American College and University: A History* (New York: Random House, 1962), Frederick Rudolph observes that "change and uncertainty were the order of the day" on college and university campuses during the 1930's. But he adds that campus protest was not part of a coherent national movement, and certainly did not mirror any widespread support of the Communist Party (pp. 465–68).

23. Daniel Aaron, *Writers on the Left: Episodes in American Literary Communism* (New York: Harcourt, Brace and World, 1961); James Burkhart Gilbert, *Writers and Partisans: A History of Literary Radicalism in America* (New York: John Wiley and Sons, 1968); Marcus Klein, *Foreigners: The Making of American Literature, 1900–1940* (Chicago and London: University of Chicago Press, 1981), pp. 39–86; Richard H. Pells, *Radical Visions and American Dreams: Culture and Social Thought in the Depression Years* (New York: Harper & Row, 1973); Milton Cantor, *The Divided Left: American Radicalism, 1900–1975* (New York: Hill & Wang, 1978); Bernard K. Johnpoll and Lillian Johnpoll, *The Impossible Dream: The Rise and Demise of the American Left* (Westport, Conn.: Greenwood Press, 1981); and Leslie Fishbein, *Rebels in Bohemia: The Radicals of the Masses, 1912–1917* (Chapel Hill: University of North Carolina Press, 1982). See also David McClellan, *Marxism After Marx: An Introduction* (New York: Harper & Row, 1979), pp. 312–31; and the discussions in William Barrett, *The Truants: Adventures Among the Intellectuals* (New York: Doubleday & Co., Anchor Books, 1982), pp. 76 ff., and Irving Howe, *A Margin of Hope: An Intellectual Biography* (New York: Harcourt Brace Jovanovich, 1982).

24. Alfred Kazin, *On Native Grounds: An Interpretation of Modern American Prose Literature* (1942; rpt. New York: Harcourt Brace Jovanovich, 1970), p. 410. In these paragraphs I am repeating an argument I also present in *The Crisis in Criticism*, chapter 5.

25. Cantor, *The Divided Left*, p. 108. Cantor's treatment of these issues is astute, and I am indebted to it. I have also benefited from Irving Howe and Lewis Coser, *The American Communist Party: A Critical History* (1957; rev. ed. New York: Frederick A. Praeger, 1962); Lawrence Lader, *Power on the Left: American Radical Movements Since 1946* (New York: W. W. Norton & Co., 1976); and William L. O'Neill, *A Better World: Stalinism and The American Intellectuals* (New York: Simon & Schuster, 1982).

26. Cf. Paul Hollander, "Intellectuals, Estrangement, and Wish Fulfillment," *Society*, 20 (July–August 1983), pp. 16–24: "The intellectuals' need to believe has crystallized in our time around some variety of socialism or Marxism. Such ideological attachments led to the suspension or discarding of what used to be regarded as the major defining characteristic of intellectuals: their critical thinking, their capacity for social-political criticism and demystification" (p. 18).

On Behalf of Theory

Frank Lentricchia

> *We build the flux out inevitably. The great question is:*
> *does it, with our additions, rise or fall in value? Are the*
> *additions worthy or unworthy?*
> –William James

I agree with much of William E. Cain's reconsideration of Richard Ohmann's *English in America* from within the context of recent developments in critical theory. He has sure-handedly isolated the points of excess and hollowness in Ohmann's rhetoric, yet in the process he will not reject what is strong and true in Ohmann's book—the argument that the study of English in the United States tends to be intellectually bloodless. Cain would situate literary study socially and historically, and make it somehow politically active in the resistance against various kinds of oppression. In other words, though a critic of Ohmann, Cain refuses to throw in with traditional academics and other voices of the New Right in Reagan's America.

Since the publication of Ohmann's book in 1976, two competing theories have dominated the American critical scene. First deconstruction and now, as deconstruction moves over the hill, a new Marxism presumably revitalized by contacts with structuralism, Derrida and feminism. Neither movement compels Cain's admiration. In what goes by the name of deconstruction, he sees a political cop-out—an elaborate theory which tries to undercut any and all justification of political choice, including the choice to work against "cruelty, suffering, and exploitation." As a theory, deconstruction (in effect, if not in explicit intention) works on behalf of quietism and political enervation. In what goes by the name of Marxism, Cain sees a mostly irrelevant criticism of literature and society—culturally obscure and even weird in the eyes of most Americans—whose vision of history and social change, when *not* irrelevant to the American scene, had already been duplicitously co-opted by Rooseveltian liberals in the 1930's. These are points that I would not quarrel with, since in *Criticism and Social Change** I make them myself.

Where Cain and I differ is in our respective attitudes toward intellectual work in the academy and on the related question of the role of theory. Theory, he says, is becoming "self-contained, a showy preserve for specialists." At another point he says that "theory has not caused members of the profession to reexamine their enterprise in fundamental ways," perhaps because, as he states at still another point, most theorists, like a great deal of Derrida, neither have been nor could be read "outside the circle of experts." The first statement is true for those who practice theory in that way. And a lot of theory—deconstruction is particularly vulnerable on this point—encourages such self-regarding ballet. Since Cain names no names, I'm not sure who he has in mind. I have my own list. As healthy counter-examples to both statements I'd offer the writing of Kenneth Burke and Raymond Williams: both have produced a body of so-called practical criticism and both regard theory itself as a "practical matter" (a practice); both show us that even if theory (this is fashionable with weary theorists) is an after-the-fact justification of what theorists do anyway as readers, when it is done clearly theory at the very least can serve the important function of teaching others how to read and think about literature in a particular way: theory in this light serves an educational and therefore a political function. In the exemplary instances of Burke and Williams—this, I'd argue, is the basis of their health as critics—literary theory is always more than literary theory. For them, literary practice is a social practice and theory is a way of critically engaging the cultural work of both literature and literary criticism within a given social whole.

Thoroughly enough pursued, theory will encourage us to consider and judge the consequences of different interpretive procedures—it will force us to ask questions about the implications of interpretation that are not literary in import (not "literary" in the narrow formalist sense of the word). Moreover, such meditation often requires its own discursive space. The questions that theory raises are complicated; they have an ancient philosophical history; they cannot easily, and sometimes they cannot at all, be successfully posed and explored in the context of the usual forms of literary analysis and literary history.

Those who, like Walter Michaels—Cain may be among them—are these days speaking against theory will say that theory deviously poses itself as transcendental adjudicator of all practices, when in fact it is either an apology for what the critic does as reader or, when it sits in judgment against other practices, it judges them from the point of view of another practice: merely opinion, masked as knowledge, fighting

---

*Chicago and London: University of Chicago Press, 1983.

opinion. I don't wish to argue that this description of theory is wrong – it seems to me, in fact, too often to be right. The sort of theorizing that anti-theorists don't like always speaks with great authority and confidence because it always knows that literature is X – and nothing but X. Anti-theorists assume this posture too, but their virtue presumably lies in their ability to say openly that literature is my X or your Y – so why argue about it, since there is no epistemological ground above or beyond the terrain of controversy? What theory does, according to anti-theorists (anti-theorists are now, perhaps unwillingly, the voice of the traditional theory-haters in the profession), and what anti-theorists implicitly claim for themselves I'd call a truncated and overly mechanical view of intellectual life, which always projects us as absurdly blithe spirits: unreflectively locked into particular belief and the practice rationalized by that belief. What we do is what we do, and when we don't do it who knows why we change our minds?

Anti-theorists today tend to call themselves pragmatists, but the father of American pragmatism, Charles S. Peirce, long ago in his essay "The Fixation of Belief" attacked the stance of the anti-theorist as one of the traditional expressions of irrationalism, a nonmethod of fixing belief (not unknown among some "theorists") with bullheaded tenacity and, at its worst, with willful ignorance. Peirce did not believe that anyone of good faith could sustain the anti-theoretical stance in practice: "The social impulse is against it. The man who adopts it will find that other men think differently from him, and it will be apt to occur to him in some saner moment that their opinions are quite as good as his own, and that this will shake his confidence in his belief." If Peirce is right, then theory is not the pointlessly specialized activity of disengaged intellectuals; it is rather the fundamental obligation to live self-reflectively and even – this is a strong implication in the work of Peirce, James, and Dewey – a condition of democratic community.

What anti-theorists leave out is the most interesting, productive and I think human moment in our work. It is the moment of unrestrained doubt, when we feel utterly *unjustified* in doing anything, when we question everything, when what we do seems to us to have unacceptable consequences or (horribly) no consequences at all for our lives as social beings, when we don't know what to put in the place of what we've been doing, when we come to distrust putting anything in place of our old habits – because we know that any set of answers will once again say that literature is. . ., and you fill in the blank. This moment of doubting is also a time of agony because it feels as though we have no well-grounded set of opinions (no theory) from which to criticize literature and society. Out of this moment of flux, of radical questioning of everything, and for reasons difficult to be precise about, we make a decision, we move toward opinion, but now chastened, understanding that what we profess "in theory" is always socially complicit and compromised because theory's real origin is not the free-floating history of ideas (Derrida talks to Hegel who talks to Kant) but ideas that are grounded in the history of our lives.

What we take from this moment of personal crisis is not (I hope) the debased humanist sentiment that all points of view are valid, but the historical consciousness that any point of view—opinion, belief, theory—about literature and literature itself are alike in this crucial way: both are bound over to contexts and forces not in their autonomous control; both express something else besides themselves; neither is freely originary. To become committed to this historical lesson means reconceiving theory and the history of theory in something like the following way: theory is primarily a *process* of discovery of the lesson that I am calling historical; any single, formulable theory is a reduced version of the process, a frozen proposition which will tend to cover up the process it grew out of by projecting itself as an uncontingent system of ideas. The history of theory is a series of such propositions in calcified form, summary outlines of what others—other places, other times—have gone through. The canonical version of the history of criticism is, then, another version of the history of ideas in which these calcified systems communicate only with one another. To study theory and its history in the way I'm advocating is to try to recover from a reading of the calcified record of ideas the real conflicts—the particular social forces and the changing social grounds which are conveyed (both reflected and shaped) "theoretically." The chief value of this kind of study of theory is that it provides a convenient, because highly condensed and highly focused, access to the historical study of society and the powers that would dominate and resist therein. The study of theory, whether one's own or the older positions, is a way of studying the involvement of culture in political power and, in the twentieth century, the specific relations of academic criticism and political power.

Probably one of the most penetrating effects of theoretical reflection in the moment of doubt occurs when it puts bluntly forward consequences of what we have been practicing as critics which we do not want, which embarrass us, and it is at that point that theory is most urgent because it can become the triggering device of a change in our interpretive practice and, correlatively, of what we make of ourselves as social creatures who happen to teach literature. At such points in our theoretical reflections we become conscious of our responsibility. Bereft of theoretical practice in the sense I've put forward here, we are very likely to remain mired in blind interpretation, a way of reading that cannot turn on itself, cannot evaluate itself.

When I claim that theory fosters evaluation and self-critique, I do not claim that theory moves us above the conflict to some value-neutral, epistemically-secured space. Theory may foster evaluation because it encourages leaps into perspectives not our own, judgments upon ourselves from the vantage of other positions in the arena of conflict, and alien measurings of what we believe to be at stake. Theory, then, should not lead us into escape but into more intimate involvement in history: not for the purpose of making us happy and tolerant pluralists—empathetic occupation of another position may teach us how destructive that position is, may push us into even more vigorous opposition—but for the purpose of helping us understand that though there is plurality in the world of argument, the causes of such plurality are only in part intellectual (ideas are not *fons et origo*), that consciousness of self as a bearer and disseminator of ideas is necessarily coterminous with consciousness of self as a bearer and disseminator of values, that as intellectuals we always act on behalf of and against others—in the interests of some, against the interests of others—and that each of our acts as intellectuals has that sort of double edge. This is what I mean when I say that theory is a social practice.

So to be against theory, in this latest, perverse version of pragmatism and American anti-intellectualism, is to court the mindless life that those who like things just as they are hope we in America's colleges and universities will continue to cultivate. To be against theory is to be against self-examination—against raising and exploring questions about how texts and selves and societies are formed and maintained and for whose benefit. To be against theory is to take everything at face value and never to be suspicious. It is not the kind of posture that any critic with interests in social change, in whatever direction, should ever countenance.

Theory is being widely disseminated in our profession from "the circle of experts" to those of our colleagues who do not consider themselves theorists, to our graduate students and into our undergraduate classrooms. It is now causing many in the profession to ask questions they don't normally ask. There are very few graduate students these days who don't want to know about theory and what it might be for. Depending on how it is conceived, theory might be one of the movers of change. We'll have to see. *Why* theory might produce change is the question. Time will not tell because of course it never does. Rather, it is our "specific acts of work" (Cain's apt phrase) that will make the difference.

In understandable irritation (which I share) at the theoretical grandeur and Olympian distance of a lot of Marxist theorizing, Cain dismisses "academic Marxism" because it is disconnected from what he calls the "real political scene." But I would say that no intellectual of Cain's disposition can possibly live with the implications of the phrases "academic Marxism" and "real political scene." If by "academic" Marxist he means one who works in the academy, that's one thing. If the implication is that such a Marxist must work elsewhere in order to achieve authenticity and good faith, that's something else. Those who scourge academic Marxism might remember that Marx saw struggles against ideas as struggles against political, material forces. Ruling ideas, he argued, are the ideas of those who run things. Antonio Gramsci crucially extended Marx's argument: the production, management and dissemination of ruling ideas are the business not only of ruling-class intellectuals but also of traditional intellectuals like philosophers and professors of literature and poets who, whatever their economic background, unselfconsciously pass on ruling ideologies in the practice of what they take to be their autonomous disciplines. If the proper place for a Marxist intellectual is outside the academy—I don't believe it—then *all* intellectuals in the academy are displaced persons: they should all be in the streets, or maybe in Washington, or someplace, anyplace else that might qualify as the "real political scene." The point is this: either the academy is or is not what T. S. Eliot called a "conduit of tradition." Either tradition has or has not something to do with the maintenance of existing social structures. Either the intellectually privileged are or are not shaped by the dominant ideas of dominant social forces and classes. Either we will or we will not generate resistance. Eliot, no radical, was on Marx's side on all these issues. If Eliot and Marx are right, and I think they are, then the academy is a good place—as good as any other—for the work of social change and/or social conservation, depending on your politics and your desires.

Having once, without guilt, accepted his or her choice of place, it becomes necessary for the theorist not to succumb to the ward heeler's version of politics. I allude to Cain's sense that real political work in the university goes on at departmental meetings, where courses, appointments and curricula are debated and shaped. But this only seems to happen. Cain is putting the cart before the horse. People act at those meetings as they act elsewhere and as a consequence of what they think. I don't discount that some thinking goes on at those meetings, that thinking can actually be influenced at such moments. In the main, however, that doesn't happen. The job of people like Cain and myself is not to try to convince our colleagues in a meeting that the canon should be opened up. I have never seen anyone of commitment change his or her mind over such weighty questions in an hour or two. We will convince and exert influence before and after and outside those meetings, in the long debate carried on in our writing, our teaching and our conferences, over what to think of canons, formalist criticism and the like. What happens at the departmental (ward) level of political activity is a consequence, not an origin, an effect within the political scene, not the scene itself. The real political scene for academic intellectuals is in our work, where we work and the impact of our work—all of this at once—here and now in America.

Feminist Criticism in the University: An Interview with Sandra M. Gilbert

Gerald Graff

GRAFF: People now complain that the only real function of "academic criticism" is to reproduce itself: literary explication has become an industry, subject to laws of industrial production, and though it pretends to high functions such as aiding the public to appreciate literature, we all know that its real "public" is mostly other professors and its real "function" to advance careers. How would you respond to the charge that academic feminist criticism, despite its claim to political importance, is really just the latest of these growth-industries? Hasn't feminist criticism evolved its own versions of the standard industry PR: its own "methodology," its network of mutual self-congratulation and back-patting, its rationalizing theories of female writing, etc.?

GILBERT: As you know, I don't basically disagree with your worried postulate about "academic" criticism. In fact, I've speculated a lot lately on the decline of the poet-critic—the person of letters who (in the tradition of thinkers from Sidney, Coleridge, Emerson and Arnold to D. H. Lawrence, T. S. Eliot, Allen Tate and John Crowe Ransom) was both a practitioner and an analyst of literary art—and I've come to the tentative conclusion that the specialized structures of the university have fostered a schism between the right brain (the creative writer) and the left brain (the critic), which leaves both halves of the communal mind engaged in activities that often seem partial, passionless, even pointless.

But look back at the list of critical/artistic precursors I just assembled! Do I need to note that it doesn't include a single woman? Of course, I could have named Elizabeth Barrett Browning or George Eliot: but would you think I should define either as a professional *theorist*/artist comparable to Coleridge, Emerson or Arnold? Probably the first major English-speaking woman of letters whom everyone would agree that I should assimilate into that lineage would be Virginia Woolf—and then maybe Gertrude Stein, maybe Adrienne Rich. What I'm getting at here, of course, is a crucial dissonance between male and female intellectual history. Where male critics may well feel themselves both belated and diminished, where they may fear, indeed, that they have fallen from a lost and glamorous wholeness into the grimy holes of academic bureaucracy, their female peers see themselves as just beginning to enter intellectual culture and, more specifically, academic society. Thus (to arrive, finally, at the heart of your question), though we feminist critics may be industrious, we don't feel ourselves to be part of an industry, at least not in the pejorative sense of, let's say, a robot-like assembly line for turning out deconstructive readings of Conrad or structuralist analyses of *King Lear*.

On the contrary, if ours is an industry, it is a *home* industry, by which I mean a fundamentally confessional enterprise in which each participant inevitably begins her intellectual work with a careful study of the house of fiction(s) in which she herself has, perhaps unwittingly, dwelt all her life. As you can imagine, such a home industry requires the development of arts and crafts whose processes and products seem far more coherent, more directly relevant to, "reality," than the procedures of the academic assembly line may perhaps appear to the hapless assistant professors who unwillingly but desperately labor in the badly ventilated factories of bibliography or (even) in the dark Satanic mills of Derrida. In other words, I suspect that most of us like working for the home industry of feminist criticism because it does allow us to begin to integrate the right brain and the left brain, the feeling self and the thinking self.

Of course, we too are subject to the great macroeconomic laws of Publish or Perish. But then, twenty or thirty years ago most of us would have perished intellectually without ever having a chance to publish. Or, worse, we might have published *and* perished. Now I think it seems to many of us to be a privilege to have been given a job in a visionary company whose long-term goals actually encourage us to rethink our past, present and future in new ways. And, yes, we do no doubt indulge in a good deal of back-patting—or "networking," as the fashionable phrase would have it—but that, too, is for us an exciting, even unprecedented phenomenon. Where men of letters from the Renaissance to the Romantic period, and male academicians from the inhabitants of Virginia Woolf's "Oxbridge" to the acolytes of the "New Criticism," have always bonded, if only to discuss their differences, thinking women, as Adrienne Rich puts it, have slept with "monsters"—with nightmares of alienation or, at best, marginalization. Now mutual "back-patting"—by which I take you to mean "community"—at least seems possible, and for us it is an important and pleasurable possibility. As Woolf wrote in *A Room of One's Own*, discussing the friendship of "Mary Carmichael's" characters Chloe and Olivia, the very existence of such "back-patting" will "light a torch in that vast chamber where nobody has yet been," the room of female friendship.

Of course, I realize our new home industry is in some ways a hazardous enterprise. Some women intellectuals are probably put off by a level of enthusiasm that sounds like cant; others may be made anxious by what looks like the politicization of everything. As for our male colleagues, I'm sure a number of them secretly believe that we're all just a bunch of bitches who ought to go back to the kitchen. But for myself, I can say that I'd rather be enthusiastic about my workplace—and I'd rather feel that what goes on there is politically crucial in the best sense—than hold down an ordinary nine-to-five job whose criteria for advancement require distance, detachment, "coolness."

As for those who wish we'd go back to the kitchen, they are, of course, the very people who inspired us to found our own factory. Just thirty years ago, in a decade when many of us who do this work were just starting college, Lynn White, Jr., then President of Mills College, wrote a book called *Educating Our Daughters*, in which he proposed a "distinctively feminine curriculum" and speculated that a "beginning course in foods"—perhaps "focusing on the theory and preparation of Basque paella"—might be "as exciting as a course in post-Kantian philosophy." To be sure, many of us feminists did in fact learn to be very good cooks (as did our husbands), but is it any wonder that, imbued with unsatisfied intellectual hungers, we decided to convert our kitchen into a study? Is it so surprising that we wanted to have an "industry" of our own?

GRAFF: I can see why you would want to have one, but what is likely to prevent feminist criticism from becoming as hackneyed as the other (male) industries?

GILBERT: At the risk of sounding ameliorative or hyperbolical, I guess I'd say *desire*—a desire rooted in personal more than professional needs, or, perhaps more accurately, a desire in which the professional can't be separated from the personal since, to paraphrase a traditional feminist saying, for us the professional *is* the personal. After all, when you talk about "hackneyed industries," you're talking about hackwork, about alienated labor. By definition, however, our labor can't be alienated from ourselves, since our project aims at a kind of personal as well as sociocultural transformation.

GRAFF: You've written extensively about the questions raised by theories of "*écriture féminine*," "women's culture," and whether writing (and reading) are gender-specific. Obviously, this is a highly complicated question, but could you sketch your general line on it? Has coediting a large anthology of literature by women [*The Norton Anthology of Literature by Women*] changed your views on this question?

GILBERT: To begin with, I should confess that the very concept of *"écriture féminine"* sounds wonderful to me. Different as they are, the French feminist theorists who have developed this idea—perhaps most notably Hélène Cixous and Luce Irigaray—are themselves remarkably witty and charismatic writers, and such texts as "The Laugh of the Medusa" or "When Our Two Lips Speak Together" have a special Mystical/Romantic glamor for all of us. What woman artist (and here I think I speak more as my poet-self than as my critic-self) wouldn't want to find some way of writing in "white ink," in the rich milk of the female body? But, as you know, my collaborator, Susan Gubar, and I have tried hard to think about all the ramifications of this idea, and finally (in an essay entitled "Sexual Linguistics," which is coming out soon in *New Literary History*), we've concluded that *"écriture feminine"* is basically a compelling fantasy about language which must be seen as part of an ongoing dialectic of (male and female) linguistic fantasies, a battle of the sexes over the possession and potency of language which has, for various reasons, become increasingly intense in the last century.

Why do we use the word "fantasy"? Clearly I don't have time here to discuss our thoughts in very much detail, but I can make a few, brief points. First, what might "writing the body" *mean* anyway? As Cixous and others surely know, the phrase itself is somehow oxymoronic. In fact, just as several generations of Woolf scholars have tried to explain to themselves precisely what Woolf meant when, in *A Room of One's Own*, she called for "a woman's sentence"—and none, in my view, has managed to come up with specific criteria that would distinguish, say, Woolf's own syntactical structures from E. M. Forster's or, even, D. H. Lawrence's—so I can imagine platoons of critics seeking in vain to find the traces of milk and blood that linger in female texts. (And what if traces of milk and blood, or sperm and blood, are found in *male* texts? What if, in English literary tradition anyway, it is artists like Whitman and Lawrence who have "written the [male] body"?)

Second, and perhaps more important in critiquing the idea of *"écriture féminine"* (at least as Susan and I have thought things out), is the fact that theorists who call for a female body-language do so on the Lacanian assumption that woman is necessarily excluded from the symbolic order—excluded by, in Lacan's phrase, "the nature of things which is the nature of words"—because little girls and boys acquire language at just the moment when they are inscribed into culture through "the Oedipus," which enforces the dynamics of sexual difference. But in fact, as language acquisition studies show, and as Anika Lemaire reminds us that Lacan himself admits, most children have learned to talk before they enter the Oedipal stage, before, that is, their psychosexual and cultural identities have been firmly consolidated.

But if little boys and girls have become language-using creatures during the *pre*-Oedipal phase, a time when their absorption in the mother has not yet been transformed by the *nom* or *non du père* which represents patriarchal strictures and structures, then little girls are no more alienated from language than are little boys. To be sure, as they grow up they will discover that as, let's say, English has evolved, its vocabulary has developed many lexical asymmetries which reflect society's devaluation of women. Certainly the connotations of words used to describe women are frequently unpleasant and sexist: for instance, we think of a "poet" as a serious artist but a "poetess" seems somehow like a trivialized, secondary being. But I don't believe that there is anything inherent in the psychosexual relationship of men and women to language which *necessitates* such pejorations. They are historically constructed phenomena which can be deconstructed without rejecting the pleasures of language as we know it in favor of some indefinable — indeed, unspeakable — linguistic *jouissance*.

All this is not to say, however, that Susan Gubar and I did not find significant evidence of "women's culture" when we assembled an enormous range of texts by English-speaking women (2500 pages of them to be exact!) for our recently-published *Norton Anthology of Literature by Women*. Specifically, we did in fact notice that female-authored literature *was* marked by what some French feminist theorists have called "gaps" and "absences." These "absences" were not linguistic ones, though; rather, they were generic, and they were particularly associated with women's poetry. When we began to write our instructor's guide for the book, we decided to include a unit on genre, and as we reviewed the poems we had collected — works by women ranging from Amelia Lanier and Mary Sidney Herbert in the sixteenth century to Denise Levertov and Sylvia Plath in the twentieth century — it became strikingly clear to us that many of the central lyric genres in which male poets have always worked (for instance, the pastoral elegy and the so-called high Romantic Ode) have been virtually ignored by female poets. There is, as we think our anthology demonstrates, a long and rich tradition of women's verse in English, but, interestingly, it's verse that tends to be explicitly or implicitly narrative, or else it's verse that appears to have some sort of "occasional" purpose. How to account for this? We've given a few preliminary answers in the guide itself, but we're really still struggling to explain what seems to be a fascinating phenomenon.

To go back to the question of *écriture féminine*, however — which, as you've seen, is a phrase that I interpret almost entirely in terms of the idea of women's language — I should add that our disagreements with the French don't mean that Susan and I believe we Americans should renounce the very real pleasures of the texts produced by contemporary French theorists. For myself, I can say with conviction that I find a joyous rage in the writings of, for example, Cixous and Clement (I'm thinking now of *La Jeune Née*) which is wonderfully liberated and liberating. So I really want to laugh *with* the Medusa, not at her!

GRAFF: But can one just laugh off stereotyping which seems sexist in its own way? As for "compelling fantasy," what about the objection that escapist fantasies have already done quite a bit of harm in this context?

GILBERT: I'm not quite sure what sort of "harm" you're talking about. Of course romantic fantasies—for example, gothic tales of brooding, black-browed heroes and "frail" but "feisty" heroines—can be and have often been debilitating for female readers, but utopian fantasies are frequently empowering: they help us extend the limits of what we can imagine; they broaden the horizons of our expectations. Certainly linguistic fantasies have functioned in such a way for male writers from Whitman to Williams, from Joyce and Eliot to Burroughs and, say, Ginsberg. And I'd say they've had similarly energizing effects for women of letters from Dickinson to Woolf and Stein—and, now, Cixous, Irigaray, and their various French, American and English acolytes. To be more specific, might not fantasies about a female body/language enable women writers to metaphorize the female body in powerful new ways? Might we not decide, in fact, that such fantasies act on the female imagination much as Yeats said the "ghostly instructors" of *A Vision* acted for him—to bring "new metaphors for poetry"?

GRAFF: Feminist criticism seems to reawaken in a new guise certain old questions about cultural nationalism. For example, some women writers may find the designation "women writer" as constraining and misleading as other writers have found the designation "Jewish writer" or "Chicano writer."

GILBERT: I should begin by saying that Elaine Showalter has written a marvelous piece ("Women Who Write Are Women") about this subject in a recent issue of the *New York Times Book Review*, and I strongly agree with her conclusion that "When women writers are told they don't write like women, because their work is so powerful or original or profound, they must respond, 'This is how women write.'" At the same time, however, I know it's true that writers are often (and quite naturally) disturbed by the categories into which critics want to fit them. As a poet and sometime fiction writer myself, I actually understand this perfectly. When you sit down with your notebook, or in front of your typewriter or word processor, you feel—you must, of course, feel—that you can write, be, do anything you want without necessarily laboring under the cloud of self-consciousness that excessively narrow self-definitions might lower over your head. You want to be free, as Virginia Woolf put it, to "write as a woman who has forgotten she is a woman" (or, conversely, you want to be free to write as a woman who has remembered—with pleasure, pain, or awe—that she is a woman). Thus what the writer needs not to know and what the critic needs to know may well be two very different things.

Nevertheless, I can't see how writer and critic can disagree about the fact that what is finally written is, whether consciously or not, written by the whole person. If a writer is a Jew—that is, a Jew who has grown up aware of being a Jew—then how can his or her Jewishness be separated from his/her whole being? If a writer is a woman who has been raised as a woman—and I daresay only a very few biologically anomalous human females have *not* been raised as women—how can her sexual identity be split off from her literary energy? Even a denial of her femininity, such as one sees in some supposedly "male-identified" authors, would surely be significant to an understanding of the dynamics of her aesthetic creativity.

GRAFF: To take a slightly less pugnacious approach, I note you have written that male modernist writers have treated clothing in terms of "gender-created myths," whereas their female counterparts have often struggled "to define a gender-free reality behind or beneath myth . . . ."[1] That seems rather a paradox—women's writing is gender-specific in its quest to transcend gender. I find that idea attractive, sentimental meliorist as I no doubt am. But might this view not set you against those who say any concept of "gender-free reality" is a phallocentric myth?

GILBERT: Actually, the notion that women's writing is gender-specific in its quest to transcend gender is not quite so paradoxical as it may sound. In fact, in a sense it goes back to the idea we were just discussing: a woman may not want to think of herself as a woman writer but she may not want to think of herself that way precisely because she is a woman who is a writer—that is, because the imperatives of her literary self have been created by the conditions of her personal life.

But to return to your real question: is the concept of a gender-free reality a phallocentric myth? Well, yes, I suppose it may be, especially if gender-free implies "androgynous" and the concept of androgyny is taken to mean that, as some feminists have charged, the female is subsumed within the male. I should emphasize, though, that in "Costumes of the Mind," the essay you're referring to, I'm not really espousing my own belief in the possibility of a gender-free reality. Rather, as a literary historian, I'm defining and describing the fantasies about a gender-free reality that seem to me to have (at least at times) informed the writings of women artists as varied as Charlotte Brontë, Olive Schreiner, Virginia Woolf, Djuna Barnes and Sylvia Plath.

Do I myself believe in or want to work toward such a "reality"? I don't know, and I'm not sure that my speculations are any more valuable than those of other women. Susan Gubar and I are often asked what we think or dream will happen in the future, but we're not prognosticators; we see ourselves, rather, as historians—diagnosticians, if you will. Naturally we share the vision of social justice and, more particularly, female empowerment that has energized the feminist movement, but it's so difficult for us to analyze the problems of the past and understand the possibilities of the present that we usually feel we have to leave the prediction of the female future to our women students and our daughters. Because, as we think our new anthology shows, feminism is an ongoing process whose progress since the Renaissance has been enormous, we think—we hope—our female descendants will do a good job with that future.

GRAFF: Whenever I see critics ascribing certain special characteristics to women's writing, I wonder if they could pass a blindfold test: let's present them with a dozen anonymous texts they've never seen before and ask them, on the basis of their theories, to distinguish male and female authorship. How well do you think they would score?

GILBERT: I'm not really sure. Linguists like Robin Lakoff, Dale Spender and Mary Hiatt have suggested that certain characteristics mark female speech and writing, at least in English: for instance, women are said to have a far more subtle and refined vocabulary of colors than most men do, a vocabulary no doubt often acquired from years of reading fashion magazines and Bloomingdale's catalogs. So maybe if you read a text that uses a lot of words like "mauve," "fuchsia" and "magenta" you'll be justified in speculating that it's by a woman. And of course, as Susan and I, along with such other critics as Elaine Showalter and Nancy Miller, have argued, women's novels tend to have certain kinds of covert subtextual plots which strain against their overt stories, while, as I mentioned earlier, women's poetry (in English, anyway) often reveals the absence of some major generic conventions.

Still, all these observations—even including the observation about vocabulary—can only really be made when one forms works into a canon, so that structural and thematic parallels can be clarified through juxtaposition. And how, after all, can you shape a canon that would allow you to make meaningful inferences about, say, gender and genre, without having recourse to authorial signatures? If influence is an issue— and as a literary historian I think it is—then you can be sure that writers themselves have always known who their "strong precursors" (in the Bloomian phrase) were, and known their gender too. Even such literary male impersonators as George Sand, Currer Bell, George Eliot, Vernon Lee and—to take a more recent example—James Tiptree, Jr., soon became known as the women they were, and women readers who knew these writers were women would not only have recognized the recurrent female themes their works inscribed, they would also have responded to

118

them and, if they were writers themselves, they would have revised and reinscribed them.

In this regard, James Tiptree, Jr., seems to me to be a particularly interesting case. As a pseudonymously "male" writer, she was thought by some critics to be a kind of science-fiction Hemingway, but when she was "unmasked" as a woman the powerfully female—indeed, feminist—concerns in her work became clear to everyone! So maybe asking feminist theorists to discuss women's writing without the contextualization provided by signatures would be like asking people to analyze the series 8–14–23–34–42–53 without letting them know that these numbers represent train stations on the IND subway line in New York City. The numbers don't exist in an abstract mathematical relation to each other; their coherence is both an historical fact and an historical construct.

GRAFF: Does the trend toward "literary theory" intersect with or go against the grain of academic feminist criticism? Again, a complicated question, but maybe you can address it briefly.

GILBERT: Both. On the one hand, "theory" intersects with feminist concerns because it has forced us all to think about the nature and function of literary texts, to interrogate the authority of a received canon and to consider—as we were doing a few questions ago—the essential characteristics of the language out of which texts are woven. On the other hand, however, because "theory" often tends to be ahistorical, it goes very much against the grain of much feminist criticism, at least of much of the feminist criticism practiced in America today. Moreover, because "theory" has assumed an especially privileged role in the contemporary academy, with its practitioners often seen as members of a priestly elite in possession of a sacred, semi-secret vocabulary of terms, tools, and allusions—"*différance*," "*sous rature*," "defamiliarization," and so on—it sometimes seems to many feminists like the last humanistic bastion of masculinist authority, an intellectual Men's House where specialized ritual volumes are guarded by initiates who have learned to speak what Walter Ong has called a "*patrius sermo*," an occult "father speech" whose virtue is precisely that it is unavailable to those who have only been taught to talk in that lowly vernacular which Thoreau once defined as our "brutish mother tongue."

To be sure, a number of American feminists have hailed deconstruction for its "antiphallologocentrism." But what does it mean when Derrida claims that he is (in some mysterious sense) a "woman"? For those of us who *are* women, the word "woman" has a specific empirical meaning that goes far beyond playful metaphors of marginality! And if we say *we* are "women," that doesn't seem, somehow, to have quite the glamour that Derrida's statement does. One has to wonder why.

To be sure, too, many theorists think it's in our (female) interest to hail the "death of the author" and celebrate the pleasures of texts which have been liberated from the oppressive weight of that originary phallologocentrist who just happened to compose them. And perhaps that's all very well if the originary phallologocentrist was called "Homer" or "Milton" (though even in those cases I myself would consider the signature of some interest). But what if the originary "phallologocentrist" was called "Elizabeth Barrett Browning" or "Emily Dickinson"—two women writers whose texts seem to me to reflect pains and pressures that have been until recently quite forgotten? Those of us who haven't had a history—for instance, women—naturally would prefer to recover that past before we celebrate its demise! And besides, who really profits from the death of the author? *Cui bono*, as the old adage would have it? Why of course it's the priestly critic, the one whose textual *jouissance* exhibits his (and I use that pronoun advisedly) hegemonic power, his exuberant skill with arcane terms and themes!

Finally, it seems to me not at all irrelevant that Geoffrey Hartman, one of our best and wittiest exponents of "theory," has very sensibly said (in *Saving the Text*, his brilliant gloss on *Glas*) that "in the deconstructive activity the monuments of unaging intellect are not torn down." No, of course they aren't; the property rights are merely transferred from one *Blütbruderschaft* to another.

GRAFF: To go back to your point about the decline of the poet-critic, which you trace, in an *American Book Review* article, to the academic division of labor and the separation of creative writing from scholarly programs: you yourself are a poet-critic, and one thinks of Adrienne Rich and perhaps others. Might feminist criticism be a force for reviving the poet-critic?

GILBERT: I hope so. As I began by saying in response to your first question, I do find the virtual disappearance of the poet-critic a strange and interesting development, one that I'd also associate with the rise of the sort of "theory" we were just discussing, and one that I'm inclined to attribute to the compartmentalization fostered by academic bureaucracies. To give you an example of the peculiar schizophrenia I'm thinking of: last summer at the School of Criticism a well-known theorist, celebrating the "death of the author" and advocating the "reversal of hierarchies" implicit in the "privileging" of the interpreter/reader, declared that nowadays most literary people would very likely subscribe to his views. When he was asked whether he believed that most contemporary poets would also define themselves as "textualists" in his sense, and particularly whether they'd repudiate what he rather scornfully called "the mysterious power of creativity" in which writers and readers alike used to have faith, he hesitated, then, with little or no irony, made the somewhat surprising claim that poets are not in any case "literary." A mild ripple of laughter swept through the audience—but it quickly dissipated, perhaps because most of those present would themselves have agreed that, despite their indefatigable production of increasingly unread literary texts, most contemporary poets are *not* really "literary," not literary, anyway, in the sense of being self-consciously "literary-critical"—i.e., "theoretical."

Of course it's true that in journals like *Field* and *American Poetry Review*—or in the various essay collections produced by Denise Levertov, Donald Hall, Diane Wakoski and others—a number of poets offer prose reflections on their own aesthetic experiences and assumptions. On the whole, though, such pronouncements seem to me to be largely technical and confessional, as though most of these writers fear that they're ill equipped to make large judgments of either tradition or the individual talent. And while it's also true that a few contemporary poets (for example, Robert Pinsky, Alan Williamson and David Young) do write what we might call "professional" criticism—textual analysis or evaluation that's neither primarily autobiographical nor principally technical—in its way, their criticism tends to be as particularized (indeed, as non- or even anti-theoretical) as the confessionalism of poets who define themselves more exclusively *as* poets. It's surely no insult to the scholarly and critical achievements of, say, Pinsky and Young, if we concede that in America today the major "theoretical" names—Bloom, Fish, Hartman, Miller, Culler et al.—are as divorced from what has traditionally been considered "the mysterious power of creativity" (that is, the power to write poetry) as the major poetic names—Bly, Rich, Levertov, Ashbery, etc.—are from so-called "critical theory."

How and why is the university to "blame" for all this? I suspect that an intensification of professionalism is both cause and consequence of the splits I've been describing. During the fifties and sixties, critic-poets were rapidly assimilated into American institutions of higher education, and as this happened they must have found it increasingly necessary to evolve in specialized ways in order to differentiate and define themselves for academic administrators. So—and I may as well just quote my *American Book Review* piece here—"the person-of-letters with a somewhat dominant left brain, who might once have read Hegel and written sonnets, now read Hegel, Nietzsche, Freud, Lacan, and Derrida—and became a professional critic. At the same time, the right-brain-dominant soul, who might have written *ghazals* and analyzed Rilke, now wrote sonnets, sestinas, *ghazals*, *haiku* and free verse, and translated Rilke and Neruda—and became a professional poet. And now at last the university understood them both! Professor Left Brain was a theoretician; Professor Right Brain a technician. One belonged in an English department, the other in a creative writing workshop. One could be expected to write for *Glyph*, the other for *APR*. Well and good. But was there something a bit dithery and jargony, even a bit Laputan, about Professor Left Brain? Did

Professor Right Brain seem a bit too naively fixated on the mystique of the 'deep image' and the 'breath unit'?"[2] Until fairly recently, hardly anyone seems to have thought to ask. And even if one asked, what remedies might there be for this situation?

Well, naturally I'm glad you suggested that feminist criticism might be at least *one* remedy, one force for reviving what I see as a lost wholeness. In fact, I've noticed that some of the best recent prose by poets generally *is* about ideas—though not literary ones. For as professional theorists have increasingly cornered the critical market, poets have tended more and more to write not so much about books as about what we'd ordinarily call (as if it were distinct from books) "the world." Thus some of the liveliest prose by contemporary poets—work by people like Adrienne Rich, Galway Kinnell, Robert Bly, Susan Griffin and Gary Snyder—is essentially moral in intention and evangelical in style. Perhaps the contemporary poet's goal is not to change the word but to change the world? Not to teach about literature but to preach about life (if, again, we can consider life and literature two distinct categories)? Obviously, if that's the case, a number of the points I was trying to make earlier about the specially compelling status of feminist criticism as a "home industry" would be relevant here. For those of us who are feminist critics *and* poets there must inevitably be a seamless continuity between all the activities in which we engage. And it's obvious that for our male contemporaries there are matters that are equally urgent: peace, ecology, social justice— and, yes, those transformed relations between the sexes which are obviously so crucial in what we Californians sometimes call "this modern world of today." Perhaps the poet-critic will be revived, then, in a role far more ancient (and far more crucial to the making of art) than that of theorist: the role of prophetess or prophet, seer ("see-er," as H.D. once put it) and sayer of new days and ways.

GRAFF: To what degree have women's studies programs been overtaken by a ghetto syndrome in which, once feminism has been safely institutionalized as a "field," the rest of us don't need to bother listening to it any more? Are there ways of avoiding this?

GILBERT: I think women's studies programs often started *out* with what you call a "ghetto syndrome"—a feeling, usually quite justified, of powerlessness and marginality, or of, at best, tokenism. But I also think, contrary to what you're saying, that at least in a number of institutions these programs have been or are being increasingly "overtaken" by a surprising centrality. (Of course, that is by no means universally the case; at many colleges and universities, including the school where I've taught for the last decade, the women's studies program, if it exists, doesn't yet have a single FTE and has no more than a few thousand dollars for its entire annual budget!)

122

At those institutions where women's studies have prospered, however, what are the consequences of this moderate success? They are, I suspect, diverse and puzzling. Women's studies directors and participants still wonder if we're experiencing tokenism—or is it co-optation? We wonder if we'll be "mainstreamed" out of existence. We wonder if, as you say, nobody will bother listening anymore. (But then, Jerry, how many of our male colleagues *ever* bothered to listen? I find your use of the phrase "any more" charming and consoling, but misleading.)

You ask if there are ways of avoiding the problems I've outlined. I would say the first way, which has always been the way for women, as it has been for minorities, is simple survival. Amnesia, whether willed or accidental, has long been a problem of feminism. Why did historians encourage us to "forget" for so many years the massive impact and enormous centrality of the "first wave" of the women's rights movement, the one that after almost a century of struggle won women in England and the United States the vote? Why did we women ourselves *let* ourselves forget? If we can remember why we have women's studies programs and so empower those programs to survive, I believe people will eventually listen to us. Perhaps I'm being Pollyannish to imagine that if you go on talking long enough people will listen, yet—as you can probably tell from my intense desire to revive the poet-critic, to reintegrate right brain and left brain—I have to believe that. I have to believe that some sort of personal and social wholeness is possible and that, therefore, action does ultimately beget transformation.

But let the last words here be those of Virginia Woolf, the woman of letters whom I defined in my answer to your first question as the intellectual grandmother of all us contemporary feminist critics. Concluding *A Room of One's Own*, Woolf describes the energy and commitment necessary to resurrect Shakespeare's lost "sister," and by implication the passion necessary to perpetuate women's studies programs: "if we live another century or so," she says, and "if we have the habit of freedom and the courage to write exactly what we form . . . then the opportunity will come and the dead poet who was Shakespeare's sister will put on the body which she has so often laid down." More crucially still, she adds, in what I regard as one of her most splendid understatements, "I maintain that she would come if we worked for her, and that so to work, even in poverty and obscurity, is worth while."

---

1. Sandra M. Gilbert, "Costumes of the Mind: Transvestism as Metaphor in Modern Literature," in *Writing and Sexual Difference*, ed. Elizabeth Abel (Chicago and London: University of Chicago Press, 1982), p. 196.

2. Sandra M. Gilbert, review of Stuart Friebert and David Young, "A Field Guide to Contemporary Poetry and Poetics," *American Book Review*, III:6 (November–December 1981) pp. 3–4.

Criticism and the State (Political and Otherwise) of the Americas

Gene H. Bell-Villada

> *Literary criticism is not your forte, my dear fellow. Don't try it. You should leave that to people who haven't been to a University.*
>
> –Algernon Moncrieff in *The Impor-tance of Being Earnest*, Act I

Some recent reflections by art historian and critic Rosalind Krauss call for an extensive look, symptomatic as they are of the state of literary culture in this Republic. Writing in *October*, No. 13, Professor Krauss singles out for something like praise and special consideration "the para-literary works of Barthes and Derrida," notably the former's *S/Z*, *The Pleasure of the Text*, and *A Lover's Discourse*. At the same time Professor Krauss harshly reproves "this country's critical establishment" for its stubborn resistance to those unclassifiable and highly original texts. Nevertheless Professor Krauss sees grounds for hope in the favorable reception and increasingly good fortunes enjoyed by Derrida, Barthes, et al., "in graduate schools, where students, whatever their other con-cerns might be, are interested in reading." Summing up her case, she asserts, "what is clear is that Barthes and Derrida are the *writers*, not the critics, that students now read" (emphasis in the original).[1]

In one sense Professor Krauss' facts are undeniable. Yes, certain seg-ments of the "critical establishment" have resisted "paraliterature," often-times out of narrow ignorance and vested cultural interest (although *other* segments of that "critical establishment" have gladly welcomed the arrival of "paraliterature" in New Haven, Ithaca and Baltimore). And yes, those Barthes and Derrida texts (less "para*literary*" than "metacriti-*cal*," it should be said) have no doubt become *the* postgraduate source-books, the treasured cult-books and *grimoires*, the secular high scriptures of an ever-dwindling population of American literary clerics-in-training.

What reservations arise have more to do with Krauss' assumed prem-ises. First, there is the privileged status she attributes to graduate stu-dents, who, in her view, have some special relationship to "reading"— whereas the ideal of a common reader, forming part of an educated general public, plays no evident role in her speculations. Second, there is her overall sense of judgment: in a time that has seen the emergence of some truly sophisticated yet accessible authors—such as Milan Kundera, Italo Calvino, Gabriel García Márquez and numerous other Latin Americans, plus noteworthy North Americans like Barthelme, Doctorow, Coover and Ishmael Reed—there is something cramped and claustrophobic about Krauss focusing on Barthes and Derrida as "the *writers*" of our day.

Finally, there are her evaluative criteria. What Krauss finds positive in "paraliterature" is its "drama without the Play, voices without the Author, criticism without the Argument," and most of all its dealing not with "the July Monarchy or love and money," but rather its being "'about' its own strategies of construction, its own linguistic operations, its own revelation of convention, its own surface." From Krauss' own description, an earnest first-time reader might suspect "paraliterature" of being some ingenious and self-absorbed phenomenon, coolly distant from ordinary life and emotions, with no light to shed on, say, love, marriage or childhood, no intuitions to share about labor strikes, race prejudice, personal bereavement or war, might even infer that it is an ephemeral fashion, cerebrally clever but at root incapable of (and its "*writers*" sublimely uninterested in) making its select readers either laugh, rage or cry—or even think.

I don't claim this to be necessarily true of such works (Barthes does deal with love), though it's the impression one gets from Krauss' publicist account. After all, what she is promoting in Barthes' and Derrida's experiments is, precisely, their *not* being "about . . . love and money" or indeed "about" anything at all. Meanwhile, those readers unfortunate enough not to be graduate students but desirous of seeing representations of "love and money," etc., in the books they read, might turn instead to the mere novelists and other *naïfs* who find or imagine such mundane concerns in their Colombian and Czech homelands and actually write "about" them.

I

I would like to address the situation of literary criticism in our country, and in particular to examine what has become a serious problem—namely, the total and often willful separation of criticism from the basic production practices, the reasons for being, and the uses and emotions of literature; its separation from the most elementary motives as to why writers write and readers read; and, finally, its separation from the broad social sphere of politics and everyday life. In addition, through brief glimpses at Hellenistic Greece, the more recent Euro-American past and the Latin American present, I hope to suggest the degree to which the literary-critical situation in the United States is not typical but very much a special case, that the enormous scale of our critical-institutional machinery, and the academic intensity of our critical-theoretical inquiries, is by no means a world-historical norm, but a locally specific formation and yet another instance of American exceptionalism.

What we call "literary criticism" today (as opposed to strict "research" or "scholarship") has come to mean the theoretical and speculative activity of professors of literature, at North American universities mostly. The objects of their speculations vary, but on the whole the texts studied tend to be an established canon of works stretching from about 1750 to 1960 (Early Novel and Pre-Romantics through Postmoderns). Notwithstanding a plurality of approaches and "schools" (and the word is quite literal here, unlike, say, "the surrealist school"), their work appears almost exclusively in academic journals, and is conceived for, and read almost exclusively by, an academic guild of critics and critics-to-be. The ideological spectrum is congruent with the national polity: an occasional vociferous rightwinger; a rococo assortment of *cénacles* on the Left; and a numerically predominant, genteel and vaguely tolerant, but ideologically frozen centrism (particularly at the elite graduate institutions).

Public involvement by academic critics is rare. Edward Said's work on behalf of the Palestinian cause stands out precisely for the oddity it is. Similarly, there is little textual engagement outside of the set academic and canonical boundaries. In contrast to their job a few decades ago, contemporary critics are seldom called upon to read new verse or fiction, formulate judgments and write modest descriptive reviews thereof. On the other hand those "paraliterary" flights do suggest some uneasiness within the given limits, some yearning for (as it were) boundary two, a search for cultural roles beyond that of being commentators on the Great Books. And yet few critics today venture with any consistency or success into poetry, narrative, reportage or other traditional creative craft. Again the exceptions are telling. William H. Gass teaches philosophy, not literature. There are Umberto Eco and David Lodge—Europe, however, is not my focus here. And actually, though Lodge is much involved with structuralist theory, his novel *Changing Places* delivers a hilarious satire via protagonist Morris Zapp (rumored to be modeled after Stanley Fish) on the personal competitiveness, hard-edged professionalism, inflated empire building and other like absurdities of American literary academe. To recapitulate: literary criticism in this nation is now something of, by and for professors, who on the whole tend to read more crit. than lit.

Until not too long ago, literary criticism used to be a feature of the general press, where occasionally there might emerge a figure of stature such as Van Wyck Brooks or Edmund Wilson. The journalistic tradition does in fact survive in the literary essays of Gore Vidal, John Updike and Mary McCarthy. There are also practical critics on the order of Morris Dickstein, Helen Vendler and Irving Howe—who ironically are full-time academics, though their common ground for two-way exchange with high theoreticians seems nonexistent.

What seems to have been forgotten, however, is that many of the founders of modern criticism were themselves more than just critics. We affix the label "New Critics" to one group, but the received rubric doesn't do them justice. The original "Fugitive" circle included Robert Penn Warren, much better known to Americans for his fictionalized portrait of Southern populism than for his criticism, and moreover a fine poet, as were John Crowe Ransom and Allen Tate. Tate also did such things as translate French Symbolist verse, crank out reviews for the weeklies and write biographies of Stonewall Jackson and Jefferson Davis. In addition, R. P. Blackmur, I. A. Richards and William Empson all published poetry and were capable of producing good verses of their own.

It is easy to carp at these critics' lyrical work and consider them "frustrated" simply because they don't measure up to the canonical standards of Eliot or Pound or Stevens. Behind such carping there lies an indifference and even contempt for the *praxis* of poetry, a failure to appreciate what is positive about regularly producing verse with some sense of loyalty to the medium, an incapacity to recognize that it is better to have made a few good poems than never to have assumed the long-term risk of writing poetry at all, and that well-crafted "minor" verse may be intrinsically more valuable than most competent minor (though modish) criticism. Indeed, Blackmur, Richards and Empson conceivably owe their achievement as critics to their having had "hands-on experience" with the humbling work of lyrical production and having "learned by doing."

But one need not invoke so ancient and intimidating an art as writing verse. There are more modest and workmanlike literary skills. Mention has been made of reviewing new novels or poetry—a much-maligned profession. As with everything else, however, literary reviewing is hard to do truly well. It's no simple task to summarize a novel, convey its specific traits and judge its strengths and weaknesses—all with vision, sensitivity and a clean, lively 500 words. So useful a job is obviously ruled out by the academic vanguardists for whom lit. crit. is no handmaiden but a free and autonomous force, and for whom evaluation is passé, something for those innocents who still read books for pleasure. I suspect, though, that most high theorists would be unable to review a novel if they had to (even with cool-cash incentives from the *New Yorker*). The weight of the past canon and the inevitable intertextual comparisons would only obstruct their vision. Moreover, their custom of addressing only other critics—a habit that has deprived them of the common touch—would probably block communication with a larger audience. Erich Auerbach notes that the reading public of the late Roman Empire "lost its contact with the lower classes, ceased to be embedded in the greater community of the people . . .with which it must maintain contact if it is to survive." Stripped of that symbiotic relationship, Auerbach notes, "no literary public can maintain its function and character."[2]

Terry Eagleton's *Literary Theory: An Introduction* is a marvelous little book. With its fast prose and many witticisms it delights even as it instructs. Staying at an irreverent distance from the multifarious "schools" it passes in review, it avoids the trap of becoming too publicist or celebratory a volume. And after a survey of great scope and thoroughness, Eagleton dares to pose the question: "What is the *point* of literary theory? Why bother with it in the first place?"[3]

Yet, absent from Eagleton's 200-plus pages is any passing reference to current fiction, drama or verse—an all-too-neat illustration of the rift under discussion here. One doesn't expect Eagleton to have cosmopolitan tastes and cite Latin American or East European fabulators (though he does mention literary theorists from as far away as Poland and Estonia). On the other hand one might reasonably hope that a British Marxist and anti-imperialist would encourage left culture by saying *something* about his own countryman John Berger (a fine novelist, social essayist, Marxist art critic and the regular screenwriter for Alain Tanner) or about Commonwealth authors like Chinua Achebe, Salman Rushdie and (why not?) the Naipauls. Eagleton's stated premise, of course, is that literature does not exist and that critics should thus widen their horizons and study, e.g., ads. And yet he does allude often enough to the grand old literary classics of the past—the implication being that literature does not exist *today*.

Behind Eagleton's and many another modern critic's blind spot stands a sad little secret: the period 1955-85 has not been an era of broad, consistently outstanding literary creativity in the U.S., the U.K. or France. Certainly in our own country there are plenty of reputable talents still developing and writing well, and individual masterpieces do crop up here and there, but, save for Mailer's uneven career, no commanding figures exist on the order of (to cite novelists only) Hemingway or Dos Passos or even Fitzgerald or Henry Miller, let alone a Faulkner. As early as the 1930's these now-classic U.S. authors were the object of high critical esteem and widespread imitation in Europe and Latin America, whereas today, our nation's global reach notwithstanding, there are no post-1945 American writers whose artistic influence or world stature can be thought of as in any way comparable (Nabokov's case being something of a curiosity).

In the absence of visible, focused, shared creative ferment in the United States, the productive and innovative ideals have inevitably shifted, *faute de mieux*, to academia, its concerns and genres. Unfortunately, the basic documentary and exegetical spadework for "canonical" Anglo-American letters is all but complete; we have literary histories in abundance, scholarly editions galore and whole libraries examining minor Romantics and chosen Modernists; moreover, in recent years the biography and the critical guide have been losing their old generic luster and are considered shopworn and naive. At the same time few members of our graduate-school elite corps are in any position to seek cultural treasure in the writings of women, blacks, Native Americans or other noncanonical folk. Caught in an intellectual impasse, lacking any strong artistic or political commitments outside of the profession, but under enormous peer pressure to "produce," they face limited options and yet find themselves in serious need of newer turf and higher claims.

What has come along to meet those very needs is vanguard literary theory, with occasionally positive results. It takes someone of Northrop Frye's lucid brilliance, religious sincerity and Toronto marginality to confront the entire Bible in *The Great Code*. On the other hand, it is only the peculiar mix of delusion, vanity and prestige in our graduate schools that can give rise to such bizarre phenomena as Geoffrey Hartman's heady declaration of independence for literary critics and his eager advocacy of "avant-garde criticism." It is only from within the privileged and cloistered unreality of affluent academe that Stanley Fish can come up with his inspired belief that the critic "brings texts into being and makes them available for analysis and appreciation," and more, that literary criticism is "absolutely essential . . . to the very production" of the literary object.[4] In an era of more generalized literary creativity such proposals would simply be shrugged off as the daftest sort of wishful thinking and silliest of grand illusions. In our skewed literary culture they're paid serious regard.

The sorry state of our literary life cannot be attributed solely to television. Germany and Latin America, nearly as media-dominated as we are, have been experiencing literary renaissances. The reasons, more complex, involve the slow and simultaneous drying up of a number of institutions. The anti-left purges of the forties and fifties deprived many a young American writer of alternative cultural and ideological foundations. The broad middlebrow readership that used to subscribe to *Look* and *Saturday Review* has fragmented into a lonely crowd of special-interest magazine consumers. Transnational conglomerates have gobbled up most publishing houses and brought about cutbacks in quality fiction and other less "profitable" product lines. Editing in the United States, once a gentlemen's profession allowing free writing time (as it still is abroad), has fallen prey to production quotas and "scientific management" directives. Bohemia has been commercialized and gentrified, ridding itself of indigent writers. Inflation has driven up everything— except authors' fees. The expatriate community in Europe is a thing of the past, and the *Paris Review* now comes out of Flushing, New York. Save perhaps for feminism, there are relatively few spiritual or material spaces today that can nurture or encourage, let alone feed the American writer-to-be.

Ironically, the one cultural institution that has survived and even greatly benefited from the "post-industrial" shift has been the University. From the big Ivies to the humblest community college, the American higher education system underwent spectacular growth following World War II. It's a familiar tale: GI Bills, federally-funded loans and research, and youth expansion during the affluent years. All things must pass, however, and the symptoms of economic and academic decline are obvious and ominous. Our pool of unemployed literati now approaches in scale that of a Third World nation. Small, unendowed colleges are merging or shutting down. The Humanities "boom" of the early sixties and seventies is dead and gone. Of course, French 101 and Freshman Comp are basic to the service industry, and English majors continue to graduate in respectable numbers, though their future reading will most likely be law journals and *Forbes* rather than Keats or *Diacritics*. Still, the University, with its pre-professional and technocratic programs, remains a prime means of upward mobility (and status maintenance) in the United States. For better or for worse, it is also the one major national setting where "literature" possesses any visible or material existence – in curricula, but also through public lectures, poetry readings and most every subsidized magazine from *Partisan Review* to *Praxis* (recently absorbed by UCLA). There is also the free time for writing and hence, not surprisingly, many poets and novelists (and composers and painters) want to have jobs there, where most critics already do.

We tend to take it for granted, but actually our university system – like our sleek skyscrapers, our automated kitchens and our telephone technology – is among the wonders of the modern world. The North American campus invariably amazes foreigners with its varieties of old and new architecture, its idyllic beauty and bucolic expanse, its fairly low faculty-student ratios and readily available professoriat, and its monumental facilities for arts, athletics and higher research. Whereas the *physical* Sorbonne consists of little more than a few big classroom buildings around the Left Bank, any typical Midwestern state college boasts a museum, a concert hall and a library collection that Parisian professors would envy. There is also the sheer scale of American academic enterprise, with close to 3,000 accredited institutions of higher learning, compared to France's 70. In academic literary studies alone, the U.S. subpopulation professionally so engaged far surpasses in numbers the *entire* combined university teaching rosters of, say, the Argentine.

That very size can be deceptive to academic employees. Because a specialist book on Shakespeare or Eliot can sell 2,500 copies, and because a talk by Stanley Fish at the MLA convention can attract audiences double that number, there is the temptation to think that what one is doing is more than in-house business, more than the rituals of yet another special-interest group jockeying within the great American pluralith, that one is achieving something culturally momentous in the world, doing not just a local brand of literary commentary but criticism itself and even "literature." Yet try as one might, one can't escape the underlying custodial function of academe, its determinative role (outside of the sciences) of transmitting the works of the past, however exotic the secondary products currently sprouting in our graduate-school hothouses. Of course, without the traditional editing or interpretive tasks to help keep those bright minds rooted in practice, the tendency is to conjure up elaborate châteaux in the air and then project them in the marketplace of "new ideas," where the most skilled illusionists and virtuoso performers draw the biggest crowds. Meanwhile the poets and novelists, who (like hapless Third World countries losing their bauxite and bananas to corporate Empire) did furnish us the essential materials in the first place, end up forgotten in their graves or their writing programs, drowned out by the supermall of discourse, their presence but a sorry trace within so much high-tech hype and software.

II

There is a remote historical parallel sometimes evoked in order to illuminate our odd situation: the Alexandrian analogy. Usually made in passing as a kind of shorthand, the analogy calls for elaboration. "Alexandrian" denotes the late Greek culture of the Hellenistic Age, which, during the fourth and third centuries B.C., flourished overseas in the great commercial city of Alexandria, Egypt. By then the renowned Athenian playwrights, poets and philosophers had receded into the past, becoming classics. In the meantime a hungry Alexandrian eclecticism encouraged free cultural borrowing from Egyptian, Asian and Minoan lore. Local artistic deficiencies were compensated for by a large-scale cultural-material apparatus, symbolized in the Mouseion (whence our word "museum"), that vast complex encompassing "lecture halls, labs, observatories, a library, a dining hall, a park, and a zoo."[5] It was there in the Mouseion that, for the greater glory of the royal house of the Ptolemies, the Alexandrian literati studied and wrote full-time. Pride of place at the Mouseion went above all to its so-called "Mother Library" of 120 catalogers and 500,000 books. Duplicate volumes were housed in the even bigger and more celebrated "Daughter" Library at the Serapeum, the one that Julius Caesar is charged (falsely, it seems) with having burned to the ground.

It should come as no surprise that modern literary scholarship had its beginnings in Alexandria. The first Greek grammar was compiled there, leading to rules of usage, often pedantically applied. Schools of literary criticism sprang up, and a librarian named Zenodotus pioneered the division of the *Iliad* and *Odyssey* into the multiple "books" known to us today. Disproportionate cultural power was wielded by the Head Librarians, whose own literary writings carried a great deal of weight. Callimachus, for example, supervised major bibliographical projects and was the leading lyricist of his day. His rival, Apollonius of Rhodes, another Head Librarian, composed the sophisticated epic poem, the *Argonautica*.

On the other hand, these Librarians' creative products, while certainly skillful and technically achieved, are but pale reflections of the great Athenian masterworks. W. W. Tarn, a leading scholar of the Hellenistic Age, notes of Callimachus that "were it not for his epigrams one might almost say he was not a poet but a learned man writing verses," and by the same token the *Argonautica* is "a learned man's failure. [Apollonius] could draw a picture, but could not tell a story."[6] There were also such "experiments" as poems written in the shape of a bird or an axe, and someone actually rewrote the *Odyssey* through systematic avoidance of the letter S. As Tarn observes, "Poetry . . . had been almost crushed to death by the weight of the great masters; none could approach them, and it was hardly worth trying. . . . Men's aim everywhere was rather to keep poetry alive than to challenge the great masters."[7] The anxiety of influence may be more a matter of a certain kind of period than an eternal burden of all poets.

Obviously the Alexandrian analogy is as pertinent to our times as is any, and worried commentators have inevitably made the connection. Randall Jarrell in his classic essay "The Age of Criticism" (a piece as fresh and relevant today as when it first appeared in 1952) employs some three times the adjective "Alexandrian." (As Jarrell himself observes, "in many ways we *are* Alexandrian; and we do not grow less so with the years."[8]) And towards the turn of the century, when the modern research university was just emerging into shape, Nietzsche (himself a product of that institution) time and again reflected, with typical sardonicism, on the Alexandrian ethos. He lamented that "Our whole modern world is caught in the net of Alexandrian culture and recognizes as its ideal the man of theory. . . ."[9] The essential figure of our era, says Nietzsche, is that of the "eternally hungry . . . critic without strength or joy, the Alexandrian man who is at bottom a librarian and scholiast, blinding himself miserably over dusty books and typographical errors."[10]

Reflecting on contemporary splits between poetry and poetics, Nietzsche cites one Wolf to the effect that "Antiquity was acquainted with theories of oratory and poetry which facilitated production [and] formed real orators and poets, while at the present day we shall soon have theories upon which it would be impossible to build up a speech or a poem as it would be to form a thunderstorm upon a brontological treatise."[11] What Nietzsche elsewhere calls our "Socratic-Alexandrian age" is unique in that "at no other period in history have the so-called intelligentsia and the artist faced each other with such hostile incompre-hension."[12] Or, in his most drastic observation, "Never has there been so much talk about art and so little respect for it."[13]

Nietzsche said much of this 100 years ago. Were he alive today he might note that never has there been so much talk about "writing" and so little interest in real writing; never has there been so much theory of "reading" and so little actual reading of novels or plays or poetry; never has the heady jargon of "narrativity" and "narratology" been more ban-died about and narrative itself been at so low a point of growth or esteem; never has there been more techno-babble about "poetics" and less interest in actual poems old and new; never have "the pleasures of the text" been so much invoked and so few texts read for pleasure. "The Death of the Author," says a fashionable, portentous, cheerfully nihilis-tic slogan, but the death has been aided and abetted by an unexpected alliance of academic critics and media conglomerates.

Our Alexandrianism, in turn, is of a piece with the broad patterns of late U.S. capitalism, with its bloated managerial and marketing and legal strata; its ever-bigger financial manipulations and merger manias; its shopping malls that gobble up good farmland; its baroque weaponry that has no relation to battlefield realities or political fact (but much to do with the semiotics of Empire); its arcane medical technologies and specialities that overshadow basic health needs; its periodic museum extravaganzas; its Music Directors whose public role eclipses that of any living artist or composer; and its high-powered schools of literary theory and the wondrously precious things they do. These outsize phenomena are the typical outgrowths of a conservative but strangely overripe soci-ety that encourages lots of make-work "change" and "innovation" of a purely technical sort, all in order to sustain a gigantic *status quo* presided over by the Fortune 500, the DOD, the AMA, the nouveau Sun Belt riches, and the academic and cultural combines—high-level mainte-nance, in a word. Our rhetoric is libertarian and individualistic, but we're all salaried bureaucrats now.

III

Nothing could differ more from our literary situation than that of the Latin Americans. Ours is an Age of Critics and Metacritics, theirs an Age of Literature that begins with the poets Neruda, Vallejo, Paz and Guillén, continues with the pioneering story writers Borges and Cortá-zar, and further endures with the novelists Rulfo, Carpentier, Donoso, Fuentes, Roa Bastos, Vargas Llosa, Cabrera Infante, Cortázar again and Nobel laureate García Márquez, to name just a few. When educated Latin Americans nowadays think "literature," they have in mind not so much settled canons and critical theories as the lyrics and narratives actually issuing forth in their homelands at this time. Novels like *One Hundred Years of Solitude* and *Hopscotch* have entered the arena of daily discourse, and the novelists are (depending on their ideological hue) either courted or criticized by political establishments or opposition groups. Traditionally a part of Latin American public life, today even more so the literary artists, together with their critics and readers, see themselves as participants in their nations' ongoing struggles and debates.

In an era of such exceptional creativity, criticism can make few special claims for itself. Literary criticism in Latin America, moreover, arises out of institutional bases the precise opposite of our own. Latin American universities survive with difficulty, set upon as they are with scarcity of funds, physical decay, illiberal governments and sometime occupation by the military. Criticism for criticism's sake could hardly be expected to flourish under such conditions, even if thousands wished it to, and needless to say there is neither the money nor the market for a Peruvian *Diacritics*. A few fastidious professors might faithfully collect sets of *Glyph* or *Poétique* and, accordingly, orientate their thought and researches toward the North Atlantic, but their own writings are mostly derivative and respond to no significant local needs. In all, the universities play a relatively minor role in Latin American literary life, so slight that a number of prominent writers have never attended college — notably Borges, whose highest earned degree is a Swiss high school diploma, or Elena Poniatowska, from Mexico, doyenne of Latin American women writers, who started out as a cub reporter the day after graduating from Catholic high school at age nineteen.

Where criticism in Latin America does command a more substantial function is in the general press. In a continent where some dailies still run fiction and verse, literary essays provide ample copy for the cultural department. Mexico City alone boasts half a dozen weekend arts tabloids published by the dailies, and there are numerous smaller periodicals as well. The mass-circulation sheets so far have furnished halfway-decent fees for their writers, who make ends meet either by free-lancing or by juggling staff and editorial positions.

Latin America's very backwardness, then, helps keep its literary critics connected with day-to-day reality. Not that their conceptual apparatus is comparably backward: on the contrary, Latin American journalistic critics are nearly as much up on current theoretical developments as any Yale professor, but at the same time they are fully engaged in such bread-and-butter activities as reviewing a variety of new works, foreign and domestic. The more ambitious among them write book-length historical or biographical studies, or pursue creative or editorial projects of their own. The man of letters is a professional species currently alive and well in South America.

A major instance of this far-ranging critical activity is the work of the late Ángel Rama, an Uruguayan whose long list of titles includes a novel, literary histories, theoretical speculations, sociological articles and countless journalistic essays on subjects as diverse as Ruskin, García Márquez and *Sophie's Choice*. Rama was also active as the general editor of the Biblioteca Ayacucho (a handsome library of the Latin American classics coming out of oil-rich Venezuela), and before that he helped edit the Uruguayan weekly *Marcha*, one of the most respected Hispanic cultural publications, roughly equivalent to the *Nation* in style and outlook. Rama was to pay dearly for his multiple involvements. *Marcha* was shut down by the Uruguayan military dictatorship in the 1970's. Fleeing the repression, Rama ended up teaching at the University of Maryland, only to be denied residency by the Reagan State Department. (Among the few specific "charges" brought to light: didn't Mr. Rama visit China during the 1950's?) Effectively deported, Rama left for Europe on a Guggenheim fellowship; he and his wife then met a horrible death in the 1983 Avianca air crash outside Madrid. A man very much of this world, Rama nevertheless could speak without a hint of embarrassment about "the beauty, truth, and pleasure of works of art"—a set of notions now deemed uninteresting and naive in our graduate-school subculture.

Perhaps the most impressive in-depth study by Rama is his 300-page *Transculturación narrativa en América Latina*, an astounding instance of "total" criticism. As suggested by the title, Rama shows how narrative fiction becomes acculturated and transformed in a South American environment. Approaching literary genres not as eternal essences, as universals living in splendid aesthetic isolation, Rama instead applies a broad but lucid theoretical vision that brings in Amerindian ethnography, urban sociology, structural anthropology, physical geography, economic history and a nonsectarian Marxism together with stylistics, semiotics, theory of fiction and traditional literary scholarship—all with a view to capturing the complex process of historical development of narrative in Latin America since 1810. Rama penetratingly demonstrates how literary works and movements grow out of shifts in regional imbalance, class power and successive importation of literary forms via imperialism—those issues of domination and resistance. Rama further caps his performance with a first-rate biographical examination of Peruvian novelist José María Arguedas and a thorough analysis (narrative, linguistic, historical, mythical and even musical) of Arguedas' legendary novel of conflict between Quechua Indians and Hispanic whites, *Deep Rivers*. In sum, Rama's book both reconstructs a continental history and "reads" an individual text, and thereby shows what a nonspecialist literary criticism can do by combining Marxism with a knowledge judiciously gathered from all social and literary disciplines.

Aside from Rama's bold achievement, the most vital and stimulating criticism in Latin America comes from the authors themselves—from poets like Octavio Paz and novelists like Mario Vargas Llosa, from all-around men of letters like Borges and activist voices like Ariel Dorfman. Their insights and artistry place them within that ongoing tradition of author-critics that includes Coleridge, Baudelaire, Henry James, T.S. Eliot and Sartre. Nonfiction from the pen of these South Americans is but another aspect of their creative production; their critical prose comes into being primarily because it responds to and nourishes their literary needs; and their chosen subjects emerge not from academic premises but from the inner reasons and compulsions of their artistic practice.

At the same time, precisely because its own chief practitioners do reflect and write regularly on matters of their trade, the art of fiction and verse maintains a lively public presence and spiritual authority in Latin America. Paz's critical essays, for instance, are encountered not only by literature students and scholars but by Mexican writers across all generations and by general educated readers who feel concerned about the cultural condition of their society. Such issues as the day-to-day uses and special joys of literature, the relationship between current writings and past texts, the ever-shifting standards of literary taste, the possibilities inherent in language and form, the place of Latin American culture in the larger world, and the subtle links between art and politics—these and other like topics are commonly enunciated and heatedly discussed as urgent questions in a live and open forum, rather than as the abstracted and hyper-sophisticated formulae of an exclusive professional guild.

The prime Hispanic example of the practitioner-critic is also the grand old man of Latin American letters: Borges. Ever since his start in the 1920's, Borges' distinctive way was to craft hundreds of brief, loving cameos, affective but thoughtful miniatures that memorialize some essential feature of their selected subject—Flaubert's epistemology, Kafka's prehistory, Wilde's clarity and wisdom, Valéry's and Whitman's respective poetical personalities, and much more. Whether writing about H.G. Wells or the Kabbalah, Borges invariably enjoys himself as he ranges freely and intelligently, quotes things by heart (like a modern Montaigne), and shares with us his appreciation of authors and works that are as real to him as his flesh-and-blood friends and relations. His essays are classic illustrations of—to cite another autodidact, R.P. Blackmur—"the formal discourse of an amateur." Nevertheless there is method to Borges' hedonistic musings. In those scattered and innumerable fragments he perceives and constructs a fantastical tradition stretching from Shakespeare and the Gothic romances on through Flaubert, Kipling, and Chesterton—a nonrealist aesthetic obviously of a piece with his own nonrealist art. The Borges of the mini-essays is also the Borges who forged a revolutionary mode of fabulation as well as its narrative theory.

Outside of Borges, the Latin American author-critic best known in the non-Hispanic world is Octavio Paz, whose prose *oeuvre* would merit attention even were he not the greatest living Mexican poet. The range of Paz's themes is as encyclopedic as is Borges'. His 1972 Norton lectures at Harvard, *Children of the Mire*, bring in such matters as pan-European Romanticism and Modernism, modernity and its notions of time, and the economic condition of Latin America, all with a wealth of specific reference. In a more abstract vein, *The Bow and the Lyre* is a luminous 250-page meditation on each and every aspect of lyric verse—from its linguistic building blocks, on through its creation and reception, culminating in a final "Shelleyan" sixty pages that reflect panoramically on the dialectic between poetry and history. This leads us to Paz the generalist, whose *Labyrinth of Solitude*, an extended sociocultural essay on Mexico from the Aztecs to the present, has sold in the hundreds of thousands and is required reading in the Mexican schools. Paz's critical work further includes numerous incidental articles on film, painting, Surrealism and individual literary figures European as well as Hispanic. The reigning author in his country, Paz inspires respect rather than pride or affection. A man of the Left until recently, his elderly neo-conservatism makes him a less positive presence to the young, but it is a foregone conclusion that he will occupy in Latin America's pantheon a standing analogous to that of Eliot in ours.

Mario Vargas Llosa is acquiring increasing renown in the United States for his full-bodied novels of Peruvian life, but in the Hispanic world he is equally recognized as critic and journalist. When his 600-page book on García Márquez came out in 1971, it was at the time the most thorough study of the Colombian novelist then available. His shorter *La orgía perpetua* (*The Perpetual Orgy*), a study of Flaubert and *Madame Bovary*, is in some ways a much more engaging book. One of the best modern introductions to the literary hermit of Croisset, it furnishes detailed biography, close formal and stylistic analysis, narrative theory and a general summing up of Flaubert's place in world letters.

What immediately catches the reader's attention, however, is the introductory 45-page memoir recounting Vargas Llosa's own personal relationship to *Bovary*, including an evocation of his reasons for loving the book. (Among those reasons is a fact infrequently acknowledged by our jaded critics: the book's melodramatism and its potent mix of "rebellion, vulgarity, violence, and sex," which, of course, made the novel such a sensation in the first place.) For Flaubert is Vargas Llosa's chief mentor. Many of Flaubert's most renowned traits—the rigorous objectivity, the careful attention to fact, and the search for technical perfection—are also those of Vargas Llosa. The Peruvian's elective affinity for the Frenchman is therefore a living and organic bond that has consistently borne him fruit, somewhat like Eliot's revival of Donne, or Mailer's and Doctorow's narrative lessons learned from Dos Passos. In Vargas Llosa's own production, the social panorama of *Conversation in the Cathedral* is his answer to *Sentimental Education*, the satire of *Captain Pantoja* corresponds to *Bouvard and Pécuchet*, the outsize tapestry of *The War of the End of the World* is a tropical *Salammbô*, and all of his novels ultimately build on the episode of the livestock fair in *Madame Bovary*.[14] Hence a "classic" European author lives on through Vargas Llosa's public discipleship as artist and critic, and consequently more South American readers follow his example and are led to rediscover Flaubert.

In a similar way, Vargas Llosa's *Entre Sartre y Camus* compiles twenty years of pertinent articles that trace the Peruvian author's fluctuating loyalties to the two Frenchmen. Graceful and eminently readable, Vargas Llosa's book dwells with pinpoint accuracy and writerly sympathy on such essentials as Camus' lyrical gifts, *pied noir* identity, fertile provincialism and limitations as a philosopher, and Sartre's intellectual brilliance, idiosyncratic leftism, authoritative status in France and limitations as an artist. Vargas Llosa thus concerns himself predominantly with matters of intellectual and social substance rather than with the purely formal qualities of these authors' works.

In the end, Vargas Llosa sides with Camus. Somewhat like Paz, the Peruvian has shifted ideologically from New Leftist to American-style centrist. And yet, despite his change in public stance, in his literary and political analyses he still routinely deploys Marxist concepts. Similarly, though he is now openly hostile to Third Worldist rhetoric, Vargas Llosa the subtle essayist repeatedly alludes to the peculiar dynamic that arises whenever he, a Third World author, encounters North Atlantic texts—that old familiar issue of cultural imperialism. Virtually every modern South American critic of repute feels compelled to grapple at some moment or other with the fundamental and monstrous fact: Latin America as product of the West but not of it, as target but never the beneficiary of foreign plunderers. Five successive centuries of control by Spanish, British, French and United States imperialists are the reality always lurking subliminally in any South American discussion of the glories of North Atlantic civilization. Though armed with full knowledge and coherent understanding of the West, Latin literati remain ever-conscious of their problematical relationship thereto. But this very awareness of being "peripherals" is what immunizes them against the abstract eternalism and blandly deceptive universalism of our Alexandrian culture.

Inasmuch as they acknowledge their peripheral and colonial position, Latin American literary intellectuals, even avowedly anti-Marxist ones, basically accept Marxist theory, particularly when examining questions of imperialism and the arts. The exiled Chilean novelist Ariel Dorfman has gained a steady reputation in the United States with his candid reflections on popular culture for National Public Radio ("All Things Considered") and the *Village Voice*. During the years of the Allende presidency (1970–73), when Dorfman involved himself in slum-education projects in Santiago, he also was to achieve international notoriety as coauthor of *How to Read Donald Duck*, a witty and insightful analysis of the social message embedded in those seemingly innocent Disney comics. More recently, in *The Empire's Old Clothes*, Dorfman has trained his literary Marxism on such Western cultural belwethers as *Reader's Digest*, Babar the Elephant and the Lone Ranger. South American Marxism also turns up in places as unexpected as *poésie pure*: Françoise Pérus, a Frenchwoman living in Mexico, has a judicious and lucid Althusserian-Marxist account of the Hispanic aestheticist movement of 1880–1920. Hers is one of the first books in any language ever to flesh out the concrete socioeconomic contexts of the phenomenon of "art for art's sake," and it was granted the prestigious Casa de las Américas prize (Cuba) in 1976.

To Latin American literati of every political stripe, then, Marxism furnishes a theory not only of history but also of the relations between society and art. Academic criticism in our country, by contrast, while having assimilated all sorts of doctrines that account for the autonomy, the textuality, the self-referentiality and the "literariness" of literary texts, has long been without a comparable assortment of ideas that would equip our critics to see literature as something socially created, distributed, experienced and shared, enable them to consider the poet and novelist as participants in social change—sharers in the adventure of human history. In our century we have witnessed the rise and passing of Van Wyck Brooks' liberal progressivism, Irving Babbitt's conservative humanism, Edmund Wilson's *marxisant* intuitions, Eliot's and the New Critics' feudal nostalgia (obscured during their 1950's hegemony) and Lionel Trilling's Arnoldian ideals of mannerly civilization. Today, among the confusing array of critical methods being marketed and promptly mainstreamed in academe, what is notably absent (aside from a primitive, turgid semiology) is anything like a general sociology of culture—in the broadest possible sense of a set of principles that, while mindful of formal and aesthetic beauties, can transcend formalism, can render intelligible the social process of the arts and evaluate its products.

This, I believe, is one of the fundamental lessons that critics here in the United States can learn from their Latin counterparts: a sense of literature's existence in society. In addition, much as South American literary intellectuals customarily do, we might assess more critically our own relationship to Europe and to the world at large. Having originally emerged out of Western colonialism, as a nation we now dominate the globe (as well as outer space), and our imperial culture exhibits that disturbing innocence, that provincialism peculiar to all empires: a tendency to lose sight of basic realities and ordinary distinctions, and regard our elaborate ideas and obsessions (including literary ones) as universal concerns. Even as American enterprise exports its mass culture to every last corner of the earth, it equally readily imports (with some time lag) most every overseas high-cultural product from Bauhaus and Max Weber and Freud to Buddhism and Dodecaphony and Deconstruction, and then (much as it did with pizza and now with croissants) quickly Americanizes the artefacts, remakes and readapts them for local demands and tastes.

What forces and lacks are there at work in our society to bring about this dual dynamic and unequal exchange? And conversely, what happens to ideas and movements that may have oppositionist functions elsewhere, but here become simply more merchandise up for sale in our business civilization's cultural bazaar? As I mentioned earlier, when a modern Peruvian or Mexican critic reads a French or English book, he remains cognizant of his status as a "colonial" who stands in the intimidating but alluring shadow of the "imperials." A similar awareness, it might be recalled, was actually rather commonplace among U.S. writers before World War II, when we were far less central a country, semiperipheral, and when expatriate subculture still played a substantial role in our literary life. Today's expatriates, by contrast, are university personnel, and when an American academic latches onto Barthes or Derrida, how much recognition is there of his or her status as an intellectual from a former European "colony" now claiming texts as a functionary of "empire"? How much self-awareness is there of the "imperial" citizen now taking on the products of a country with history and traditions very different from his or her own?

Beyond this, once might reexamine the status of academic lit. crit. itself. It's a fact most striking that the continent now blessed with the greatest creative excitement also has no "critical establishment" to speak of, no Yales, Cornells, or Hopkinses whose literary high priests presume to a wisdom surpassing that of the poets. As we already noted, literary activity in Latin America remains part of the larger social life, is inextricably bound up with the movement of history. And whereas in American universities most every "school," from the New Critics to Deconstruction, has been premised on denial of history and on strict separation of social from aesthetic (or, worse still, on appropriation of the historical by the aesthetic), our classic modern authors viewed things quite differently. At one time or another novelists like Dreiser, Dos Passos, Hemingway, Fitzgerald, Faulkner and Steinbeck, as well as critics like Edmund Wilson and Alfred Kazin, all wrote with knowledgeable sympathy and authority about the ways in which the Civil War, the Reconstruction, white racism, the rise of new capitalists, labor struggles, the First World War, 1920's wealth, the Red Scare and the 1930's Depression were shaping American lives. Even genteel and ostensibly apolitical writers like Henry James and Edith Wharton did capture—to a degree unmatched by any historian—the intimate textures and nuances of soul of our socioeconomic elites, and they dramatized those European-

American cultural differences that often elude today's theoreticians. The sharp methodological disjunction between written texts and lived contexts is a relatively recent doctrine, one that became general orthodoxy only with the phenomenal growth of literary academe after 1945.

From conservative educators today one hears noise about "getting back to basics." Liberal-left sectors in the literary academy, rather than summarily dismiss that noise as so much reactionary sloganry (which it often is) would do well to respond with a "back-to-basics" program of their own. We commonly deplore our students' prodigious ignorance of history and of its most elementary facts, but our literary-critical *apparatchiki* have lent their support to such ignorance by preaching a formalism that exorcises history and discounts its interpretive and cognitive worth: even as historicism fades into bourgeois society's "heroic" past, so does any shared sense of the historical. The American literary-critical guild today suffers from a kind of social amnesia; its members badly need to reestablish contact with our country's past and present, to relearn what the expanding frontier, the Monroe Doctrine, the World Wars, the Cold Wars, the Bomb, and the rise of what Frederic Jameson calls "the media society" have been about, and, equally important, to rediscover the role which successive collective struggles have played in altering our social order. And again, much as the Latin American literati are ever-mindful of their history as colonials, their Yankee counterparts must come to grips with the hemispheric, then global, and now potentially dangerous, empire that is their nation, one whose elected Chief of State can make casual jokes about launching genocidal nuclear war.

These elementary rediscoveries are to be achieved not by entertaining the latest theories of discourse but by pondering certain "basics" easily to be found in dependable volumes of historiography, in serious progressive reportage and quality journalism, and in classics of modern social research by, e.g., C. Wright Mills, Harry Braverman or Barrington Moore. Our universities (the late C.P. Snow notwithstanding) are divided not into Two Cultures but actually three: Scientific, Literary and Social. The rift between the latter two has been baneful to both: solipsized Alexandrians in one group and soulless technocrats in the other.

Finally, besides regaining sight of the history of their country's past, present and future, American literary critics are in some need of reencountering literature itself. Northrop Frye once drew an ingeniously seductive analogy to the effect that, just as a physics student claims to study "physics" rather than "nature," literary critics should see themselves as learning "criticism" rather than "literature" or "art."[15] To an ironic and depressing extent, Frye's view has become an all-too-accurate and prophetic assessment of the life and habits of our literary critics, who, faced with the inordinate growth of the profession, tend increasingly to read lots and lots of criticism and a great deal less literature. (To his credit, Frye has also been committed to his own national literary project—unacknowledged anywhere south of Lake Huron—of commenting on and promoting Canadian fiction and poetry.) Given the institutional setup of U.S. academic literary studies, there is an overwhelming structure of incentives for the critic to be up on every recent development in criticism and theory, with correspondingly negligible stimulus to read poems or novels outside of those few dozen "canonized," respectable names that comprise one's chosen national/chronological/ generic subspecialty. Some hardy pioneers do venture off and stake a claim in, e.g., children's literature or detective fiction, but this only further exemplifies that inexorable dynamic of specialization, fragmentation and accumulation which dominates the academy.

Many a critic originally wound up in literary study because, in some distant past, he or she had come under the spell of Shakespeare or Dostoyevsky or Baudelaire. Professional training eventually dispelled such naive and precritical responses, and verbal skills were effectively rechanneled into learning diverse theories about maybe just one of those fine authors (again, according to special field). If American literary critics are to bring more cultural nourishment to literary academe, they might consider a "natural" diet consisting of more literature and less criticism. By such a recommendation I don't have in mind anything like "back to the text," but something broader and simpler. Sitting on the Borgesian racks of our labyrinthine libraries and lustrous bookstores are thousands of novels, plays and poems that ultimately matter far more than this winter's greenhouse crop of readings of *The Waste Land* or next fall's high fashion of theories of *différence*. Our critics would be performing a concrete service to literary art (and I daresay to their own souls) if they started reading more current verse and narrative, more past authors who aren't frozen and trapped within the Anglo-American curriculum, and more German, Italian, Slavic, Hispanic, and African plays and fiction.[16] (Foreign literature in translation suffers from notoriously poor sales in this country, which is slightly scandalous, given our "pluralistic" self-image and rhetoric of "openness.")

Moreover, as a means of getting "back to the basics" of criticism proper, American literary critics and American culture conceivably might gain from the revitalization of a dormant but venerable old tradition: instead of laboring exclusively over yet another scholarly article, the concerned critic might inquire occasionally at local newspaper offices about the possibility of reviewing a book of stories, popular history or literary biography (foreign or domestic). At first the results may be frustrating, what with few immediate consequences, lowered "productivity" and published pieces of a sort held in low regard by upper academe, but anything that can help lead literary criticism away (literally *e-ducare*) from its ivied impasse of exquisite little cults can't be completely bad in the long run.

142

As for those who wish to see the pluralist drift and theory "boom" in post-Vietnam lit. crit. as a sign of renewed vitality, that is a mirage. Save for the opening to Marxism incidentally allowed by pluralist tolerance and the concomitant recognition now occasionally granted to social reality, the brisk traffic in theory-transplants is mostly a mark of decline, its savorless fruits spawned by a subculture that has lost its larger sense of purpose and turned inward, and whose civilized, erudite laborers toil and produce almost exclusively for one another. This unhappy condition reflects the overall malaise in the American late-capitalist polity and its depressed industries, dismal voting rate, urban shantytowns, circus politics, reactionary mass stirrings, hollow-headed leadership and third-rate Hollywood thespian turned tinsel-glitz *caudillo* (with ex-quarterback Jack Kemp already warming the GOP benches for 1988). Many observers expect things to worsen the next decade or two, with increased military jingoism, financial troubles and some native-style repression. Meanwhile, in the face of a domestic sociopolitical panorama that begins to look vaguely "Latin American," plus certain South American "friendly régimes" that behave more and more Nazi-like, the only response that the U.S. "critical establishment" can come up with is its elaborate paraliterary schemes, its wars on referentiality and its preachments that "History is Fiction, Trope and Discourse." The families of several thousand Salvadoran death-squad victims may entertain other thoughts about history.

A citation from Antonio Gramsci enjoys a kind of underground cult status today: "The old is dying, and the new cannot be born. In this interregnum there arises a great diversity of morbid symptoms."[17] The Modernist revolution is all but dead in our Northern climes, there is no alternate culture visibly taking shape on our horizon, and literary academe now forms part of our gloomy interregnum.

---

1. Rosalind Krauss, "Poststructuralism and the 'Paraliterary,'" *October* No. 13 (1980), pp. 36–40.

2. Erich Auerbach, "The Emergence of a Literary Public in Western Europe," in *Sociology of Literature and Drama*, ed. Elizabeth and Tom Burns (London: Penguin, 1973), pp. 427, 421.

3. Terry Eagleton, *Literary Theory: An Introduction* (Minneapolis: The University of Minnesota Press, 1983), p. 194.

4. Geoffrey Hartman, *Criticism in the Wilderness* (New Haven: Yale University Press, 1980), passim. Stanley Fish, "Demonstration vs. Persuasion: Two Models of Critical Activity," in *Is There a Text in This Class? The Authority of Interpretive Communities* (Cambridge: Harvard University Press, 1980), p. 368.

5. E.M. Forster, *Alexandria: A History and Guide* (Garden City: Doubleday & Co., 1961), p. 19.

6. W.W. Tarn, *Hellenistic Civilization* (London: Edward Arnold & Co., 1930), pp. 242, 245.

7. Ibid., p. 238.

8. Randall Jarrell, "The Age of Criticism," in *Poetry and the Age* (New York: Farrar, Straus & Giroux, 1953), p. 77.

9. Friedrich Nietzsche, *The Birth of Tragedy*, trans. Francis Golffing (Garden City: Doubleday & Co., 1956), p. 109.

10. Ibid., p. 112.

11. Friedrich Nietzsche, *We Philologists* (entry No. 60), trans. J.M. Kennedy, in *Complete Works* (London: T.N. Foules, 1911), Vol. IV, p. 143.

12. Nietzsche, *The Birth of Tragedy*, p. 122.

13. Ibid., p. 135.

14. For further elaboration see Katherine S. Kovács, "The Bureaucratization of Knowledge and Sex in Flaubert and Vargas Llosa," *Comparative Literature Studies*, Vol. 21, No. 1, (Spring 1984), pp. 30–51.

15. Northrop Frye, *Anatomy of Criticism: Four Essays* (New York: Atheneum, 1968), p. 11.

16. On the marginal existence of foreign literatures in the United States, see Walter Cohen and Peter U. Hohendahl, "Marxist Literary Critics: Problems and Proposals," *Humanities and Society*, Vol. 6, Nos. 2 and 3 (Spring and Summer 1983), pp. 161–77, but especially pp. 168–69.

17. Quoted in Karl Marzani, *The Promise of Eurocommunism* (Westport, Conn.: Lawrence Hill & Co., 1980), p. 296.

III. Inside and Outside the Industry

Journalism and Criticism

Morris Dickstein

Even to link the words *journalism* and *criticism*, as I have in my title, goes against the grain of our tendency to think of criticism as an ever more specialized activity. The twentieth century has seen important advances in our technical understanding of how works of art are put together. This has accompanied a new kind of complexity and difficulty in the works themselves, and brought in its train a great many technical terms, refined concepts and subtle strategies of critical attack. Literary criticism, which used to be the bastion from which the educated generalist held forth not only about books but about life itself—society, morals, politics, religion—has become so professionalized that even scholars in other fields like history and sociology complain that they can no longer understand it. This is a surprising reversal from the time when critics, priding themselves on their guardianship of the language and their access to a general audience, regularly attacked social scientists for their jargon-ridden obscurity, pseudo-scientific aspirations toward system, and unduly narrow professional identification.

But even before criticism took on this special academic coloration, its difference from journalism was marked and considerable. The word journalism suggests a day-by-day thing, as ephemeral as the paper it's printed on. Though the journalist himself may lead a feverishly active and adventurous life, in his work he is expected to be the passive conductor of the world's ongoing business. The critic, on the other hand, whose daily life may be that of a gentleman in an armchair, is engaged in an activity whose root meaning involves making judgments, and brings to bear criteria that are enduring rather than ephemeral. A critic is expected to intervene in his material far more drastically than the journalist. Strictly speaking, journalism is simply information, and cultural journalism, which has been with us since the eighteenth century, is information about books, performances, exhibitions and other cultural events. The development of cultural journalism is interwoven with the

147

growth of the press itself and the development of a large, anonymous reading public – new to culture, unsure of its own taste, and eager for guidance through a tangled maze of cultural artifacts.

"Modern journalism," writes Leonard Woolf, "saw its opportunity to meet this demand for information about new books and invented reviewing and the reviewer."[1] From early on, this reviewer was expected to make critical judgments about the books before him, and this is where journalism and criticism begin to intersect. Critical journalism becomes important when art leaves the court and the salon and enters the marketplace. The history of reviewing – a largely unwritten history, surprisingly – develops in tandem with the history of advertising, in a culture which depends less and less on patronage, more and more on publicity. Reviewers are key links in a commercial chain which connects the modern producers of culture with its potential consumers. Even today, books which are not reviewed in certain key periodicals like the *New York Times Book Review* are sometimes said not to exist: bookstores might not stock them, libraries will not order them, publishers may not advertise them and other periodicals are less likely to review them.

With this kind of low commercial origin, reviewing has generally been assigned a low cultural status. If even the critic is a parasite on the body of literature, the reviewer is a parasite on the publishing industry and the miscellaneous public. Since most of what's published each year is worthless, the reviewer who begins with a sense of high purpose and a real love of books is quickly dispirited or reduced to a hack. George Orwell has described this demoralizing process in a keen article called "Confessions of a Book Reviewer," where he notes that "the prolonged, indiscriminate reviewing of books is a quite exceptionally thankless, irritating, and exhausting job. It not only involves praising trash . . .but constantly *inventing* reactions towards books about which one has no spontaneous feelings whatever. . . . [The reviewer] is pouring his immortal spirit down the drain, half a pint at a time."[2]

Orwell was writing in 1946. The kind of professional reviewer he was describing, the person who actually makes his living from reviewing a hundred or more books a year, is a vanishing breed. This is not simply because of the reduced importance of books in the postwar cultural scene. After all, Orwell's jaundiced remarks could just as readily be applied to professional movie critics and drama critics. Reviewers have declined because reviewing outlets – newspapers especially – have disappeared and the producers of culture have developed high-powered forms of publicity, notably television, which involve no risk of criticism whatsoever. Instead of selling books themselves, publishers have learned to peddle the personalities of authors. The "Today Show" is the standard author's tour raised to the nth power and constricted to seven minutes. Only "quality" books with fragile commercial possibilities still depend on reviews.

Newspapers and magazines have responded to this *People* magazine climate by integrating reviews into their new Style sections and surrounding them with interviews, gossip, feature stories, ads and listings. Accounts of book and movie deals, paperback sales, production problems and the private lives of authors and performers have increasingly taken the place of critical judgments in the form of reviews. It is still possible, occasionally, to see a book or movie roasted in one column while being promoted uncritically as a glorious event on the other side of the page. But this schizophrenia has become too stressful even for reviewers to bear; it's far easier for them to join the chorus of celebration before passing on to the next undying masterpiece. Reviewers have become television performers themselves, peddling their personalities in bite-size chunks like actors on talk shows. Even in print, reviewers can often be seen pleading for attention, pirouetting with factitious liveliness to hook the reader's elusive interest. The successful reviewer becomes a talked-about figure, like the people he writes about. (This has happened most recently with film critics.) The others remain mere appendages to the commercial scene. In this light, it's hardly any wonder that the status of reviewers remains low by any traditional standard.

But the overheated media scene of the present moment is not an accurate index to the underlying links between journalism and criticism. In "The Function of Criticism Today," Alfred Kazin reminds us how many of the greatest critics of the past did their best work for periodicals — provoked at times by bizarre occasions and harried by difficult journalistic pressures — lack of time and money, the specific demands of editors and audiences:

> Have we forgotten under what conditions so much of the most powerful criticism originated? Poe wrote his greatest critical essays for general magazines, in the same way that Coleridge and Hazlitt wrote for newspapers. Sainte-Beuve wrote his greatest pieces week after week for newspapers. Eliot wrote his best early essays as a reviewer for English weeklies. Proust wrote his own first essays for frivolous Parisian papers. . . . Go back and recall that Emerson's great essays were popular lectures, that Henry James's famous essay on "The Art of Fiction" appeared in a popular magazine, as did his best fiction, that Howells's essays on realism and his marvelous essay on Mark Twain all came out first in magazines. . . . This kind of critic sees himself not as a hack, but as a man seizing the largest possible audience for his ideas, and in the weekly dialogue he holds with his readers he establishes standards, and sets up a forum around which ideas gather, where neglected important figures can be revived and new writers recognized.[3]

In another essay, "Writing for Magazines," Kazin points to Chekhov as a writer who especially enjoyed writing for magazines, where he "was allowed to be *easy*. . . . [T]he classic style of the European *feuilleton*, the style of conversation, of intimacy, of pleasure and the cafés, was Chekhov's delight and his genius."[4]

Since both these essays appeared in an immense collection of literary journalism, *Contemporaries* (1962), Kazin can perhaps be accused of painting an idealized picture or writing personal apologetics. But his reminder is a timely corrective to the other picture we get from academic histories of criticism, especially those written under the influence of the New Criticism. The impression we get from Wimsatt and Brooks, from Wellek and Warren, and from most of Wellek's multivolume *History*, is that modern criticism is indebted to everything from Plato and Longinus to German idealism — everything, that is, except the long tradition of critical journalism that began with the founding of the *Edinburgh Review* in 1802; the *Revue des Deux Mondes* in Paris; the *North American Review* in the United States; the great Victorian periodicals like the *Saturday Review*, the *Fortnightly Review* and the *Cornhill*, and continued down through all the modern literary quarterlies and book-review organs like the *TLS* and the *New York Review of Books*.

Though some of these early magazines were relatively popular, others cultivated a reflective, highbrow mode deliberately at variance with the hurly-burly of newspaper journalism. Many were edited in a frank party spirit that added vinegar to their literary coverage. Though writers like Wordsworth and Keats were violently assaulted, under cover of anonymity, from meanly partisan motives, the results were sometimes a significant contribution to the critical spirit. Francis Jeffrey's notorious attacks on Wordsworth and the Lake Poets were sometimes based on sheer snobbery, combined with an eighteenth-century sense of poetic decorum:

> The poor and vulgar may interest us, in poetry, by their situation; but never, we apprehend, by any sentiments that are peculiar to their condition, and still less by any language that is characteristic of it. The truth is, that it is impossible to copy their diction and their sentiments correctly, in a serious composition; and this, not merely because poverty makes men ridiculous, but because just taste and refinement are rarely to be met with among the uncultivated part of mankind.[5]

This is Jeffrey at his priggish worst, a hidebound representative of a timid Whig liberalism. But all of Jeffrey's reviews make sharp and accurate points against the affected simplicity of some of Wordsworth's characters and language, points to which the poet responded with numerous revisions only after they were echoed in the trenchant pages of Coleridge's *Biographia Literaria*. Unlike Coleridge, Jeffrey vitiates what he says by leaving out the other side of the picture. He saved his tributes to Wordsworth for drawing-room conversation, leaving himself open to a charge of hypocrisy. When he told Crabb Robinson, many years later, "I was always an admirer of Wordsworth," the poet's friend couldn't resist replying, "You had a singular way of showing your admiration."[6]

What is not well understood today is that Jeffrey attacked Wordsworth not simply for political or strategic reasons or out of the limitations of his taste and judgment. Literary historians have collaborated with Wordsworth in conveying the impression of an enormous uphill battle for public acceptance, impeded by the obtuse reviewers who represented the reigning taste left over from the eighteenth century. In fact Jeffrey attacked the Lake Poets because their revolution had quickly succeeded; Wordsworth had almost immediately been recognized as a great and moving poet, though an idiosyncratic one. Reviewing Wordsworth's *Poems in Two Volumes* (1807), Jeffrey admits that "the Lyrical Ballads were unquestionably popular; and, we have no hesitation in saying, deservedly popular,"[7] but it is clear that, in the main, he sees the mission of the *Edinburgh Review* as the correction of popular taste, which he *prides* himself in controverting. So sure is he that the new volumes confirm all of Wordsworth's worst faults that he announces, with great fanfare, that he is willing not simply to trust to the judgment of posterity—the usual court of appeal, evidently, for a highbrow quarterly—but to wager on the public opinion of his own time.

This is only one way in which the Edinburgh reviewers foreshadow the acerbic, dissident tone of Eliot in the twenties, *Scrutiny* in the thirties, *Partisan Review* in the forties and fifties, the *New York Review* in the sixties, and neoconservative journals today. "Mass Civilization and Minority Culture," Leavis called it in an early polemical pamphlet, whose title was an emblem of the strange combination of conservative values and radical rhetoric in the highbrow culture of the modern era. The "Advertisement" in the first number of the *Edinburgh Review* contained many other elements which were prototypical of the later, fully developed quarterly mold. The magazine promised to be more discriminating than existing journals, to run fewer and longer reviews, really essays, and to allow books to ripen in the reviewer's mind without regard to the pressure of booksellers and the dates of publication.[8] Existing reviews like the *Monthly Review* and the *Critical Review* tended to be strictly informational and to publish large numbers of summaries and abstracts of new books. As John Clive, the historian of the early years of the *Edinburgh*, has written, "scores of hacks and penny-a-liners were completely dependent on the mercy of editors in their turn dependent on booksellers who financed the reviews in order to advertise the books they printed and sold. This meant that praise and blame were invariably bestowed on the basis of commercial rather than literary criteria. The venality that inevitably resulted put book reviewing as a profession into such bad odour that those who thought themselves gentlemen took it up only as a last resort."[9] The Edinburgh reviewers, on the other hand, by and large middle-class professionals, were gentlemen in every way, down to their Whig prejudices and ambitions, their snobbish. airs, and their enlightened liberal opinions on many social and political questions—enlightened, that is, in an England that still had a slave trade and an unreformed Parliament. The Whigs were out of power for nearly all the early period of the *Review*, and this helped give it a critical edge which its Tory counterpart, the *Quarterly*, mimicked in its ferocious attacks on liberals and radicals like Hunt and Hazlitt.

Thus a period of sharp political (and literary) polarization helped put criticism on an entirely new footing in England, far from the world of both Grub Street hacks and abstruse aesthetic speculation. Criticism was a hard-hitting enterprise deeply enmeshed with political pamphleteering and the emergence of new classes of readers, who were also new players in the political arena. This was a time when taxes and government-required stamps made the cost of newspapers artificially high as a way of depriving the restive working class of incendiary reading.[10] The kind of "impure" criticism produced under these volatile conditions evidently holds very little interest for the modern historians and theorists of criticism. The New Criticism, despite its political origins among the Agrarians, was another step in the shift towards aesthetic criticism which had begun in the late nineteenth century but remained incomplete in Arnold, Pater, Wilde and Yeats.

The New Criticism was also a highly theoretical movement; it aimed to overthrow existing notions of the literary text and prevailing habits of impressionistic, historical and philological criticism. It was no mere method of explication, despite its emphasis on pedagogy. Writers like Ransom and Tate, Richards and Empson, Warren and Brooks, Wimsatt and Wellek, Blackmur and Burke were at once critical practitioners, historians of earlier criticism, and theorists who, early and late, tried hard to codify their own practical procedures. This is something that more journalistic critics, who aimed at a general audience, almost never tried to do, whether they wrote for newspapers or *Partisan Review*, for the *New Yorker* or the *New Republic*. A book like Stanley Edgar Hyman's study of modern criticism, *The Armed Vision* (1948), written under the influence of the more theoretical wing of the New Criticism, is a revealing document of its time—the same period when the academic histories of criticism were being written. Hyman's book begins with a set of villains—popular, historical critics like Van Wyck Brooks and Edmund Wilson—and gradually slides across the ideological spectrum toward a set of heroes, Blackmur, Empson, Richards and, above all, Burke, Hyman's mentor.

In many ways this is a refreshing set of emphases; Hyman is bracingly opinionated and fun to read, especially for his irreverence toward the sacred cows of middlebrow writing and academic system building. But one main thrust of his book is to eliminate cultural criticism, journalistic criticism, and personal, intuitive criticism—free of self-conscious "method"—entirely. This comes out most clearly in his furious attack on Edmund Wilson, which was later suppressed from the paperback edition. As far as I know, Wilson did not respond to Hyman directly. Instead he collected three decades of literary journalism into *Classics and Commercials* (1950) and *The Shores of Light* (1952), which was far more devastating than any reply. There it was; he had done the work; his articles held up. His judgment, his eye for new talent, the crisp simplicity of his writing, were amazing. Taken together, the pieces formed a vast literary chronicle of the era—though, in the postwar climate of professionalization, it took some time for Wilson's standing as a critic to be restored and for him to become the reigning man of letters he was when he died in 1972.

By that time the world had gotten tired of the New Critical emphasis on interpretation rather than judgment, on the text rather than its contexts, on pedagogic Method rather than individual sensibility. The rising reputations of Wilson and Trilling after their deaths, the ascendency of successors like Howe and Kazin, Kermode and Donoghue—all writers who had figured only marginally in anyone's standard history of modern criticism—testified to their rare personal qualities of mind and style, yes, but also to many features of journalistic and cultural criticism which had begun to evoke new respect and attention. These were the qualities of the old-fashioned man of letters, the generalist—supposedly, according to John Gross, an almost extinct species.[11]

The modern version of this figure is not the same as the old pipe-smoking amateur spilling out his impressions on the page. Even a century ago this image was inaccurate if we look at the prodigiously varied and productive lives of Victorian prose writers—not just the Carlyles, Ruskins and Arnolds, but figures like G. H. Lewes, Frederic Harrison, John Morley, Walter Bagehot and Leslie Stephen. Of course there were many genteel bookmen of a milder stamp, especially in America, as young radicals like Randolph Bourne and Van Wyck Brooks were later fond of pointing out. The contemporary man of letters has been through the tempering furnace of Marx, Freud, the Holocaust, Sartrean existentialism, and the *Kulturkampf* of the sixties. Yet as a critic his work is likely to share many of the qualities of the great journalistic critics of the past, from Poe to Henry James to Edmund Wilson.

Journalistic criticism differs from academic or theoretical criticism in a number of crucial ways, some of which bring it much closer to the buried mainstream of the history of criticism—the very history from which it has all but been excluded by academic chroniclers. Journalistic criticism is practical criticism, brought into being by an occasion—usually the publication of a new book—which is both communal and immediate. Sometimes it is victimized by the occasion: when the book is trivial, or minor, or below the author's own best standard. The good reviewer who wants to generalize about a writer and observe the shape of his career may feel that he's trapped inside the wrong book. Or he may be forced to give the reader so much information that little room is left for criticism or ideas. But in being obliged to meet the reader's immediate needs, the reviewer must create through his language what we often fear no longer exists: a community of shared literary values and social concerns. Good book-reviewing is always relevant and contemporaneous, never merely antiquarian. Lionel Trilling was sometimes criticized for his use of the first person plural; but at its frequent best his "we" spoke not for an in-group of the critic and his friends but for an acute sensibility attuned to the rhythms of the *Zeitgeist* and the nuances of the social mood.

Henry James in his journalism was a master of this kind of nuanced apprehension. Writing of Matthew Arnold, George Sand or Trollope, James tells us exactly what made them seem so fresh twenty years earlier and why they have come to seem somewhat less so in the twilight of their careers. We understand from him that each book not only has its place in an unfolding career but interacts unpredictably with a cultural moment and an individual reader. Thus, at one and the same moment James describes the shape of a career, the history of his own reading, with its nimble shifts of generous enthusiasm, and the changing literary climate, which the subject himself, with his earlier work, may have done much to alter.

James' reviews demonstrate how the needs of the common reader encourage the journalist-critic to be especially vivid and dramatic. Writing constantly about new works to readers unlikely to have read them, the reviewer must try to flesh them out as effectively as a fictional character. James goes further; he tries, as all the great critics have traditionally done, to catch the essential flavor of a writer, to discern the figure in the carpet and lay bare the essential project. Of George Sand he writes, for example:

> She was an *improvisatrice*, raised to a very high power; she told stories as a nightingale sings. No novelist answers so well to the childish formula of "making up as you go along." Other novels seem meditated, pondered, calculated, thought out and elaborated with a certain amount of trouble; but the narrative with Madame Sand always appears to be an invention of the moment, flowing from a mind which a constant process of quiet contemplation, absorption and reverie keeps abundantly supplied with material. It is a sort of general emanation, an intellectual evaporation.[12]

This is just the kind of writing that the New Criticism and academic criticism have shunned. It seems old-fashioned for being so impressionistic and lyrical. Yet James gets a great deal done here. He characterizes a writer's essential stance in a suggestive and lively way, though one not easily subject to precise verification. As much by metaphor as anything else, he makes what Leavis would call an implicit limiting judgment of her work in the very act of praising it. He suggests that there is something childlike and merely "natural" about her work; that it is meandering and, though perhaps inspired, not profoundly structured; and that its method differs as drastically as possible from his own more calculated procedures—a contrast which makes him feel both envious and superior. James' criticism is at once personal and detached, biased and objective.

James had before him the precedent of writers as different as Johnson and Hazlitt, Sainte-Beuve and Arnold, for this kind of experiential criticism, which depends on the accents of the personal voice, whatever its claims to impersonal authority, and centers on the interior drama of reading, responding and apportioning praise and blame. Their comments on literature were rooted as much in the vibrations of sensibility as in any 'objective' set of principles and standards. Even Sainte-Beuve, who was later attacked by the younger generation for his frigid biographical method, could rise to lyrical celebration in the presence of genius. One of his late *lundis*, "To Love Molière" (July 18, 1863), is a brief series of almost incantatory variations on the title phrase. What does it mean, he asks, to love Molière, or to prefer Racine or Corneille, or to respect Boileau (for "surely no one loves Boileau")? How must such affections, if we take them seriously, alter our whole outlook, not simply our literary judgments? In a mere three pages, Sainte-Beuve provides a fine example of how literary journalism can reach epigrammatically towards the core of a writer's world and of a critic's feeling for that writer. It tells us that to love writers is to be transformed by them, so that nothing else feels quite the same again, and each paragraph of the article is a brief inventory of a writer's unsettling intervention in our mundane lives: "To love Molière is to rid oneself of complacency and excessive admiration for man. . . . [T]o prefer Racine is to risk overindulgence in what in France we call 'good taste,' which in the end leaves such a bad taste."[13]

Much of modern criticism, by veering towards either the explication of themes or the analysis of formal structures, loses the intimate, experiential dimension that we feel in James and his forebears, and that survives best in journalistic criticism. Gerald Graff has described such interpretive criticism as "textual rationalization," the pyrotechnics of showing that—in a text, at least—whatever is is right. He points out that the early exegetes were reacting "against a crudely judicial criticism which especially condemned modern and experimental literature by arbitrary stylistic and doctrinal canons."[14] Evaluative criticism can easily devolve into obtuse dismissal or hazy appreciation. But interpretive criticism can turn just as easily into a mechanical process, a routinization of the imaginative. Critical journalism at its best combines the wide-ranging freedom, the gifted *un*professionalism of Victorian criticism, with a more modern textual attention and an awareness that a reading is not the Truth but only a quick take upon it, a singular perspective. Critical journalism is an epigrammatic shorthand awaiting completion by the reader, or a lone voice listening for an answering echo, which can only come from another reading. Sainte-Beuve's own metaphor for this in his article on Molière is striking: "I am only giving the key and the theme; it is up to the reader to carry on from here."[15] This is in keeping with the musical structure of the article itself.

Critical journalism is almost by definition partial, even fragmentary, taking the form of short flights rather than large, comprehensive works. Many modern critics, from Benjamin and Adorno to Trilling and Rahv – all weaned on the heroic phase of modernism – are attracted to the fragmentary dynamics of the essay for the way it accords with our fractured sense of contemporary reality. Literary journalism is criticism by fits and starts, bound to the moment, happily unable to systematize itself or break free from either its cultural setting or its very specific relation to readers and the marketplace. In newspapers – the cheaply printed anthologies which have been described as the verbal equivalent of the modern city – criticism must vie for attention with everything else, all the topical stimuli so characteristic of contemporary life. In "The First Edinburgh Reviewers," Walter Bagehot wrote that because of the larger and more miscellaneous reading public, journalism and criticism had grown more rapid, lively and instructive; but the very essay in which he said this was remarkably leisurely by modern standards.[16] Bagehot was partly sardonic about this development, as he was about almost everything, but he could also see its virtues. In our time, when the cultural scene often seems merely trendy and frenetic, it's much harder to strike that balance. The professionalization of criticism, heightened recently by the growth of specialized theory, has abridged the public space of literary discourse and made cultural journalism and the public style in criticism seem methodologically naive and academically suspect.

In reaction to this devaluation of public criticism, I have sketched perhaps a slightly idealized picture here, taking cultural journalism in its higher reaches rather than its mediocre norm. The best journalistic critics have always been properly scornful of the average performance of their colleagues and stringent advocates of more rigorous critical standards. Poe attacked publishers' reviewing cliques "which, hanging like nightmares upon American literature, manufacture, at the nod of our principal booksellers, a pseudo-public-opinion by wholesale."[17] (Apparently some things never change.) He mocked the reviewers who find an easy substitute for the labor of criticism "in a digest or compendium of the work noticed, with copious extracts."[18] On the other hand, he satirized the typical highbrow quarterly reviewer "who loves the safety of generalities" and "is a sworn enemy to all things simple and direct."[19] Poe held out for a criticism that would be both aesthetic and disinterested, "an absolutely independent criticism – a criticism self-sustained; guiding itself only by the purest rules of Art; analyzing and urging these rules as it applies them; holding itself aloof from all personal bias; acknowledging no fear save that of outraging the right; yielding no point either to the vanity of the author, or to the assumptions of antique prejudice. . . ."[20]

Like Poe fifty years earlier, Henry James described the criticism around him in the 1890's as a mass of vacuous fatuity. With bitter wit he castigates "periodical literature" as "a huge, open mouth which has to be fed" and assails "the practice of 'reviewing'" as "a practice that in general has nothing in common with the art of criticism." In James' eyes, the eyes of a lifelong reviewer as well as an impassioned artist stung by obtuse reviews, "the critical sense is so far from frequent that it is absolutely rare, and the possession of the cluster of qualities that minister to it is one of the highest distinctions."[21] Like Poe, James combines a grand vision of the potential of criticism with a jaundiced view of its current journalistic practitioners. In a similar vein, Edmund Wilson in 1928 wrote: "It is astonishing to observe, in America, in spite of the floods of literary journalism, to what extent the literary atmosphere is a non-conductor of criticism."[22] Herman Melville had uttered the same complaint in his essay on Hawthorne: "American authors have received more just and discriminating praise (however loftily and ridiculously given, in certain cases) even from some Englishmen, than from their own countrymen. There are hardly five critics in America; and several of them are asleep."[23]

These comments were written out of a sense of the value criticism could have, not as an academic specialty but as a contribution to the health of a culture and the well-being of writers. What Wilson wanted was the sight of "the intelligence fully awakened to the implications of what the artist is doing,"[24] and he called his prescriptive manifesto "The Critic Who Does Not Exist." Wilson, like Poe and James, was clearing a space for a reviewer-critic very much like himself. He saw around him a set of competing schools of writers and journalists, each pouring out scorn on the other and defending its turf. He was sure "that our contemporary writing would benefit by a genuine literary criticism that should deal expertly with ideas and art, not merely tell us whether the reviewer 'let out a whoop' for the book or threw it out the window."[25] Merely judicial criticism is not enough; it must be a true practical criticism attentive to both the particulars of the text and the general questions it raises. Otherwise it defaults on what it can do for both writers and for the culture at large. Judicial criticism can never be entirely set aside without ushering in a narrow academicism. The almost forgotten journalism of a century ago remains a model of what criticism might yet become, a totality of response to works of art that is both scrupulous and committed, intensely private yet intensely public. James in 1868 gave some of the purest formulations of the critic's function when he wrote that "the critic is simply a reader like all the others—a reader who prints his impressions." "Nothing will ever take the place of the good old fashion of 'liking' a work of art or not liking it. The most improved criticism will not abolish that primitive, that ultimate test."[26]

---

1. Virginia Woolf, *Reviewing*, With a Note by Leonard Woolf (London: Hogarth, 1939), p. 29.

2. George Orwell, "Confessions of a Book Reviewer," in *The Collected Essays, Journalism, and Letters of George Orwell*, ed. Sonia Orwell and Ian Angus (Harmondsworth, England: Penguin, 1970), IV, p. 217.

3. Alfred Kazin, *Contemporaries* (Boston and Toronto: Atlantic-Little, Brown, 1962), p. 504.

4. Ibid., p. 472.

5. Jeffrey's reviews are reprinted in *The Romantics Reviewed*, ed. Donald Reiman (New York and London: Garland, 1972), II, p. 217. See also John O. Hayden, *The Romantic Reviewers, 1802–1824* (Chicago and London: University of Chicago Press, 1969).

6. John Clive, *Scotch Reviewers:* The Edinburgh Review, *1802–1815* (London: Faber & Faber, 1957), p. 157n.

7. Reiman (ed.), *The Romantics Reviewed*, II, p. 429.

8. See Hayden, p. 11.

9. Clive, p. 32.

10. For many provocative insights into the history of British journalism, see *Newspaper History: from the seventeenth century to the present day*, ed. George Boyce, James Curran and Pauline Wingate (London and Beverly Hills: Constable, 1978).

11. See John Gross, *The Rise and Fall of the Man of Letters* (London: Weidenfeld & Nicolson, 1969), a lively book which suffers from its own journalistic limitations. Though it devolves into a series of individual profiles, it is the closest thing we have to a critical history of reviewing in England.

12. Henry James, *Literary Reviews and Essays*, ed. Albert Mordell (1957; rpt. New York: Grove Press, 1979), p. 133.

13. C.A. Sainte-Beuve, "To Love Molière," in *Sainte-Beuve: Selected Essays*, ed. and trans. by Francis Steegmuller and Norbert Guterman (Garden City: Doubleday & Co., Anchor Books, 1964), pp. 126–27.

14. Gerald Graff, unpublished essay.

15. Sainte-Beuve, "To Love Molière," p. 126.

16. Walter Bagehot, "The First Edinburgh Reviewers," in *Literary Studies* (London: S.M. Dent & Sons, 1911), I, pp. 1–35.

17. Edgar Allan Poe, *Essays and Reviews*, ed. G.R. Thompson (New York: Library of America, 1984), p. 1025. This superb volume makes Poe's critical journalism widely available for the first time.

18. Ibid., p. 1029.

19. Quoted by John Paul Pritchard, *Criticism in America* (Norman, Okla.: University of Oklahoma Press, 1956), p. 85.

20. Poe, *Essays and Reviews*, p. 1025.

21. Henry James, "The Science of Criticism" (1891), in *Literary Criticism: Essays on Literature, American Writers, English Writers*, ed. Leon Edel, with Mark Wilson (New York: Library of America, 1984), pp. 95, 98.

22. Edmund Wilson, "The Critic Who Does Not Exist," in *The Shores of Light* (1952; rpt. New York: Farrar, Straus & Giroux, 1961), p. 369.

23. Herman Melville, "Hawthorne and His Mosses," reprinted in *The Shock of Recognition*, ed. Edmund Wilson (1943; rpt. New York: Farrar, Straus, and Cudahy, 1955), p. 197. Though confined largely to what our best writers wrote about each other, this volume is probably the best single anthology of American literary journalism. Its idiosyncratic choices are full of exciting rediscoveries, including Poe, early Lowell, and D.H. Lawrence's then-neglected writings on American literature.

24. Wilson, *The Shores of Light*, pp. 367–68.

25. Wilson, p. 372.

26. Quoted by René Wellek in *A History of Modern Criticism, 1750–1950*, The Later Nineteenth Century, IV (New Haven and London: Yale University Press, 1965), p. 217. Wellek's commodious *History* is the only one which gives any substantial attention to the mass of critical journalism, though he too concentrates on major figures. What is needed is a sociological and critical study of the growth of literature as an institution and the many-sided role that reviewing has played in that development.

158

The Two Worlds of Cultural Criticism

Mark Krupnick

I

Why is it that American literary academics interested in a generally left-wing critique of culture are so indifferent nowadays to America's native tradition of radical criticism? More particularly, what happened to induce would-be oppositional critics in this country to look for direction to Frankfurt intellectuals such as Theodor Adorno and Herbert Marcuse rather than to American contemporaries of the Frankfurt School critics such as Lionel Trilling, Philip Rahv and Harold Rosenberg? It seems odd, on the face of it, that academic critics well informed about the debates centered on Gramsci, Benjamin and Bakhtin should know next to nothing of the early Van Wyck Brooks and Edmund Wilson or of the New York intellectuals associated with *Partisan Review* in the thirties and forties.

One obvious explanation is that the present generation of literature-and-society academics is, however vaguely, "Marxist," and the New York intellectuals were not. Trilling and Sidney Hook and Clement Greenberg may have started out as Marxists, but they gradually turned away not only from Marxism but from political radicalism altogether. More recently the New York critics' liberal anti-communism of the 1950's has modulated into neoconservative anti-radicalism in the intellectual monthlies edited by Norman Podhoretz (*Commentary*) and Hilton Kramer (the *New Criterion*). It seems to become easier every day for New York writers to overcome the radical piety of their progenitors.

But the conservative mood of some of the New York intellectuals doesn't by itself explain the neglect of Trilling, Rosenberg, et al. in academic literary circles. There is nothing to stop left-wing academic critics from retrieving New York criticism in its more vigorous, more radical phase, between, say, 1935 and the beginnings of the Cold War. Critics have shown themselves able to distinguish between the John Dos Passos of the radical trilogy *U.S.A.* and the later, more conservative Dos Passos. Why, then, the neglect?

The main reason, I think, has to do not with the specific positions of the New York critics but with their intellectual style. Many elements of that style distinguish it from contemporary academic criticism. Above all, the New York style in criticism is unabashedly secular and worldly in outlook, alert to the movements of opinion and aggressive in staking out positions. The pressures of politics make themselves visible in the texture of this writing, which more closely resembles the work of Wilson and Orwell, say, than Blackmur and Barthes. New York-style criticism is freewheeling and speculative and gets bored easily. It is bored by the close reading of texts; sometimes it is too easily bored with sustained argument altogether. It relies for its authority on the critic's own voice, not on impersonal method or system. It avoids the fetishism of technique in academic criticism and at its best it also avoids the sometime gentility and mandarinism of the professors.

One of the most important distinctions between criticism in the universities and the older New York criticism is the latter's relative indifference to technical philosophy. In the thirties the Marxism of the American left literary intellectuals was a rough-and-ready affair, philosophically thin and based on a skimpy knowledge of the socialist intellectual tradition. Nowadays, the emphasis in academic Marxist theory is on "theory" as much as on "Marxism," and the new academic Marxism, like the Marxism of the Frankfurt School, is very much a philosophical critique. It is the relative indifference of the *Partisan Review* circle to technical philosophy that separates them from their Frankfurt contemporaries.

Of the most important New York intellectuals only Sidney Hook was a philosopher, and Hook came to Marxism by way of John Dewey rather than by way of Hegel. The German philosophical tradition, as it runs from Kant and Hegel to Nietzsche and Heidegger, was the core of the Frankfurt intellectuals' culture. For Hook, on the other hand, much of that tradition represented simply a collapse into obscurantism and irrationalism. To say that German philosophy was central to the work of the Frankfurt critical theorists is not, of course, to say that they endorsed the tradition without qualification. One has only to think of Adorno's detestation of the post-World War II cult of Heidegger, whom he attacked in his late book *The Jargon of Authenticity* (1964). But Adorno thought it necessary to deal with Heidegger; the New York intellectuals, with the exception of William Barrett, hardly mention him.

One way of measuring the distance between the intellectual styles of Frankfurt and New York is to compare Adorno's philosophical treatment of authenticity with Lionel Trilling's much more literary approach to the question in *Sincerity and Authenticity* (1972).[1] Trilling's book deals with Rousseau, Hegel, Nietzsche and Sartre, but it is "philosophic" only in the discursive way of the English-speaking man of letters. It's symptomatic that Trilling doesn't even cite Heidegger or Adorno's book on him. Sartre is more to Trilling's point than Heidegger because, like Trilling himself, Sartre was as much a man of letters, a *politique et moraliste*, as a metaphysician.

Enthusiasm for philosophy among the New York intellectuals probably reached its peak in the thirties, when Hook emerged as the leading American exponent of Marxism and, only a few years later, as its most formidable philosophical adversary, in his attack on the idea of the Marxist dialectic. William Barrett, Hook's successor in the philosophy department at New York University and as resident philosopher at *Partisan Review*, became better known as a popularizer of existentialism and as a man of letters than as a technical philosopher. The best-known of the New York critics were not philosophers at all but full-time literary men, and practical critics at that, rather than aestheticians. Nowadays academic theoreticians celebrate Kenneth Burke, the most dauntingly philosophical literary man of the thirties. Meanwhile, once-popular critics like Trilling are discounted because of their lucidity.

The irony is that the New York critics prided themselves on their zeal for ideas, in contrast with what they thought of as the intellectual vacuity of genteel academic scholarship. Neither did they subscribe to the theorized anti-intellectualism of their chief rivals, the New Critics. Those critics, the progeny of John Crowe Ransom, took their stand in opposition to generalizing intellect and "abstraction" (which they associated with science and technology), in favor of "imagination" and "sensibility." The New York intellectuals were like the New Critics in being drawn to concreteness, but they were not shy about abstract ideas and the inevitable connection of ideas with ideology. Despite their interest in general ideas, however, by comparison with philosophical academic critics of a later generation, the New York intellectuals seem in retrospect to have always had about them a touch of the journalist. "Journalist" is a term of opprobrium in academic literary circles. But after twenty years of floating about the skies of philosophical abstraction, criticism would do well to touch down and recover contact with the concrete, ground-level virtues of the older literary journalism. Criticism has forgotten recently that, like literature itself, it must ultimately derive its strength from contact with the earth.

In the 1970's the Frankfurt intellectuals became a substantial presence in American academic literary theory. The rise of the new academic Marxism, championed by younger critics like Fredric Jameson, helped to put Adorno and Walter Benjamin on graduate school reading lists. At the same time the rise of the Frankfurt School was matched by the falling influence of the New York intellectuals. The decline of the New Yorkers' prestige in academic circles was not totally a surprise. Rahv and Howe had always been rather neglected, and Trilling, the most respected of the New York group in the universities, had never been a model for advanced academic criticism. The reason is probably that Trilling had no critical method that could be easily imitated. He had, instead, a certain style, tone, quality of intelligence. Such gifts are not transferable. Many critics have thought to inherit Trilling's mantle, but it has been with him as with F. R. Leavis in England: there have been no true successors.

It was hardly to be expected that Trilling's Arnoldian gracefulness would make him central in a specialist academic culture of professionals and technicians. But there was something new in the seventies. There had always been a small number of academic critics, like W. K. Wimsatt, Eliseo Vivas and Murray Krieger, who were almost exclusively devoted to theoretical issues. But in the seventies "theory" took on a broader implication and became the focus of advanced criticism. Every academic critic who wanted to be taken seriously was obliged to be concerned with ideas at the highest level of philosophical abstraction.

The change was devastating for the old New York intellectuals, whose general ideas were rarely presented in the language of formal philosophy, and who were more often concerned with practical questions of culture and society than with abstract questions of method and interpretation. These intellectuals were more disposed to deal with large ideas in a glancing way than to engage in sustained theoretical argument. Irving Howe has described the New York idea of the intellectual life as "free-lance dash, peacock strut, daring hypothesis, knockabout synthesis."[2] That seems to me a caricature of the New York critical style, but it does suggest the influence on the New York critics of writing for nonspecialist magazines of opinion. The important thing at *Partisan Review* was to be lucid, lively and "brilliant." It was left for professors to be scholarly, thorough and (presumably) dull.

The New York intellectuals have sometimes described themselves as if they had been born out of the Depression and the radical movement of the thirties. In fact, they were carrying on the central tradition in American criticism, which has always been more or less culturally oriented and journalistic. As Geoffrey Hartman has recently observed of the literary situation in the twenties and thirties, which the New York intellectuals inherited: "it was not the universities at all but the journals and magazines that spread what literary culture there was." The result, as Hartman adds, is that what grew up between the world wars was "a culture of journalism, not yet a culture of criticism."[3]

Hartman means to point out the limitations of that culture. His point about the American journalist-critics is something like Matthew Arnold's about the English Romantic poets: they did not know enough.

Hartman's point seems to me valid. No one is likely to argue that Stuart Sherman and Ludwig Lewisohn possessed the learning or critical acumen of Paul de Man or Hartman himself. Still, that old journalistic criticism has its own virtues. One thinks especially of the passionate sense of nationality and the feeling for the textures of American life that are to be found in the journalistic criticism of successive waves of New York literary intellectuals since the time of Van Wyck Brooks and the young Edmund Wilson.

The question at present, when academic criticism seems to be moving toward the left, is whether "theory" can be adapted to the cultural concerns of that older American tradition of literary-intellectual journalism. We won't know until it's been tried, but we may get a better idea of the difficulties faced by contemporary criticism if we consider what has been happening since the sixties, when "theory" first began to dominate academic literary studies.

II

The situation of cultural criticism today may be illuminated if we compare it with the situation twenty years ago. For my contrast of then and now, I mean to take as my representative figures Lionel Trilling and Edward Said. For all their marked political and cultural differences, Trilling and Said do share a distinctive New York intellectual style. And it's convenient for the contrast I wish to show that Said is now the leading literary intellectual at Columbia University, as Trilling was up to the time of his death in 1975.

Trilling was born in 1905 and formed his characteristic stance as a critic during the ideological battles over Marxism in the 1930's. Although Trilling was teaching at Columbia in the thirties, the university was not his whole world. In that decade the avant-garde was still a minority culture and a genuine alternative to the official culture of the universities. There were the true producers of art and culture, and opposed to them were the professors of literature, fuddy duddies such as hardly exist any more in a pure form. The professors of old were gentlemen scholars piously defending "civilization" against barbarism. By the mid-sixties, all this had changed. The decorous spokesmen for "traditional values" were more likely in the sixties to be found among the contributors and editors of nonacademic middlebrow magazines than among the ranks of influential academic critics. And professors of literature who wanted to think of themselves as "radical" or "advanced" no longer were obliged to look beyond their own campuses. Everything—creative writing, continental theory, radical politics—was taking place within the university. Demographic shifts, together with capitalism's success in diffusing—and diluting—the styles of modernism, had brought about a mass youth culture. In this great democratic nation the young were all in the universities, and the most fractiously antinomian of them seemed to be taking Lionel Trilling's course in modern literature at Columbia.[4]

Suddenly the university had become the world. The introduction to *The Liberal Imagination* (1950) shows that Trilling had been concerned in the late forties about the bureaucratization and Stalinization of the liberal mind. As the Cold War got underway, politics was something more than the politics of one or another theory of interpretation, which is what politics often means in recent academic criticism. Trilling's major essays after 1948 were written in the shadow of great spy trials like the Hiss-Chambers case, which was hardly an academic affair. His singleton novel *The Middle of the Journey* (1947) had uncannily prophesied just such an ideological confrontation as was later exposed by the Hiss-Chambers case, and the split within the intellectual community that was a consequence of that case.

Compare Trilling's introduction of 1950 with his introduction to *Beyond Culture* (1965). That introduction speaks of the Chancellor of the University of California system and his grandiose vision of the super-university to come. In 1965 Trilling was worried not about Stalinism but about the cultural imperialism of the new American multi-university, where everything, including the old culture of subversion, was being institutionalized and legitimized. Trilling wrote uneasily of "the new circumstances in which the adversary culture of art and thought now exists." His anxiety about the university as the new focus of intellectual life only increased after 1965.

Trilling spent fifty years of his life at Columbia, with very few breaks from his freshman year in 1921 to his death in 1975. Yet up to the sixties he never wrote about teaching or about the academic context of literary studies. Nothing seemed duller to *Partisan Review* intellectuals than problems of pedagogy. They were "intellectuals" in their self-conception, not school teachers. But in the sixties Trilling was able to overcome his embarrassment about taking seriously the academic context of criticism. Half the essays in *Beyond Culture* are about problems of teaching and learning, and there is a similar preoccupation with the humanities and the problems of teaching literature in the essays published posthumously in *The Last Decade: Essays and Reviews, 1965–75.*

It may also suggest Trilling's shift of focus that he published no fewer than four textbooks for the college classroom between 1967 and 1973. These include two anthologies jointly edited with Harold Bloom: *Romantic Poetry and Prose* and *Victorian Prose and Poetry*; another anthology, *Literary Criticism: An Introductory Reader*; and, most important, *The Experience of Literature*, a 1300-page reader with longish commentaries by Trilling on many of the selections. This textbook, which had been over ten years in the making, sums up in canonical form Trilling's taste and the taste of an entire generation of New York critics. Now that the politics of canon-formation has become a popular subject of criticism, Trilling's reader is worth another look. It's indispensable for anyone concerned with how modernism was transformed from a genuinely adversary culture into an academic tradition.

What happens when the university becomes the whole world? I think the case can be made that Trilling's turn to pedagogy was not a flight from the great world to the ivory tower. For the university in the sixties was no longer a sanctuary from the worldly world and its corruptions. It was the decisive context of intellectual life, as the Communist Party had been in New York thirty years before. Still, the university is not really the whole world, and Trilling's writing in the sixties revealed a certain abandonment of the large political-cultural issues he had discussed in the forties. More and more Trilling's literary criticism forfeited its grip on contemporary society in shifting its focus to "the self." His writing suffered a corresponding loss of concreteness and vividness as it came to be haunted by Hegelian abstractions. There was a price to be paid for the academicization of criticism.

One might suggest that price by referring not to any literary theorist of the sixties but to a novelist, John Barth, and his most representative fiction, *Giles Goat-Boy* (1966). This is a comic novel about the university as world, which, not coincidentally, is also a novel about narcissism, solipsism and the price of living exclusively in your own head. Barth was typical of the new academic culture in that his brilliant inventiveness, his proliferation of fictions, was not deflected to the slightest degree by the resistance of politics, history or social actuality. Confined within itself, whether as fun house or prison house, the mind can enjoy the fantasied omnipotence inseparable from its actual impotence. Literary theory, inspired by renewed interest in the great Romantic mythmakers, showed a similar preoccupation with the gap between art and life and a similar turn to pure subjectivity. Blake and Shelley had by no means been indifferent to the situation of English society, but their North American academic expositors took over the High Romantic faith in imagination as redemptive without adequately acknowledging the historical world that needed to be redeemed. Harold Bloom's postmodern gnosticism shared with T. S. Eliot's incarnationist Christianity a profound revulsion against history and nature alike.

III

One difference between the generation of critics influenced by T. S. Eliot and the generation of critics influenced by Harold Bloom is summed up in the word "theory." In speaking of the present generation of critics, I have in mind a group of men and women born between 1930 and 1950 whom we can associate with two major tendencies of the sixties: the emergence of continental theory in university departments of literature and the revival of radical politics. Edward Said is a senior member of this group and came to the new theory largely on his own. His first book, a phenomenological study of Joseph Conrad, appeared in 1967, only a few years after Geoffrey Hartman's important phenomenological study of Wordsworth. And *Beginnings* in 1975 established Said as a pioneering figure among American critics mediating the new French theory.

Said the literary critic has frequently been dealt with severely by critics distrustful of his specific political aims. There is reason for caution. Said has shown himself to be a tough and provocative spokesman on behalf of Palestinian nationalism. It's probably true to say that at some level all of Said's writing promotes that cause. I think, however, that his literary work exists at a different level than his political pamphleteering and deserves to be treated on its own terms.

What we see when we approach Said without prejudice is that his early work emerges from the hypertheoretical context of sixties academic literary studies. His Conrad book, originally written as a doctoral dissertation in Comparative Literature at Harvard, is markedly different in its theoretical assumptions from the criticism of Harry Levin, Harvard's chief comparatist in those years. But the book is not really very threatening. It is marked by an apolitical, sixties-ish academic concern with personal identity summed up in its title: *The Fiction of Autobiography.* It largely stays away from politics.

Neither is Said's next book, *Beginnings: Intention and Method* (1975), directly polemical in the manner of his more recent writing. The book is full of virtuoso readings of nonliterary figures like Freud as well as canonical figures such as Milton and Dickens and Hopkins, but the strongest impression the book leaves is of an ingenious mind as much drawn to problems of theory as to literature itself. The problem for such a mind is going to be how to free itself from the trammels of its own impulse to abstraction. Putting forward a politically minded theorist like Foucault in opposition to an unrelievedly ironizing theorist like Derrida, as Said does in *Beginnings*, is not going to solve his problem. That problem is to overcome the critical heritage of the sixties and find a language for talking about politics and the common world. The problem, as I would put it, is how to reconcile the theoretical sophistication of academic criticism with the political-cultural savvy of the old New York intellectuals.

Orientalism (1978), which is Said's best book so far, is one approach to such a reconciliation. This book is an ambitious critique of Western scholarship on Islam since the time of Napoleon. Apart from its interest as a revelation of European sterotypes about the Arabs, it has been very influential in directing critical attention to the history and ideology of literary studies as an institution. As advanced academic critics in English and Comparative Literature grow more and more self-conscious about the circumstances of their own profession, the book's influence can only become more pervasive.

When the book appeared, Said's relentless attention to the "discourse" of Orientalism caused him to be widely regarded as an American epigone of Foucault. In fact, however, Said's study may be less close in spirit to Foucault than to the classic humanism of German literary philologists such as Auerbach and Curtius—and to the American variant of that humanism in the work of such New York writers as Trilling. Said turns out to be a traditional humanist in denying that impersonal systems of language and power can explain Orientalism as a discursive system. His final appeal is always to human agency and efficacy. Also, whereas Foucault relies on a philosophy of language that stresses difference, Said's chief objection to Western scholarship on Islam is that it makes the Arabs out to be *too* different and thereby denies their common humanity.[5]

Said's "humanism" mixes oddly with his Nietzchean-Foucauldian emphasis on power and may be thought evidence of his lack of philosophical rigor. It can also be seen as an attempt to rescue the foundation of a positive politics. For if language does all the work, it's hard to see how men and women can bring about historical change. Whatever the reasons may be, the effect in Said's writing is a new methodological eclecticism, wholly unlike the rigor of theoreticians such as Foucault, Derrida and de Man. Like Trilling in his best essays, Said now uses whatever helps him deal with the job at hand: New Critical close reading, Frankfurt-type ideology critique, psychobiography, cultural anthropology, old-fashioned history of ideas.

Said's most recent book, a collection of essays entitled *The World, the Text, and the Critic* (1983), shows where he may be coming out. These essays don't achieve the concision and pointedness of Trilling's essays in *The Liberal Imagination*. Nor would Trilling much care for Said's political attitudes. But the books have a great deal in common. Said's struggle to bring his philosophical interests to bear on immediate cultural issues is bringing him ever closer in method and tone to New York-style cultural criticism and setting him apart from an increasingly ghostly theoreticism, including Marxist theoreticism,[6] in the university.

What Said seems to be working toward is suggested in his complaints about recent criticism on Jonathan Swift:

My impression is that too many claims are made for Swift as a moralist and thinker who peddled one or another final view of human nature, whereas not enough claims are made for Swift as a kind of local activist, a columnist, a pamphleteer, a caricaturist. . . . It is as if critics assume that Swift really wanted to be a John Locke or a Thomas Hobbes, but somehow couldn't: therefore it becomes a critic's job to help Swift fulfill his ambition, turning him from a kind of marginal, sporty political fighter into a pipesmoking armchair philosopher. (p. 77)

Now, the fact is that Said himself is some way from achieving the "sportiness" he praises in Swift. Rather, his collected essays reflect the difficulty for an academic critic of our moment to get out from under the burden of theory and method. Once the social-historical world is lost to criticism, it's not so easy to recover it.

Perhaps that's why "world" appears so frequently in these essays. The thesis statement appears early and often: "texts have ways of existing that even in their most rarefied form are always enmeshed in circumstances, time, place, and society—in short, they are in the world, and hence worldly" (p. 35). It's a measure of academic criticism's loss of the world that such a truism should need to be repeated so many times. Said complains of contemporary criticism that "it has achieved its methodological independence by forfeiting an active situation in the world" (p. 146). A few pages later, he says that "contemporary critical discourse is worldless."

But what is this "world" to which criticism is being recalled? It's striking that a critic whose life has been shaped by the traumas of international politics should be so abstract in setting out his agenda for a politically and culturally oriented criticism. Nothing appears more difficult, in the present age of theory, than the recovery of the old, unselfconscious conviction of the world's actuality. In his abstractness Said is representative of the situation of contemporary criticism. Even in moving toward the flexible, worldly style of the old New York intellectuals, he carries the burden of academic theoreticism. He is abstract in arguing against abstraction and theoretical in decrying the excesses of theory.

Certainly criticism needs to move worldwards. The danger is that when American literary intellectuals get involved with politics they often betray their vocation as intellectuals in their zeal to be toughmindedly practical. The record of radical criticism in America is marred by excursions into simple-minded progressivism and American-style Stalinism. Despite misgivings, however, one welcomes the new, more worldly criticism. It has been forty years since the New York intellectuals provided America with its last important body of social-cultural criticism written from the point of view of unspecialized men and women of letters. During the past two decades the dominant forms of literary criticism have offered very little encouragement to anyone concerned with the material circumstances of art. With the exhaustion of the recent wave of aesthetic formalism, academic critics have the opportunity now to retrieve the mainline American tradition of cultural criticism. Inevitably, in an academic milieu, the older style of criticism will be to some degree academicized and subjected to theoretical elaboration. It's hard to imagine any contemporary academic critic saying again what

T. S. Eliot once said, that the best method for the critic is simply to be very intelligent. But there is at least the possibility that American academic intellectuals may be able to restore criticism to a larger, more confident role in the general life of the culture.

---

1. In a recent essay Geoffrey Hartman comments on the affinities of Trilling's theory of modern culture with the "critical theory" of Adorno and the Frankfurt School. See "The Culture of Criticism," *PMLA*, 99 (May 1984), p. 385.

2. Irving Howe, "The New York Intellectuals," *Decline of the New* (New York: Harcourt, Brace and World, 1970), pp. 241–42. The essay originally appeared, in a shorter version, in *Commentary*, 46 (October 1968). Howe's description of the New York intellectual style hardly describes his own plain, sober writing. Nor does "free-lance dash, peacock strut" adequately describe Trilling or Rahv or Greenberg, although these epithets do have some aptness in connection with the art critic Harold Rosenberg.

3. Hartman, p. 377.

4. See Trilling's "On the Teaching of Modern Literature," *Beyond Culture* (New York: Viking Press, 1965).

5. On Said's humanist assumptions, see James Clifford's untitled review-essay on *Orientalism* in *History and Theory*, 19 (1980), pp. 204–23.

6. See Said's essay "Reflections on American 'Left' Literary Criticism," in *The World, the Text, and the Critic* (Cambridge, Mass.: Harvard University Press, 1983).

Criticism and the Academy

Donald Davie

If I have anything to contribute to a debate about the "academizing" of literary criticism, it may be because I know the situation in the United Kingdom as well as the United States. For the phenomenon is common to both sides of the Atlantic, but the form it takes on the British side is in several ways instructively different from how it is with us.

To start with, before we begin deploring what "academizing" has done (and certainly lamentations are in order) we need to consider what the alternative might be; and that is easier to envisage from looking at the British scene. For in Britain the nonacademic critics are still quite thick on the ground; they have an assurance, not to say belligerence, such as their American counterparts have lost, and also it must be said the British free-lance is likely to be better informed, better educated, and with a better command of the resources—trenchant on the one hand, insidious on the other—of English prose. The mantle of Cyril Connolly, of George Orwell—of, behind them, Desmond MacCarthy and even Edmund Gosse—has not in Britain been trampled underfoot; it is still worn, and quite flamboyantly too, by persons so different in temperament and authority as Geoffrey Grigson and C. H. Sisson.

When I was young, the taunt that we threw at such people was "belletrist"—a word nowadays seldom met with in Britain, and in the U.S. so uncommon as to be, I dare say, largely meaningless. What we were taught to look for and to revile in the belletrist—I speak of the 1940's, and of those of us who attended to the philippics of F. R. Leavis—was the belletrist's habit of speaking about the books in his library as about the wines in his cellar; he was a connoisseur of literature, as others (including himself at other times) were connoisseurs of vintages. We were taught to recognize and deplore the *unfeelingness* of the connoisseur—Leavis' example, I remember, was Gilbert Osmond in James' *The Portrait of a Lady*: his unfeelingness, that's to say his glacial detachment—but also, behind that and the motivation of it, his presumption in supposing that the agonies and exaltations of poets and others through the centuries served their purpose in providing him with a range of pleasures that he could languidly choose among according to his mood. In present-day England a critic like C. H. Sisson isn't in fact unfeeling or presumptuous; but his assumption of the anti-academic mantle, along with the airs and impudences that go along with it, make him seem what he is not.

Sisson, however, an unabashed elitist and politically an ultra-Tory, is an anomaly. As a rule the belletrist, like every other sort of Englishman (the Welsh and the Scots have their own fish to fry), has had to adapt himself to the resolutely egalitarian England that came into being in 1945 and has gone unquestioned ever since, alike under allegedly conservative as under socialist administrations. No longer, therefore, does he refer to his wine cellar. On the contrary, if he is old enough, he will recall his dallyings with the Popular Front pre-1939: "In my youth people discussed endlessly the problem of bringing art to the masses, and in the case of Shakespeare, Ibsen, other drama, that is precisely what is being done today." Thus Julian Symons, biographer and crime-writer but also belletrist and influential reviewer, justifying his participation in a BBC television program called *Shakespeare in Perspective*: "I was invited to discuss *Macbeth* because I write crime stories, and the producer made it clear that he did not want an academic or historical view of the play. . . . I was asked to remember also that the television audience of millions was not the same as a theater audience of hundreds or thousands. Most of the television watchers would not know the play, many might be watching a Shakespeare play for the first time. Hence . . . it was desirable to suggest the course of the play in general, although of course not to show it in detail."[1] What Symons describes without apology, his televised introduction to *Macbeth* – this is *criticism*? An American analog of sorts might be Alistair Cooke's PBS causeries before episodes of Masterpiece Theater. Certainly readers of *TriQuarterly* will in the first place understand by "criticism" something altogether more elevated and abstruse. Yet if Julian Symons and Alistair Cooke are not on such occasions practicing criticism, what are they doing? And if they *are* practicing criticism, does not their practice acknowledge the undeniable facts about functional literacy in our societies, whether British or American, in a way that loftier and more pretentious critics quite signally and lamentably fail to do? If the critic has a responsibility towards the society that he operates in, do not Cooke and Symons recognize and fulfill that responsibility better than Professor Bloom or Professor Hartmann? I at all events have no wish to deride Julian Symons, whose excellence among belletrist critics is shown precisely by his awareness that his practice needs to be defended, and by his readiness to defend it.

All the same, the belletrist is what he is. Under the thin cloak of his social concern, we still find the hauteur of Gilbert Osmond. Consider only those "masses" to which art must be "brought." Or reflect upon another place where Julian Symons is refreshingly frank: "Was there any point in filming up at Cawdor Castle and out on a fairly blasted Scottish heath, it may be asked, couldn't the same things have been said, the same points made, by talking direct to camera in a studio? Yes, but then, given the fickleness of the television audience, how many people would have been watching?" Symons' scorn for the fickle mass audience he is addressing is patent; culture, literature, is something that he dispenses, in contemptuously graduated doses, *de haut en bas*. And the unavoidable implication is that his own possession of the goodies that he thus doles out is inviolably secure, beyond the possibility of argument or self-doubt. When we rage at the ineffable complacency of Professor X or Associate Professor Y, we need to remember that the only alternative which the historical record of modern times provides us with is the even worse complacency of the belletrist.

Do Americans, in all their justified fury at the academic takeover, want to return to the conditions of 1912, when Pound could say: "America of today is the sort of country that loses Henry James and retains to its appreciative bosom a certain Henry Van Dyke"?[2] The belletrist, for all his private and sometimes public haughtiness, is the slave of the marketplace. So far as he is concerned, literature is for consumption, like the wines that his predecessor laid down. Accordingly, a recherché taste, like that for Henry James in his lifetime, is what he cannot countenance; and as he, become a social democrat, casts wider the net of his admissible dinner guests, the surer it is that he will applaud only those writers who cater to tastes already well-established, the more certain it is that he will dismiss with knowledgeable flippancy those writers who must create the taste by which they can be judged. I conclude therefore that when the judgment and explication of literature passéd from the belletrists into hands academically insulated from the pressures of the marketplace, this was, or it ought to have been, sheer gain. And if that is not how it has worked out, what can we think except that the academic profession has failed to live up to the responsibility thus thrust upon it?

That failure we may take to be self-evident. And the causes of it are not far to seek, except that they are to be found where for a variety of reasons we are not prepared to look: that's to say, in economic necessity and social ideology. At least since 1945, and probably from long before that, the profession has been grossly overmanned; departments of English have been ludicrously too many and too large. The ability to instruct in literary criticism is much rarer than any one wants to acknowledge; and the ability to profit by such instruction, whether it is proferred through print or in the classroom, is rare also. After all, literature is one of the fine arts. We do not expect that music criticism or art criticism or dance criticism should be practiced by any but a few of our fellow citizens; why should we suppose that criticism of poetry should be on the contrary a skill attainable by any undergraduate who turns up in the appropriate classroom, there to be instructed by some one as little fitted by nature to criticize poetry as to criticize dance? The answer seems to be that there are compelling economic reasons why a large proportion of our youth should be kept off the labor market until they are in their middle or late twenties; and having them sweat over books that they cannot understand is the way that our societies have found for keeping them occupied in the meantime. Because the medium of the literary arts is language, something that instructor and pupil alike are confident of being able to handle in its inartistic uses (as newsprint, road signs, biology or geography textbooks), it is easy to con them into thinking that they can manage it also as a medium of art. But the con is a cruel deception on them, and in the short run disastrous for the literary arts they have been deluded into thinking they can master or at least enter into. For the truth is, of course, that precisely because the medium of literary art is used also for utilitarian ends, literary art is not easier but harder to get into focus than the other arts. However, the confidence trick, cruel though it is, cannot be dispensed with, for it serves ideological ends also, in a society which believes as dogma that the highest cultural goods are or should be available to every citizen. Since it is abundantly evident that the finer points of music or dance are not thus available, it's that much more crucial that the finer points of literature are, or should seem to be.

In the not very long run, the students and their instructors begin to suspect that they have been tricked. But looking for the confidence trick anywhere but where it is – that's to say, in the pretense that what is very hard is in fact, with practice, easy – they buzz with conspiracy theories, about how literary study subserves the ideology of the ruling class, or of the male citizen against the female, or of the English speakers against the Third World. Who can blame them? They *have* been deceived, though not in any of the ways they suppose.

Meanwhile, in English departments thus grossly overmanned, there grows up a hierarchy: between the lately appointed Assistant Professor slaving night by night over his scores of ungrammatical freshman papers, and the nationally known eighteenth-century scholar, there exists a gulf quite inadequately represented by the distinction between tenured and nontenured faculty. The gulf – the width of it, and the painfulness of it for those on the wrong side – is registered, as everyone knows, in "publish or perish." The tenured professor demands of his or her junior colleague that he or she, in the midst of correcting freshman papers, produce and get accepted for publication articles or books in his or her "field." Ah, "field." There is the real mark of the academic beast. Did Dryden or Johnson, did Coleridge or Arnold or Landor, did even Cyril Connolly or Edmund Wilson, have "a field"? But in Academia you'd better have one, or find one double-quick, or you're in trouble.

Nothing so much rankles with disgruntled instructors of some spirit. And they have found a brilliant way of subverting the notion of "field" to suit their ends. Incapable of finding out what literary criticism is, or how they might practice it, and rightly suspicious of their tenured colleagues' pretense that they practice this sacred mystery all the time, they some years ago (with help from French philosophers, psychologists and semioticians) contrived a field of their own, called "How Criticism is Impossible." (It is called, more decorously, "Theory of Criticism," but its true name is the one I have given it.) This has been a brilliant success story—to the extent that the junior instructors who first dreamed it up are now the most eminent and sought-after of professors. And no wonder. For it has everything: a logic-chopping rigor such as your senior "eighteenth-century man" never dreamed of; an arcane jargon accessible only to initiates; and, above all, a stamping ground for the innumerable people in departments of English (also of French, of German, of Classics) who have energy and intelligence but no literary sensibility.

For this state of affairs our "eighteenth-century man" must share the blame with his colleagues, "the Renaissance scholar," "the Victorianist," "the Americanist" and (perhaps most culpable of all) "the Modernist." By segmenting the course of literature—in English and in other tongues—into specialized "fields" defined as time spans, the Academy has made impossible precisely what should be its principal concern: literary history, a history that does not stop and start, or ring down the curtain on one show only to raise it on another, but a seamless continuity from first to last. The figure of a river, with all that that implies—of a current running now fast now slow, of tributaries, of eddies, even of oxbow bends—is surely inescapable; yet it is belied every time we pretend to find, as every curriculum committee does, a massive dam or barrage built across the course of the river in 1660 or 1798 or 1914. This shibboleth of field-by-period, ineradicable now because so many professional reputations have been built on it, means that the Academy is powerless to avert or cure what I'm inclined to see as the most heinous failing of all current literary criticism, alike at its most abstruse and exalted and at its most pedestrianly pedagogical—that is to say, a drastic foreshortening of historical perspectives back from the present day. The belletrist, with all his faults, did not fail in this way: Edmund Wilson and Cyril Connolly were as ready to talk of Ovid as of the memoirs of Ulysses S. Grant, and indeed to illuminate the one by shafts of light thrown from the other. The scholarly conscience suspects that if they were adept in one of these fields, they hardly could be in the other; and yet it's remarkable how seldom scholarship has been able to substantiate its suspicions. (The representative case may be the abortive attempt by Latinists to nail Ezra Pound on the score of his Propertius.) Connolly and Wilson, we may agree, lived dangerously; they took risks, knowing full well that they were not *au fait* with the latest scholarship, had not mastered "the secondary material." And we tell our graduate students that they must never take such risks, construing as scruple what in fact is timidity. What we hold out before them as the reward of such pusillanimous self-denial is the chance or certainty of their being impregnably secure, and therefore arrogant, within that short time span which they will agree to define as their "field." Accordingly, when Charles Tomlinson, professor but also poet, in his Clark Lectures (*Poetry and Metamorphosis*) shows the current from Ovid's *Metamorphoses* still flowing in *The Waste Land*, he is assailed alike by the graduate students and by their professors. He has broken all the unformulated rules.

Timidity is still the distinguishing feature of the academic critic, just as it always was. And yet what has irked some of us in recent years has been, on the contrary, his effrontery, his presumption. However, as we have just seen, the one proclivity by no means precludes the other. Let the academic critic lay down the rules of the game so that he shall be exercised only on those matters where he knows himself secure, and he will of course be dogmatic and overbearing. A particular case of this, I'm afraid, is that academic specialist whom I have called, as he calls himself, "the Americanist." He was unheard of before 1945; and his emergence since then has done much to foreshorten historical perspectives. For American literature, as we all know, has a "colonial period"; but we all know too that courses offered in that period attract few students, and that publications concerned with that period attract few readers—those few necessarily concerned with the history of ideas more than with literary history, since Cotton Mather and Jonathan Edwards and the deplorable Philip Freneau can figure only lamely in a literary perspective. Accordingly, study of American literature *as literature* hardly can, and never does, hark back to any date much before 1840. No call to blame the Americanist for this; the material he has engaged to deal with enforces upon him such a *terminus a quo*. And yet, what a recent date it is! What a drastically foreshortened perspective 140 years represents! What way is there to reconcile such a short and accelerated time scale (however fertile and productive the literature of that time span, as undoubtedly American literature was) with the quite differently calibrated time scale in which we take the measure of Virgil or Ovid, the Gawaine poet or even Ben Jonson? The damage that is done we apprehend when we read even such an exceptionally learned and scrupulous critic as Helen Vendler, one who has admirably refused to be corralled into a "field," reviewing collections of contemporary American verse, and judging them by standards that reach back no further than Ralph Waldo Emerson: major poets start from under every stone, or rather (since Professor Vendler is neither irresponsible nor a fool) there is no way, because there is no standard, by which she can distinguish a creditable performance from one that is, or may be, momentous. Poet and reviewer alike will be glad to think that no such distinction can be made, except at the behest of whim; and to the degree that a longer perspective makes such a distinction seem possible, to just that degree it will be resisted and ruled out of court.

And yet, behind the pretensions of Americanist, Victorianist, Mediaevalist, there is another pretension that underwrites theirs: the pretension that literary criticism is, or can be, a profession. Teaching the young about literature may be a profession—in terms of its discernible results, perhaps a shabby one—but criticizing literature cannot be. Rather it is a vocation, a calling: one to which many are called, though few are chosen. After all, the critical essay—one thinks of Poe's, of Allen Tate's, of Pater's, of Dryden's prefaces—is itself a genre of literary art. How then can one think to incorporate one's self in that company by paying dues to the Modern Language Association? But of course very few who pay those dues have any such illusion or aspiration. Though such a litany of honored names is for the most part politely borne with, as from time to time ritually proper, most of those who listen to the litany believe in their hearts that Dryden and Pater and even Tate belong, in criticism, to a horse-and-buggy age that has been decisively superseded. Here too we seem to see the workings of social ideology. For those critics who aim above all at "professionalism" are only reflecting, in their own chosen sphere, the assumption that underlies Schools of Business Management, and the big corporations that recruit from them: the assumption that many minds systematically trained and collaborating will always outstrip one mind, self-trained, proceeding on its own with dedication and flair. (How much more Dryden could have achieved in criticism if he had been enlisted in an organization that would have required him to collaborate with John Dennis and Nahum Tate!) Here too crops up the same combination of timidity with arrogance, for the operative or manager is meek on his own account, but overbearing on account of the corporation, the "organization," that he represents. A cast of mind so endemic and inevitable in twentieth-century "advanced" societies cannot be eliminated, and insofar as that cast of mind is now entrenched in academic literary criticism, the faults of that criticism must be thought to be incurable.

On the other hand, if it is true that worthwhile criticism is not and never has been a corporate activity, if our belief that it might be is what has reduced us to our present sterility, it follows that for criticism, considered as something other than the writings of this critic and that, we need have no concern at all. Criticism as an institution does not, and never did, exist. There exist, here and there, critics worth listening to. Mostly, the state of the labor market for literary intellectuals being what it is, these few will turn out to hold a post in some college or university. But they are not "academic critics" in the sense I have written of. On the contrary, it will be found in almost every case that "the profession," so far as it takes note of them, looks on them askance as unpredictable and often irascible loners. I am describing, I realise, my own *beau idéal* of a modern critic, the late Yvor Winters. If Winters could hold to his own incorruptible standards in his lifetime, so can we in ours—with the mournful acknowledgement that the strain of unremitting resistance, which destroyed Winters' judgment before the end, may be even more wearing for us.

---

1. Julian Symons, "The Case for a Double Standard," *PN Review*, 30 (1982), p. 23.
2. From "Patria Mia" in *Ezra Pound: Selected Prose, 1909–1965*, ed. William Cookson (New York: New Directions, 1973), p. 114.

The Political Economy of Criticism

Patrick Colm Hogan

University faculty are termed "professionals" and certainly enjoy a different status from proletarians. However, the internal relations of the university, most particularly productive and distributive relations,[1] put the junior professor, instructor and graduate student in the position of the proletarian or, possibly more exactly, the position of the salesman, though the less elevated and more "proletarianized" salesman of, say, Kafka's fiction (rather than the upwardly mobile and managerial salesman we envision today).[2] An enormous body of unemployed laborers in the field of literary studies makes the future of every graduate student dubious and renders the position of every junior faculty member precarious; furthermore, it solidifies the position of the regents, deans and chairmen, allowing them, like capitalists and managers, to demand greater and greater productivity and to define such productivity not in terms of quality but of salability.

Specifically, graduate students and part-time instructors serve the function carried out by women and children in nineteenth-century English factories. Departments of literary study admit, abuse and dismiss graduate students often with only the most arbitrary, ineffective and perfunctory attempts at placing them (in other exploitative positions). Of course, some departments make admirable efforts in this area; most do not. And in many the efforts are of a perverse nature—much like the hiring process itself. In other words, departments seek students for their own survival—graduate students allow faculty to teach advanced classes and, along with part-time instructors, themselves take over the undesirable courses, making these latter courses highly "cost efficient" due to the miniscule salaries which the students (and instructors) receive for teaching them. Upon completing their degrees, then, these students are faced with a job market which is arbitrary and, most often, a departmental placement committee which is uninterested—except, possibly, in the students in which one or another of the members of the committee has a *personal* interest. Sadly, I could adduce examples of incomprehensible actions on the part of placement (and hiring) committees all too easily, as, I suspect, could most of my readers, but I think the point is clear enough without this recourse to personal anecdote—the arbitration of one's professional work is arbitrary and whimsical. One discovers early in literary studies that in this profession, just as in the manufacture of breakfast cereals, quality does not define salability—but salability does define success. Little wonder alienation in literary studies begins already in the graduate programs, if not earlier, for one must choose rather soon whether one will write for salability, and thus make literary study a mere means,[3] or one will write for truth (which I take to be an end in itself), and risk swift, or slower, academic death.

It is interesting to remark in this context that recently, and predictably, an ideology justifying these conditions has arisen, and given itself the name of liberation and the overcoming of ideology. What I have in mind is, of course, deconstruction, through spurious arguments in which truth is discounted as an ideological "centrism," to be replaced by the disseminative play of difference. The "reasoning" here is that the notion of truth entails the notion of absolute authority, of absolute knowledge and of absolute presence, and, thus, the notion of truth is nothing other than the notion of *dogma*—if there is truth then there must be a perfect and indisputable statement of the truth which derives from the absolute authority in his (phallocentric, of course) absolute knowledge due to absolute presence. But, of course, truth is not ideology, and any reasonable notion of truth, any notion of truth which has been seriously defended through serious argument, not only does not presuppose the dogmatics of such ideology, but quite explicitly and necessarily opposes them. If Stalin thought he had absolute knowledge because of "Marxist science," he was wrong—and that was the problem; in fact, we can oppose Stalin only through a notion of truth, and, of course, the work to achieve the truth which that notion presupposes, but never allows to be imagined complete. Stalin's problem was not that he believed in truth, but that he believed that he had *all* of the truth, and *nothing else* either. The disseminative free-play of deconstruction will not in any way help us to correct Stalin's errors. Strictly speaking, it will not even allow us to assert that they were errors or that Stalin ever believed or enacted anything in particular. On the other hand, the free-play of deconstruction does help us to open up the free market of intellectual commerce, as instanced in journals, symposia, books and so on, and thereby ideologically reenforces the criteria of salability.

Assistant professors are only slightly better off than graduate students and part-time instructors in terms of salary and work load (although this difference is not negligible); however, in certain ways their alienation is likely to be more critical—their position is weak and the pressure to produce is immense. Most importantly, "production" here is precisely what it is in industry—the production of salable commodities, in this case, articles, books and the like. Departments and deans are concerned not with the quality of professional work, no matter how much they protest—they are concerned with the *acceptance* of the work. Once again, one finds oneself faced with the dilemma that one cannot say what one believes, that one cannot endeavor to write what is true, *because* one believes it or finds it to be most justified. For, even if one's views should happen to coincide with the fashionable views, one finds oneself in circumstances which demand that one conform one's writing and speaking to those views *not* because one holds them but, rather, because they are salable, and salability leads to tenure. Of course, there is not one single fashion at any given time and, as fashions are multiple, one who excels in a certain sort of fashionable discourse, but at the wrong university, suffers no less than someone whose discourse eschews contemporary fashions. Again, like the worker, the academic in a department of literary study cannot, quite generally, choose his work as an end in itself, for his circumstances transform that work into a mere means.

Associate professors are in no ideal position either, of course, for the concern for promotion is still present, and justifiably so, considering the pittance paid to some associate professors at even major universities. More importantly, they have gone through the tenuring process and seen both how arbitrary it is (again, who cannot tell stories of ignorant half-wits tenured at major universities and of widely published, influential and sometimes even fashionable critics who are denied tenure at even lesser institutions?), and how costly the process has been to their lives. In effect, the associate professor has devoted a decade of his/her life to a dubious success—producing salability, of him/herself and of his/her work. Whatever he/she ultimately thinks of the value of that work and of its object, both have been produced in circumstances which demanded them, in circumstances which transformed them into means, both means for personal monetary and (in the broad, Marxist sense), reproductive ends, and means for the, in many ways, opposed aims of the university and its administration. Again, it is not the work itself and its truth-value, but the *fact* of the work and its market value which have been essential (to advert to Anscombe's fact/substance distinction).[4]

Of course, in many ways such alienation is equally prominent in, for example, the physical sciences, where research is a highly ideological and often enough capital-intensive affair—as even a cursory glance at the history of cancer research in this country shows clearly. However, truth is even less of a value in literary study than it is in our dogma- and ideology-riddled sciences, principally because there are rather clear and broadly accessible criteria for success or failure in the physical sciences, criteria which are almost entirely absent from literary studies. Put crudely, no matter what the power of an ideology supporting a certain theory of aerodynamics, if the airplane cannot be got up into the air, the theory which says it can will suffer, at least in the minds of the passengers, if not the aerodynamicists. Of course, this is not universally true, especially in the less "exact" biological sciences—such as medicine—as is indicated by the continued bamboozlement of doctors and patients alike in the area of cancer treatment. However, at least this particular case can be explained by a number of factors: 1) the great success of contemporary treatments for certain types of cancer, 2) the poverty of the alternatives (itself in large part the product of ideologically guided research), 3) the near-mythical status cancer has achieved in our society and the frantic demand for some hopeful treatment which it both elicits and derives from, and 4) the supposed difficulty of defining what is to constitute a cure for cancer—and, thus, what is to count as a therapy which fails.

The point is not that the physical and biological sciences always operate according to principles of truth, but simply that, in their applications, there are gross, observable phenomena which *tend* to confirm or disconfirm given theories, phenomena which have no analogs in literary interpretation. This is not to say that literary interpretations are not subject to adjudication—I believe that they most certainly are; it is to say, rather, that the application of a literary theory cannot be said not to "work" in the clear and straightforward sense in which it can be said of the application of a theory of aerodynamics. At least in part as a result of this situation, literary criticism allows of much greater ideological determination. I must emphasize again that I am not arguing that science is not ideological. I am arguing, rather, that the ideology of science is to a degree limited by applicative factors absent from literary studies. In other words, literary interpretation is not a technology and the result of this is twofold: on the one hand, greater ease in bypassing criteria of truth in adjudicating interpretations, and, on the other hand, limitation of the community of adjudicators to the community of producers. One might say that in literary studies there is not only no airplane, there are not even any passengers—only aerodynamicists mulling about on the landing strip.

There results a situation in which all literary critical adjudication is *interested*, and interested in such a way that truth or falsity is irrelevant to the fulfillment of the interests in question. In other words, a situation comes about in which interpretations are adjudicated almost entirely by interpreters, or rather by interpreters/workers (i.e., interpreters who interpret within the context, ends, etc., of capitalist economic relations), and thus by individuals to whose concrete advantages or disadvantages those adjudications redound; furthermore, the advantages are not, at least in any general and systematic fashion, a function of the *truth* of the interpretations in question. More specifically, the interests of interpreters/workers concern certain effects upon salability entailed by specific adjudications and the criteria of adjudication which they imply. Clearly, commodities prove most salable when there is demand and, in addition, most profitable when capital investment is small. In the case of interpreters/workers, investment is always equivalent to labor, and, like the proletarianized salesman, the academic produces, labors *to sell*. It follows, then, that the adjudicative concerns of the interpreters who compose the body of workers *and* consumers would tend towards establishing—in a tacit and ideological fashion—criteria of adjudication which open markets, presumably by obsolescence, and reduce capital outlays. It also follows, as noted above, that the establishment of such criteria will be facilitated by the absence of gross criteria of applicative success or failure. To put it crudely, critics will value precisely those varieties of interpretation and criteria for adjudication which, whatever their plausibility, allow them to produce more salable interpretations more simply and less laboriously, and these valuations will not be hindered by the results of technological applications.

In accordance with this, for almost two decades academic critics have been searching for a set of interpretive principles which would obsolesce New Criticism, as well as more traditional historical, biographical and other approaches, while preserving the efficiency of New Criticism. Specifically, New Criticism required attention to the work *per se*—it minimized labor seemingly as much as it could be minimized. However, the machinery of New Criticism was cranking tediously on to an ever-diminishing audience, with ever-diminishing numbers of New Critical ideas. There seemed to be less and less to say in a New Critical mode, while the volume of work in this mode was increasing drastically, for not only did one have to read tomes of secondary criticism before one began to eke out some marginal difference in one's interpretation, one had actually to learn the meanings of the words used in the works, the allusions and so on, and one had to do so with little or no knowledge of Greek and Latin.

Structuralism provided a solution to the first problem, but it required both rigor and historical knowledge. (Those who criticize structuralism for its ignorance of history simply know nothing of Lévi-Strauss' work, for the historical and cultural context is always crucial to his interpretations—as he himself repeatedly emphasizes.) Phenomenology also provided a possible solution but it was so vague as a methodology that it was difficult to say precisely what one was supposed to do with it. It seemed entirely intuitive, and, if one had the intuitions, one could just as easily have crammed them into New Critical terminology as into that of Phenomenology. Furthermore, like structuralism, phenomenological interpretation, with its ambition to reconstitute the author's "noesis," required massive labor, from understanding Husserl to reading the entire canon of the author in question, including letters and other biographical information, before even beginning on an interpretation of an individual work.

An important exception in the case of structuralism was Roland Barthes, who introduced a "playful" method of semiotic interpretation which was at once textual yet not New Critical, and which required so little labor that it even encouraged ignorance with regard to historical word-meaning. (In his highly regarded *Sur Racine*, Barthes cheerfully interpreted Racine's words as if they had been spoken by Parisians in 1960!) However, in order to emulate Barthes' approach, even if one does not need to attend historical word-meaning, etc., one does need to attend to systematic, structural and semiotic relations within the text—a rather technical matter. Furthermore, in the Barthesian method, one has no clear idea of precisely what one is to look for. New Criticism had neatly provided us with irony, image-patterns and the like, but Barthesian "codes" were composed of altogether too impalpable stuff. In other words, even Roland Barthes seemed both too constrained and too intuitive for easy appropriation.

Deconstruction, however, suffers no such limitations. Though based upon a complex and difficult analysis of meaning and a critique of phenomenology, deconstruction has been perceived as a method oblivious to history and thus possessing perfectly simple applicability. As a Derridean acquaintance of mine recently remarked to me, "When structuralism arrived, we had to read all this anthropology and linguistics that we couldn't make any sense of—we were trained to read literature, not mathematical symbols. But then Derrida came along and it was like a breath of fresh air, because he showed us that we didn't have to read all that stuff, because he proved that all those people had fundamental flaws in their systems." Though only one person has ever said such a thing to me, I believe it to be as generalizable as this convert's "we" would indicate.

Deconstruction limits capital investment drastically. Baldly put, if you do deconstruction, then you need not read anything else because it is all wrong, anyway. Deconstruction makes New Criticism *and all other critical methodologies* obsolete, announcing as it does the isolation and dismantling of the logophonophallocentrism which has marked *all* previous western thought and, hence, *a fortiori*, all previous critical theory. Indeed, deconstructive method, as it has evolved popularly, provides straightforward principles of interpretation, even a thematics: "Begin by isolating contradictions; this may be done by uncovering ambiguities in the text (for which we are all well trained, of course) or by wordplay or by ignoring historical meanings or by overlooking literary conventions. (If stuck, attend to any discussions of writing, speech, books, letters, postcards—that sort of thing.) From one of the contradictions, establish a hierarchy. Identify this hierarchy with writing/speech. Return to the text and elaborate along similar lines," etc.[5]

183

Deconstruction, as popularly understood and practiced, is a godsend for the market; it is no wonder that deconstruction has achieved such phenomenal popularity—it is, in a sense, the assembly line of literary studies. Of course, other factors enter here as well. For example, the narcissistic appeal of a critical theory which, no matter how absurdly, terms itself "feminist," has been crucial to the success of deconstruction. However, these other factors are not our present concern.

If, then, the criteria of adjudication actually, if only tacitly, in operation conform to the dictates of an economic system which only serves to alienate us from our labor and the objects of our labor, what is the proper response, what should be done about this? I suspect that there is no way for the structure of the university to be changed in isolation from the structure of the society at large; however, I should like to turn very briefly to the question of establishing more adequate criteria for interpretive adjudication, even if these criteria may be useless within the present economic system and most particularly the subsystem of the university. Specifically, I take it that criteria of adjudication are criteria for certain ends, in the present instance the end of increasing the salability of the interpretive product. Before concluding, I should like to look for a moment at what might be more appropriate (less alienating) ends for criticism and, hence, what might be more appropriate criteria of adjudication.

Quite generally, I take the appropriateness of ends to be determined by responsibilities. As human beings, no matter what our profession, we have broad ethical responsibilities. In the case of the literary interpreter, I take these responsibilities to include not only ethical behavior, but attention to the ethicality of the work or works in question—their ethical evaluation, including, prominently, ideological critique. As literary interpreters, however, we have more specific responsibilities which concern most clearly and directly our students and our colleagues. Students enter our classes (or are entered therein) in order to learn; a sophomore, when he/she enters a literature survey, may be able to understand only very little of *Hamlet* or the *Prelude*. Our first task, of course, is to increase his/her understanding. But clearly our teaching is useless if it remains confined to our own dicta about the works in question. On the assumption that a work is never fully interpreted, and cannot be fully interpreted, the few words we say about a poem should be only the beginning of interpretation for the student, should he/she attend to the work at all upon leaving our class. Furthermore, the few works we speak of should not become the only works which the student can understand. Our teaching must be such that it develops the student's capacities for interpretation independent of instruction.

Now as it is literature we are teaching and not, say, finance, we have a second self-evident responsibility in this area—to aid our students, however we can (which may be almost not at all), in enjoying literature.

184

There seems to me little enough point in abstracting image patterns from a poem, if reading the poem gives no pleasure. Enjoyment is, I think quite clearly, essential to the work of literature. But, again, as with understanding, our teaching should aim to develop capacities of general applicability and not remain confined to a handful of exempla. Thus our responsibility as teachers is, at the least, and most obviously, to increase students' understanding and enjoyment of literature in such a way as to increase their *capacity for* understanding and enjoyment of literature. As a matter of practical note, in my own teaching this comes down not only to teaching interpretation or interpretive technique but also encouraging, examining and discussing individual response. Though I shall not argue the point here, it seems to me that as interpreters our responsibilities to our colleagues are almost entirely the same – though of course the interpretations we exchange with one another are likely to be of a different variety from those we present to our survey students – and thus I would offer the preceding statement of purpose for literary interpretation as valid in *both* cases and, with the addition of ethical evaluation, complete for literary interpretation in all essentials.

But, as regards criteria for adjudication, we see immediately that, in a sense, such criteria cannot be established for critical theory (understood as defining methodological principles for interpretation of individual works), since *any* critical theory which increases understanding or enjoyment or facilitates ethical evaluation is, by that fact, worthwhile. The only way in which we can decide whether understanding, enjoyment, or appreciation have been increased is by reference to *other* theories or studies, most particularly the theory of literature (or, broader, related theories, such as theory of meaning), aesthetical theory (or, if simple enjoyment is intended, *possibly* theory of response), and ethical/political theory.[6] In other words, a critical theory should be valued insofar as it increases our understanding and enjoyment of literature while making us aware of its ideologies and ethical concerns, no matter what else that theory involves. Thus in itself critical theory is radically pluralistic and ultimately limited only by other studies related solely to its results. For example, even should we find the "semes" and "sememes" of Greimas implausible semantical posits, and thereby invalid in, say, a theory of literature, should their use lead to instructive readings by the lights of our theory of literature, or increased appreciations by the lights of our aesthetic theory, or incisive critiques by the lights of our ethico-politics, then their ontological implausibility becomes irrelevant – they are part of a valuable critical theory in any event. Critical theory is, in this way, heuristic – but it is responsibly heuristic, responsible to our students and colleagues and to their understandings, appreciations and ethical evaluations.

There is, I believe, in these responsibilities and in such responsible heuristics a genuine and worthwhile purpose for literary critics. Sadly, this purpose is little in evidence today. More sadly still, within the alienating economy of the university, it may not even be a real possibility.

---

1. I allude here to the classical Marxist trichotomy of economic relations; I ignore the supposedly definitive *ownership* relations—their importance seems to me slight here, due to the ephemeral nature of the academic 'products.'

2. Some of the points made here and below are anticipated in Gerald Graff's "Teaching the Humanities," *Partisan Review*, LI (1984), pp. 850–54. See also his *Literature Against Itself* (Chicago: University of Chicago Press, 1979), most particularly Chapter 4 and the references cited therein, and "Who Killed Criticism?" *American Scholar*, XLIX:3 (Summer 1980), pp. 337–55. I am grateful to Professor Graff for suggestions on an earlier draft of this essay.

3. The present essay concludes a book-length manuscript. Elsewhere in the manuscript, I argue that classical Marxist analyses of alienation (from the Fichtean analysis of objectification to the 'economistic' treatment of 'fetishism' in terms of the three spheres of economic relations) are inadequate, and that a more Kantian analysis in terms of actions, the objects of which are ends in themselves, and actions, the objects of which are mere means (with some important qualifications), must be adopted in their stead.

4. "On the Grammar of 'Enjoy,'" *Metaphysics and the Philosophy of Mind* (Minneapolis: University of Minnesota, 1981). I take this distinction to be crucial to a full understanding of alienation in the sense of note 3.

5. A sterling example is Derrida's own recent reading of *Ulysses*, presented to the IXth International James Joyce Symposium (Frankfurt, June 1984); in this reading, Derrida takes Bloom's elliptical thoughts, such as "I think I" ("I think I. Yes I. Do it in the bath," etc.) as complete sentences—in this case asserting the cartesian cogito, of course (SOPHIST WALLOPS LUSTFUL LEOPOLD SQUARE ON THE LOGOCENTRISM. DUBLINERS GNASH MOLARS. PARISIANS VOW PEN IS CHAMP). More revealing, however, is the general response to the reading, well-exemplifed by the response of one colleague of mine who, when faced with the objection that Derrida had misunderstood the ellipsis in the passage, replied, "Oh, but he's *transcended* all that!"

6. In the opening chapter of the manuscript which this essay concludes, I divide literary studies into ethical evaluation, aesthetical evaluation, theory of literature and theory of criticism (or critical theory). The first two are, I think, clear enough. The third is the study of structures, devices, etc., of literature *per se*—it concerns, for example, general defining characteristics of narrative, their relation to broader cognitive capacities and so on. The fourth, our present concern, attends rather to the methodological principles appropriate to the interpretation of individual works; it does not provide a theory about symmetries across a set or sets of works, but rather provides "discovery procedures" capable of yielding up particularities of individual works.

IV. Pedagogy and Polemics

Back to History

E. D. Hirsch, Jr.

About three years ago I gave the following talk as one of the lectures that inaugurated the Center for the Humanities at Stanford University. Since I shared the podium with another speaker, Professor René Girard, I kept my remarks brief. From this original context the reader will understand why the paper is directed to a general rather than a scholarly audience, why it is short, and why it still refers to a then-much-publicized controversy concerning the English department at Cambridge University, a flap that may now be sinking into the oblivion it deserves.

Most people interested in literary criticism have heard about the Great Literary Theory Debate. It broke out of academic cloisters into the international news recently, when it publicly disrupted the English department of Cambridge University. Statements were made to reporters by Professor Christopher Ricks on the one side and Professor Frank Kermode on the other. Public meetings were held, aspersions were cast. The conflict, as described in British newspapers and magazines and on television, has been made to seem a debate between two parties, which for simplicity I will call "the Ancients" and "the Moderns." The Ancients, led in Cambridge by Christopher Ricks, are those literary professors who want to teach the old authors in the old, historical ways. The Moderns, led by Frank Kermode, are those who want to teach the old authors in new ways. The eruption of this conflict is not really an isolated event, confined to a British university. It is the British version of a debate that has been going on in recent years in literature departments in this country, as well as in France and Germany. In this essay, I will touch on some of the underlying issues in the debate and on their implications for literary study in the 1980's.

In its nontrivial form, the debate is about a very practical matter: how should literature be taught and how should it be dealt with in our culture? On this practical question, the Ancients have this to say: the proper starting point for teaching the literature of the past is to recover its past meaning. Before we decide why Wordsworth is valuable or isn't, before we say what his poetry means or doesn't mean to us today, we first need to understand what Wordsworth *meant*. The Ancients view the literary texts that have come down to us as past speech acts which need to be understood as historical events. They therefore believe that a teacher's first job is to help students recover that historical meaning. That was why they trained themselves as historical scholars—to keep alive in the present the meanings of the past. Like the Moderns, they wish to accommodate the past to the present, but to do so without distorting the past. Their aim of historical recovery could be called "primary interpretation."

The Moderns, for their part, repudiate this historical approach, first of all on cultural grounds. Primary interpretation, they say, is a deadening enterprise. It turns the great works of literature into museum objects, like dead butterflies mounted on pins. The real job of a teacher is to respeak, or revitalize, the texts of the past, and *make* them mean something to the present. The true aim of criticism is secondary interpretation, or what Foucault calls "*resemanticizing* the text." The historical approach is also to be rejected because it is philosophically naive. Secondary interpretation, the creative respeaking of texts, is not only the more valuable activity, it is also, philosophically, the only realistic activity for teaching and criticism. The Ancients are just kidding themselves if they think they can understand Wordsworth in a nineteenth-century way. They cannot escape their own time. They are merely creating their own Wordsworth out of their own cultural experience, and then calling that idea "Wordsworth." Like every modern reader, they too are *respeaking* Wordsworth; they are just doing so in a particularly deadly and naive way. Thus the Moderns have launched a two-pronged attack. They say that what the Ancients want to do cannot be done. Secondly, they say it should not be done in any case. The Modernist objections to the Ancients are both theoretical and cultural.

British newspaper commentators have interpreted this debate in terms of personalities and temperaments. They see the Ancients as conservative spirits who stand (rightly or wrongly) on the side of tradition and British common sense. They see the Moderns as adventurous (perhaps foolishly daring) spirits, ready to meet the challenge of new ideas emanating from France and Germany.

But the Great Literary Theory Debate, I would like to suggest, may also be seen as the ideological manifestation of an interest conflict. Those historians who like to expose the sociological foundations of ideas should have a field day with our present literary scene, for if I am right in my observations, the debate between Ancients and Moderns corresponds to an interest conflict between professors and undergraduates. The Ancients see themselves as spokesmen for the needs and interests of undergraduates, while the Moderns speak for the institutional advantages of secondary interpretation in the sphere of professorial publication. This explanation is borne out by the evidence of the published commentaries on the Cambridge debate that ran recently in the *Times Literary Supplement* (London). These included just one contribution from an undergraduate—a letter:

> Impressed as I was by your formidable symposium on the crisis facing the teaching of English at Cambridge, and presumably at other universities as well, I found myself regretting that not only was no student asked to contribute an opinion, but also that the interests of the student body as a whole were often forgotten. . . . The honorable exception was Malcolm Bradbury who clearly has the students at heart when he suggests that "many . . . come into English to engage with the humane pleasure of particular books, and are not always delighted to be instructed in the modes of deconstruction of texts, of engaging a universalist narrative grammar, and of amassing literary theory." For myself, as a recent graduate of Cambridge, I can only say that Bradbury's suggestion is entirely accurate. . . .[1]

In my experience, this is an entirely representative attitude of undergraduates who want to study literature. They want to discover the primary meanings of literature, and engage in primary interpretation. They want to know what the great authors meant, and why their works have been and still are considered to be great. They want to know the best that is said and thought in the world, as it was said and as it was thought. At the very least, undergraduates want to possess those primary meanings before they go on to engage in the secondary permutations involved in "*resemanticizing* the text." Most undergraduates, I would claim, are Ancients, until informed that Ancients are naive. The Ancients are more interested in primary than in secondary interpretation. And until very recent years—about ten years ago—their professors shared and encouraged their preference for primary over secondary interpretation.

The Moderns, on their side, are skeptical of these naive aims. They adopt an attitude that was expressed as long ago as 1790 in Goethe's *Faust*, a work that may contain the first known version of our current debate between Ancients and Moderns. In one of the early scenes Faust is being addressed by his assistant Wagner, who undergraduate-like has been eagerly poring over the texts of the past in order to master the wisdom that they contain. To this the disillusioned Faust replies:

> Die Zeiten der Vergangenheit
> Sind uns ein Buch mit sieben Siegeln.
> Was Ihr den Geist der Zeiten heisst,
> Das ist im Grund der Herren eigner Geist,
> In dem die Zeiten sich bespiegeln.[2]

(The times of the past are to us a book that is sealed with seven seals. What you call the spirit of the past—why that's your own spirit reflecting back at you.)

Faust, in this comment, is the first of a long and distinguished tradition of Moderns — a tradition that includes such names as Nietzsche, Heidegger, Foucault, Paul de Man and Stanley Fish. The very oldness of the tradition is highly significant for my claim that extra-theoretical issues lie behind the debate. The skeptical, Faustian view has been so brilliantly represented for so long that we need to look for some *external* element to explain why it has become so exceedingly popular in the past ten years. In the long view of intellectual history, the Modernist position is a well-known and well-trod development from Kant; hence the current enthusiasm for secondary interpretation probably comes from some extra-theoretical impulse.

I said that one extra-theoretical element is the interest struggle between professors and undergraduates, but that is just the effect of a deeper institutional cause. Anybody who is old enough is in a position to guess what the institutional explanation is. Professors have recently become more interested in the endless frontier of secondary interpretation because they believe that the frontier of primary, historical interpretation is closing down. Primary, historical interpretation began to be pursued intensively about thirty years ago, when a new institutional concept began to dominate the study of literature at the universities. It can be named "the law of interpretation." According to this influential principle, introduced by "New Criticism," the only truly legitimate activity of a literary professor is the activity of interpretation. Under the dominance of this new law, literary teaching and scholarship began to be overwhelmingly devoted to the practice of primary interpretation. Moreover, the law of interpretation entailed a still further restriction. Not only was interpretation to be the only really legitimate activity, but its preferred focus was to be the interpretation of major authors like Shakespeare, Milton, Blake, Wordsworth, Goethe, Schiller, Heine, Kafka, Molière, Racine and Rousseau. This account of academic study over the past thirty years can be documented by two brief statistics. First, out of the thousands of publications on literature since 1950, fully 8/10ths consist of primary interpretations. Second, since 1950, 7/10ths of all literary publications have been devoted to 1/10th of the authors listed in the scholarly bibliographies. A relatively small number of authors, in other words, have received a great many primary interpretations. For over twenty-five years, the chief writing activity of literary professors has been to interpret the primary meanings of canonical works whose primary meanings had already been much interpreted.

Nonetheless, in the face of this, many literary professors both Ancient and Modern still (unwisely) accept the law of interpretation as governing academic literary study. Professors have continued to publish more primary interpretations in the last thirty years than in the entire previous history of literary scholarship. But there is a limit to the possibilities of primary interpretation. Each new reading of "The Tyger" by William

Blake, if it is significant and true, must decrease the chance that the next reading can be significant and true—and new. So, given the law of interpretation, and given the institutional imperative to publish, professors have recently turned to secondary creative interpretation, with its limitless frontier, to satisfy the institutional need for limitless publication. That is the source of the interest conflict between professors and undergraduates. Both parties are caught up in the vortex of institutional homeostasis, i.e., the instinct of the academy, like any other institution, to maintain itself as it is—no matter how adversely this homeostasis affects the educational purposes of the academy.

But these sociological observations do not settle the genuine theoretical issues that were first raised by Faust, following his intellectual master Kant. Recent history explains only the timing of the current debate and its intensity. The theoretical issue itself is a different matter entirely. The theoretical issue arises from the claim that Faust was right, that primary interpretation is not possible, and that all criticism must be secondary interpretation. If this claim were just an argument to the effect that we need to accommodate past literary works into our present culture, there would be no disagreement between Ancients and Moderns. Moreover, if the Moderns simply warned us that it is difficult to practice primary, historical interpretation, and that we often fail, then, again, there would be no disagreement. The theoretical issue boils down to the very specific one whether it is or isn't possible to understand and accommodate past literary texts starting from their own historical terms.

The structure of the modernist argument is as follows: we are so rooted in our own cultural situation—our own "historicity," to use Heidegger's term—that we cannot really enter into the cultural situation of the past. Any attempt to understand that past would be in terms of our present categories, and these categories are what *we are*. They are the unrevisable gridwork through which we see, and by which we create what we perceive. We exist in what could be named the "cultural a priori." As I mentioned, this is basically an idea from Kant, who said that we see the world in terms of built-in forms such as Space, and Time, and Causality, and that these a priori forms of experience are our own unchangeable contribution to perception. No matter what the world is really like, we must see the world in terms of our own a priori categories. The Moderns are cultural Kantians who hold that we see the texts of the past in the way Kant said we see the physical world. We pre-understand our texts. We interpret them only in and through our cultural a prioris. (Foucault, in his version of this theme, uses the term "the historical a priori.") For the modernist, the historical interpreter is like the apprentice of Sais in the story by Novalis. He tries to uncover veil after veil, reaching back farther and farther into the cave of the past, but when he throws back the last veil to reveal the meaning of the text, what he discovers is—himself.

This idea of the cognitive a priori is the underlying foundation of the Modernist position in all of its forms. It underlies the theories of Roland Barthes, Michel Foucault, Hans-Georg Gadamer, Jürgen Habermas, Frank Kermode, Paul de Man and Stanley Fish. The cognitive a priori is the essential ingredient in the school of Derrida. It is essential to all the many splinter groups that advocate secondary interpretation on theoretical grounds. Because of the Modernist's commitment to the a priori, his only question is not whether we should *resemanticize* the text (since we must do so), but whether we shall do it valuably and interestingly. The only issue is how well we shall *recreate*. "No longer," says Stanley Fish, "is the critic the humble servant of texts whose glories exist independently of anything he might do; it is what he does . . . that brings the texts into being."[3]

Now if there were not a good deal of truth in the Modernist position it wouldn't have been held by so many brilliant thinkers from Goethe to Foucault. Intellectually it is irrelevant that current enthusiasm for the Modernist view may be owing to institutional causes that are neither intellectual nor admirable. The actual position is of the highest respectability. Anyone who has read widely in primary interpretation will have found examples of unconscious distortions of original meaning owing to cultural presuppositions.

But there is a world of difference between the common-sense view that we are sometimes imprisoned in our cultural categories, and the radical view that we are always trapped beyond the possibility of correction. This distinction between "sometimes" and "always" is the bottom line for theoretical debate between Ancients and Moderns. The genuine intellectual issue, quite apart from cultural and institutional issues, lies in the debate between a radical and common-sense version of historicity. Most of us think that historicity is a difficulty that we sometimes must struggle to overcome. The Modernist says that no amount of boot-strapping can ever lift us out of our cognitive a priori, which is always with us and constitutes everything we know. To which common sense gives the reply of Karl Popper: the doctrine of the cognitive a priori "simply exaggerates a difficulty into an impossibility."[4] Between the Ancients and Moderns that is the only genuine cognitive issue. Is historical interpretation a difficulty or is it an impossibility?

To examine the question in its most imposing form we need to turn to Kant himself. The cultural a priori is an entirely post-Kantian idea that derives its sanction from the analogy to the Kantian description of knowledge. Kant said that our ideas of space, time, and causality are prior to our experience, and must permanently constitute our world. By the same token, the cultural Kantians say that our linguistic and cultural categories must permanently constitute our cultural world. On the surface, Kant's argument seems immune from any decisive refutation, and in his own day no one could possibly find empirical grounds on which to refute him. No one could point to examples in which we had changed or corrected our so-called "a priori" cognitive structures.

But this immunity of the Kantian argument to empirical refutation is only apparent. In some fields outside literary and cultural studies, the a priorist is now in full retreat. That is because the a priorist sometimes unwittingly makes empirical predictions that turn out to be testable. Kant, for instance, assumed and therefore predicted that the forms of Space and Time must be permanent features of our world. He also predicted that we must always interpret events in the world as being causally connected. The collapse of these claims in the twentieth century has called into doubt the whole foundational principle of the Kantian a priori.

This recent difficulty in the perceptual a priori must also embarrass the cultural a priorist. For no *cultural* world is more deeply and permanently ingrained in us than our world of space, time and causality. It's implausible to claim that we cannot change our cultural premises far enough to understand Wordsworth, while admitting that we can change our most fundamental world concepts to understand relativity and quantum mechanics. Moreover, our physical world concepts of space and time are themselves learned, cultural categories as well as perceptual ones, and in our own century we *have* been able to revise these deep categories. We now inhabit a non-Kantian world where space is curved, parallel lines do meet, and where subatomic events occur spontaneously, without determinate cause.

Philosophers close to these empirical developments have not failed to draw their anti-Kantian conclusions. As long ago as 1920, when Heidegger was developing his version of the cultural a priori, Hans Reichenbach published a book called *Relativitätstheorie und Erkenntnis Apriori* (*Theory of Relativity and the Cognitive A Priori.*) In it he analyzed in detail the embarrassments for the Kantian position caused by the new insights into physical reality. Reichenbach's books, and those of his student, Hilary Putnam, have not yet entered into the traditions of humanistic studies. But perhaps in the 1980's they will.

Equally embarrassing to the cultural a priorist is recent work in neuropsychology. The following remarks were made by Leon Cooper, a Nobel prizewinner in physics, who has turned to neural science and heads a research center in that field. Cooper says:

> It is an old and I think, tired conjecture that certain ideas and concepts are built into our mental apparatus. It has been sponsored at one time or another as far back as Plato's Meno that our notions of space, time, causality, or even certain aspects of grammar are determined genetically. . . . This idea of built-in mental concepts is old, and occasionally reappears in high fashion. . . . The strongest argument against such higher level built-in concepts seem to me to be that they are premature and ill-defined. Where they can be defined, concepts such as time, space or geometry seem not to be built-in, but more easily explained as a conse-

quence of the interaction of a relatively unbiased mental apparatus with some of the most basic ordering of our environment. . . . A child seems willing to accept any connection, marvelous or trivial, if it is a repeated part of his world. . . . Whatever limits there are to human imagination would seem to be those we have placed [temporarily] on ourselves by culture, training, and experience . . . . Mathematicians or physicists have no difficulty at all in working with Einstein's time or any number of space dimensions. . . . Engineers and physicists who design high-energy machines have developed a fingertip intuitive notion of Einstein's time and space that is applied as a matter of everyday routine in their work. Yet they switch without any apparent mental anguish to ordinary concepts of space and time before they reach home. . . . The conceptual limits we feel so painfully are not those of nature but . . . those of training. They are there not because of how our heads are made, but by what circumstances and education have put in them. Understanding and use of new concepts or ideas requires retraining the old generation. . . . What is required is a newborn head, not a newly designed head.[5]

Cooper speaks of retraining people to give them new perspectives and ideas. In this he speaks as a good humanist. He identifies the practical issue in the debate between Ancients and Moderns, which turns out to be a cultural rather than theoretical issue, because at the theoretical level the Moderns are simply wrong. They have exaggerated a difficulty into an impossibility. The real issue is whether we *should* try to retrain ourselves and our students to new ideas (i.e., new for us) from the past, whether we ought to do primary instead of secondary interpretation, whether we ought to go back to history. The central purposes of the humanities are linked to history. Primary interpretation gives us access to the best that has been said and thought in the world. The humanities, as historical studies, can also do something more: they can provide a corrective principle in our culture. The main cultural value of humanistic study is precisely that it helps overcome our cultural a priori. It helps us to actualize perspectives that do not happen to exist in our present schemes and values. Historical study in the humanities shows us directions we might have missed, and can spare us stupidities that others have already committed. The historical study of literature has the bracing virtue of the not-self and helps to save us from the complacent fallacy of thinking that latest is always best.

Under this view of the humanities, the Ancients are really Moderns, and the Moderns are old hat. Historical study takes an interest in what is really new—that is, in what is unlike ourselves. In 1981 it is not really a great novelty to find that Wordsworth can be seen as a modern existential skeptic. Of course, it seems a *scholarly* novelty to hold that Wordsworth is just like ourselves. But it is not a spiritual novelty, and it is not even true. For us the spiritual novelty of Wordsworth is his exemplification of a human possibility that is real, impressive and unlike ourselves. That is how the humanities yield the corrective principle in culture.

A few remarks in conclusion. In this talk I have come out firmly for the Ancients—at the present time. We need to strike a balance in our culture between the present and the past, the self and the not-self. In the sixties and seventies we began to lose our balance. We gave too much play to the self, the present, and the attractions of the irrational. In the 1980's we need to restore the balance. I hope the needs of our students are going to be met, and that the historical imperatives of the humanities will be fulfilled. Although that means a return to history, it does not necessarily mean a return to historical interpretation. We have had a superfluity of interpretations in literary studies, both primary and secondary. Imaginative scholars will find other kinds of significant historical study to pursue.

I'll end with a brief summary of the views I have expressed. I've argued that the truth of the Modernist theoretical position has been greatly overrated. It had its origin in a post-Kantian idea about the unchangeability and a prioricity of our cultural categories, but this idea is simply wrong. I argued also that the new interest in this cultural a priori is largely institutional rather than intellectual in origin. It arises from an institutional need for published interpretations, and just now only secondary interpretations seem able to fill that insatiable need. This has put professors in an interest conflict with undergraduates, who want and need primary interpretations. But the cultural a priori, on which secondary interpretation is based, is a highly vulnerable idea. We should not be disconcerted by its imposing claims, or made to think that we are being naive when we try to pursue historical study. Far from being naive, historically based criticism is the newest and most valuable kind of literary work for our students (and our culture) at the present time.

1. *Times Literary Supplement* [London] (February 20, 1981), p. 199.

2. *Faust: Part I, Book II*, Robert Petsch, ed., *Goethes Werke*, 18 Vols., V.V. (Leipzig: Festausgabe, 1926), pp. 575–79.

3. Stanley Fish, *Is There a Text in This Class? The Authority of Interpretive Communities* (Cambridge, Mass.: Harvard University Press, 1980), p. 368.

4. Karl Popper, "Normal Science and Its Dangers," in *Criticism and the Growth of Knowledge* [Proceedings of the International Colloquium in the Philosophy of Science, London, 1965, Vol. 4] (Cambridge: Cambridge University Press, 1970), pp. 56–57.

5. Leon Copper, "Source and Limits of Human Intellect," *Daedalus* (Spring 1980), pp. 14–17.

English Studies,
Now and Then

William H. Pritchard

My attempt is to say something about the present state of "English," of academic criticism and teaching, by telling one man's story, then and now, as he moved from being a heady graduate student, mildly at odds with many of his peers and his teachers, to a chaired professor on the wrong side of fifty, mildly at odds with his juniors and some of his peers (his elders no longer seem to count as antagonists). Telling such a story involves dangerous temptations, mainly that of dramatizing and flattering oneself as a type of the lonely hero, persisting in stubborn though hopeless integrity of purpose: "When the forts of folly fall,/Find thy body by the wall," wrote Matthew Arnold with, he hoped, the proper disillusioned note. But perhaps the temptation may be combatted with a dose or so of humorous irony, such doses being too-often absent from academized criticism. As for resorting to the personal tale rather than to a larger, more "responsible" analysis of the profession, my justification lies in an assertion from F. R. Leavis' *Education and the University*, where he says that "literary history as a matter of 'facts about' and accepted critical . . . description" is "worthless" unless the student can

> . . . as a critic—that is, as an intelligent and discerning reader—make a personal approach to the essential data of the literary historian, the works of literature (an approach is personal or it is nothing: you cannot take over the appreciation of a poem, and unappreciated the poem isn't 'there').[1]

I make the application rather to the teaching of English in the college and university. As for objectivity, since I'm not even a member of the Modern Language Association, and since I avoid other "professional" situations—symposia, conferences, etc.—how could any pretensions to objectivity, to seeing the object as in itself it really is, be convincing? Better a tale unfold, beginning at Amherst and Harvard in the 1950's, then settling down uneasily in the present.

As an Amherst College undergraduate, I majored in Philosophy, but felt most challenged by the few English courses I elected, which were characterized by originality in their teaching and which demanded a corresponding originality in the student's work, in and out of class. There were no authorities to defer to; if the subject were a play by Shakespeare or an ode by Keats, nobody directed us to G. Wilson Knight or Earl Wasserman for the definitive analysis. What criticism I read—T. S. Eliot, a little Empson, some Kenneth Burke—was on my own and the result of picking up Stanley Edgar Hyman's *The Armed Vision*, where such critics were analyzed and judged. The teacher's originality came about especially in the "exercises" proposed on the various works we read, in which we were asked a sequence of questions designed to elicit an interesting response. It was assumed, at least so the air in the classroom suggested to me, that literature was a splendid thing (one of my teachers used to say, "Imagine getting paid for talking about books!") and that one read for pleasure, the pleasure of extending oneself. Nobody was encouraged to go on to graduate study in English, just as nobody was encouraged to become a poet. Yet some good students of literature and some good poets (you could even be both) emerged from Amherst during the 1940's and 1950's.

After a less than brilliant attempt at further study in philosophy, I went to Harvard in English, partly because some of my friends were there, partly because our teacher, Reuben Brower, had now become a professor there. Harvard provided me my first experience of the academization of literature. Hyder Rollins, the fine textual editor of Shakespeare and Elizabethan poets, lectured boringly on the Romantics by turning over his stack of file cards and giving us names, dates and the occasional anecdote. Ricardo Quintana (visiting that semester from Wisconsin) lectured on English literature, 1700–1740, with everything orderly and undisturbed by the problematic. B. J. Whiting read Chaucer aloud and made funny jokes, while Herschel Baker chatted suavely about Restoration comedy. Teachers more oriented toward what I thought of as criticism—Douglas Bush, Walter Jackson Bate, Albert Guerard—still preserved an extremely tolerant or "objective" attitude toward a variety of writers, and we were encouraged to see the particular work "on its own terms," rather than impose our terms and valuations upon it.

I was happy at Harvard, not because of anything very interesting that went on in the classroom, but because of the chance to read extensively in areas I'd never touched on, and because of the professors' willingness to let me, and others, write the sort of paper we thought we could do best. Meanwhile, one's graduate school classmates seemed in the main less than inspiring. It may just have been the snobbishness of our Amherst clique—we thought we were virtuous because we were *critics* (sort of) who made striking judgments and argued with one another about them—that helped us condescend to the young man who was preparing (for his doctoral dissertation) an edition of James Shirley's play, *The Cardinal*, or the one who was investigating further the differences between seventeenth-century Attic and Ciceronian prose. I thought it was daring of me to choose Robert Frost for a dissertation subject and D. H. Lawrence for my "major author" on the Ph.D. oral (Amherst students often failed these orals because they didn't "know enough," and B. J. Whiting defended us wittily by saying that we were no more stupid than other students). Frost and Lawrence, in 1958, were not fully accredited, and when on my oral exam Alfred Harbage, the Shakespearean scholar, asked me rather disapprovingly whether I could name any other great writer who used language as sloppily as Lawrence sometimes did in *Women in Love*, I replied with the name Faulkner. Harbage laughed heartily—as if I had unwittingly committed a joke.

Harvard's English department prided itself on its lack of orthodoxy, and it is true that for better or worse no one attempted to impose a particular methodological approach to literature and criticism (although Howard Mumford Jones insisted on a certain size of file card, a research tool I quickly learned to do without). On the other hand, such tolerance may have been little more than a convenience under which the professor could lecture a couple of times a week, give whatever writing one did B-plus or above (unless it was really awful), and get on with the book he was probably writing. My second year as a graduate course-taking student at Harvard was, except for Reuben Brower's seminar on Pope, devoid of critical life in the classroom. And aside from teaching in Brower's staff course in "close reading," Humanities 6–which he had more or less brought along from Amherst—my intellectual life as a critic and teacher owed nothing to the Harvard English department and its pedagogy, or lack of it.

When I accepted a teaching job at Amherst, it was good to go back, but I hoped also that I could go forward, through discussion and argument with my colleagues, especially within the staff courses. And there were indeed some memorable arguments about Shakespeare's *Troilus and Cressida*, Lawrence's *St. Mawr*, Tolstoy's "The Death of Ivan Ilyich"—to name but three especially remembered ones. They were arguments about the book, but also about how best to teach the book, and also—of course—they were confrontations of different personal styles and rhetorics. We always argued over the reading list (it was assumed that you started with an agreed-upon reading list), and it took some time before agreeing on teaching Lawrence, or on what Lawrence we wanted to teach (I remember our eventual selection turned out to be rather odd and interesting—*Studies in Classic American Literature*, *St. Mawr*, and *Etruscan Places*). There were some wild jumps in our "sequences" (from *Comus* to *Huckleberry Finn* one year), but we always ended up with an agreeable and I think relatively unacademic-traditional list of books. In addition to the stable items—lyric poems, a Shakespeare play, novels by

Jane Austen or Henry James—we read in this introductory course such books as Richard Hoggart's *The Uses of Literacy* and Sybil Marshall's *An Experiment in Education*, Keats' letters, James' *A Small Boy and Others*, Kenneth Burke's *The Philosophy of Literary Form*, and contemporary novels by Wright Morris and Anthony Powell and Alain Robbe-Grillet.

Something like a common purpose and shared concerns prevailed in this course until the early 1970's, when things began to fall apart. One veteran colleague, a convert to recent leftish trends in educational philosophy and practice, chose to define his subject not as literature (we were beginning with *Hamlet* that term), not Shakespeare, but the class itself, its "dynamics." He engaged with the students in role-playing, in breaking down the teacher-student division (the hated "dyadic" relationship, it was called back then), in questioning the very notion of "teaching" and its legitimacy. Another colleague dropped out of the course because his cultural and sociological interests were being poorly served by it. At one point, in a burst of agonizing reappraisal, the departmental chairman declared that we needed a daylong think session at which we might question our essential purposes as a department. Accordingly, classes were cancelled one Wednesday and the English profs adjourned to the local Hilton, where we engaged in the usual fruitless self-display and frantic wit (drinks were served at lunch). I became at least as defensive as the next person, insisting that the experience of reading Wordsworth or Yeats was the important thing, and that we were there to help students talk and write more subtly about this experience—no more, no less, than that was the purpose of "English."

Meanwhile, as the college moved slowly toward coeducation, women were hired in the department. These young and untenured colleagues (the department was, like many, by this time heavily on the tenured side) had graduated from the universities in the late 1960's and were asking different sorts of questions. Why were there not more blacks and women represented on the reading list I had suggested one year? Why should we not ask our students to read Barthes or Benjamin or Lévi-Strauss, instead of Jonathan Swift or John Updike? Was Richard Wilbur's poem "Playboy," with its possibly sexist implications, a fit object to be introduced into a classroom, and what was so good about Richard Wilbur anyway? (Too finished, not "problematic" enough.) If Philip Larkin's new volume of poetry was to be assigned, should not they also be asked to read Imamu Amiri Baraka's (Leroi Jones') poems, so as not to leave them with the assumption that Good Poetry is identical with the articulate, ironic, formal utterance of an insular Englishman?

The going phrase for this activity is "opening up the canon," about which Barbara Hernnstein Smith, Leslie Fiedler and others have recently waxed enthusiastic. Two observations occur to me in response: first, that although students in my last term's class in "Introduction to Literary Studies" (rather than, as in olden times, "Introduction to Literature") agreed it was a good idea to open up the canon (this is a liberal college where everyone praises diversity, etc.), it was also evident that they had little idea of what constituted the canon they were in favor of opening up. To no one's surprise they had read precious few of the canonical texts, largely because the English department could not agree that there were the texts which "should" be taught. What's so good, I asked my students, about "opening up" something you're not oppressed by, since you're unfamiliar with it? Better perhaps to "open it up" in the sense of getting to know it. The second observation, this one more tendentiously directed at colleagues, is that certain texts (not "books," mind you) recurred frequently enough in the discourse of the younger English professors to suggest that it might be time to open up another canon: *S/Z*, *Tristes Tropiques*; Derrida on Rousseau and Plato's *Pharmakon*; Mary Shelley's *Frankenstein*; Clifford Geertz's essay on the Balinese cockfight (that one successfully resisted by me for inclusion in a course reading list); Zora Neale Hurston's *Their Eyes Were Watching God*; Alice Walker's *The Color Purple*; Foucault on sexuality; and so on. Plenty of English majors at Amherst, now familiar with these books, remain total strangers to the poetry of Pope, to Boswell's *Life of Johnson*; to the prose of Newman, the novels of Dickens, the plays of Bernard Shaw.

At most colleges and universities, so far as I know, the teaching of literature is conducted in various ways by different individuals, who, except for the occasional exchange about a book or a method at departmental meetings, don't have to think very much about each other. At Amherst, by contrast, the presence of a large introductory staff course for freshmen called "Reading," and the presence of a required course in Literary Studies, taught at the sophomore level for all English majors and other interested students, makes it impossible to avoid seriously brushing up against colleagues who, while committed to the same texts and written exercises, are doing very different things with them in the classroom. Such brushing up has the good effect, it must be, of rousing me, and others, from our dogmatic slumbers; of making certain that I will not go on, term after term, teaching to others the works I was taught: *Coriolanus*, *Emma*, *The Portrait of a Lady*, *Walden*, *The Education of Henry Adams*, Frost's poems—just like counting our beads, as one colleague put it. At the same time, there is a point at which brushing up against a differing, an opposing, set of assumptions may be closer to laceration and more productive of sarcasm (or rage) than mutual interanimation. What, really, are the possibilities for interanimation when the participants (just to reduce them to extreme types) are an older, tenured, white, male, Anglo-American, "common-sense" evaluator of literature, and a younger, untenured or recently-tenured female, a feminist, of Continental sensibility and a deconstructive turn? I leave the question open.

I also have ambiguous feelings about what appears to be an increasing professionalization among younger colleagues. It may well be that I am simply in the grip of my own history here, of the fact that I was a graduate student at one rather than another moment in this century. Yet I remember the mixture of fear and contempt with which, at Harvard, I reacted to a fellow student's receiving back a course paper he had written, with a high grade and the comment "conceivably publishable"—also with a suggestion or two of where to send it (*Arizona Quarterly*; *Modern Fiction Studies*). Somehow, I thought, I must contrive not to step onto this treadmill, and I looked forward instead to a life of reading and teaching, with little writing for publication involved. Such did not turn out to be the case, even as I fancy that my writing is largely other than what might be called professional-academic (this is perhaps another illusion). My sense is that younger people in the profession today feel they have little choice. To receive tenure they must publish, and they are quite at home in their awareness of the journals, in their bibliographical expertise. Sometimes almost too much at home, as when I am arguing with a colleague about *Jane Eyre* and the colleague introduces another name into the discussion by telling me what XY recently wrote about *Jane Eyre* in the last issue of *Diacritics* or *Signs*. Doubtless a definitive piece, and if you're not keeping up with the right journals—if you read, as I do, the *American Scholar* or the *New Criterion* rather than *Diacritics*, then you won't be able to pull your weight in the analysis of Brontë's novel. But this respect for the authority of somebody else's book or essay rather than one's own opinion strikes me as oddly akin to what some of my professors at Harvard were engaged in back then, when we were instructed to read Tillyard on Milton or Sherburn on Pope. Of course my own career is no exception as far as deferring to authority goes. Once upon a time, I admit it, I went to the periodical room daily. I have been taken over by, then have attempted to resist, presences like Leavis, Blackmur, Hugh Kenner. But the giving of yourself to a commanding critical influence is, I think, somewhat different from too bibliographical a readiness to cite too many names and articles on too many subjects. Something about it nudges one into doubt of how direct a relation the bibliographer himself has to the art of Brontë or Tennyson.

This essay declared its personal slant at the beginning, and to press a further point, or grouse, may seem intolerably egotistic, as if the members of my profession are supposed to do as I do or think as I have done. But let me see if, as tentative generalizations, the following have any interest. First, for me the reading and criticism of poetry (I use the word to include all forms of what we used, confidently, to refer to as "imaginative" or "literary" work) went along with the listening to and criticism of "serious" music, both classical and jazz. Like the movement of a sonata, a Chopin scherzo, an orchestration by Ellington or an improvisation by Armstrong on a Hot Five recording, poetry also takes place in time—the

Keats ode has a beginning, middle and end, over the course of which something transpires. It seemed natural then to listen to the expressive curve of a poetic syntax, or the tonal range of an imagined "speaking voice" in a poem, just as one listened to and judged the Armstrong solo. Much of the pleasure in a classroom consists in helping students become more practiced and expert at distinguishing, say, Cowper from Crabbe from Collins (I did that last fall), and an important part of the experience is listening—is ear-training, to be exact.

My hunch is that more than a few younger professors of English—and of course older ones as well—tend to be what, in Frost's terms, are called eye-readers rather than ear-readers. Some of them have very good eyes indeed, and are expert at ferreting out the betrayals of this or that signifier as it vainly attempts unambiguously to designate and fix a signified. For this talent they may pay a price, that price being a relative insensitivity to the rhythms and music of poetry—to what James Guetti in *Word-Music* refers to as "aural" rather than "visual" motives. In other words, X-ray vision may go along with the possession of a tin ear. On how much difference you think this makes will depend where you align yourself as a viewer of today's scene. A further tentative generalization: is it not possible that the renewed interest in philosophy, the fact that the names of Hegel and Heidegger come readily to the lips of younger people in "English" today, may consort with a lack of "ear" or at least a disinclination to fuss much about the aural? In my own brief attempt at the graduate study of philosophy, as I fell deeply afoul of Kant (and never got to Hegel), it became evident to me that my talents lay elsewhere than in the exposition of abstract argument. This may have been merely my problem, and perhaps many professors today can be as resourceful and commanding as teachers when the subject is Hegel as when it is *The Rape of the Lock*. But I don't believe that for a minute. Something's got to give, somewhere, and that Paul de Man was the exception only proves the rule.

At Harvard, my friends and I were scornful of our teachers and fellow students who refused to risk making judgments about the worth of a poem or a novel, who were willing instead to stop with exposition of its verbal texture, or who made the move into anthropology or the history of ideas by talking about how the work had to be understood as coming from within a certain historical period or certain "other" culture. Yes, yes, true enough we said, but not enough fun. The fun lay in arguing about whether Donne's "Aire and Angels" was a better or worse poem than "The Canonization," or whether either or both could compete as an utterance with Herbert's "The Flower." How did one value *What Maisie Knew* next to *The Awkward Age* or *The Spoils of Poynton*; was it comparable in power to an early James like *The Portrait of a Lady*, or to the later novels to come? And how seriously should James be weighed against *Middlemarch* or *Anna Karenina*? These sorts of questions are what Geoffrey Hartman refers to as the "sublimated chatter" of the Anglo-Arnoldian tradition, or what Northrop Frye in the polemical introduction to his *Anatomy* reads out of court as having no place in "systematic criticism." But one of the main reasons I chose to study English in the first place was in order to engage in exactly such talk, such chatter, with colleagues and students. "Systematic criticism" might be left to expositors of Hegel, and might be located in another department.

In "Contingencies of Value" (*Critical Inquiry*, Fall 1983), Barbara Hernnstein Smith deplores the banishment of talk about value from literary studies, and wants to bring it back so the canon can be opened up, so that the Anglo-Arnoldian with his culture and his touchstones will bump against new earths, new heaven. But as I've suggested, there is another kind of "value" talk, made more or less from within the canon, engaged in interesting disruptions of accepted valuations, or interesting formulations of new valuations, which may also claim the attention— which in fact does claim my attention, and powerfully so. Unless I delude myself once again, I find less of this talk around, less interest in the kind of comparative placing and judging I'd always assumed to be a central, perhaps *the* central, fact of critical discourse. By contrast, the sort of subject that seems these days to bring people together in an engaged way might be illustrated by the well-attended session at last year's MLA (into which I snuck), the topic being "Representations and Its Discontents." Admittedly the three panelists (Richard Rorty, David Bromwich and Gerald Graff) were people you'd want to hear on any subject, more or less. But I think it no accident that in response to what seemed to me less than riveting papers, the solemn, humorless parade of questions afterwards from the audience meant that a good many people thought the stakes were very high ones, and that the subject was rather more important than, say, the novels of Anthony Trollope or Anthony Powell. It was as if by moving one step away from a particular writer or work of art, there was a guarantee of significance: these people were more than just a bunch of English teachers talking about books. (Rorty is, of course, a philosopher, but, unlike some philosophers I know, doesn't mind that "his" writers are entering the English classroom to be talked about by nonphilosophers.)

A cogent objection to everything I've been saying here is that in trying to write about "the profession" and about the younger generation of English teachers, and about what I fancy my own career has been like (a likely story!), I am practicing exactly what I preach against. By abstracting and generalizing and classifying and pigeonholing, I commit the sin I presume to detect in others. My only defense is that for the last twenty or so years I've been preoccupied, in teaching and writing, with particularities of feeling and imagination as they have revealed themselves in the language of individual poems and fictions, and in the literary careers of individual writers. For better or worse, I have avoided writing essays on The State of Poetry or The End of the Humanities (this last dreary title just picked fresh from a poster advertising a benighted conference to be held in the fall at Miami University). And I have encouraged students to acquire the reading habit, in the belief that goodness lies in the minute particulars of books and writers they've never heard of.[2] My failing and my guilt lies in the inadequate scope of my own reading, as I think of all those books still unread or unreread.

Another objection to what I've said here, apart from its possible unfairness or inaccuracy, could be mounted in terms similar to those Helen Vendler used in her address to the MLA last December, namely that critical approaches, ways of talking and reading, come and go; one generation's hero is the next one's has-been, and how should it, why should it, be otherwise? All of us are "wrong" and all of us will turn out to be old fogeys. This is good sense, taken from contemplating things under the aspect of eternity; but it's not the only way to contemplate them. I think of the stanza from Randall Jarrell's "In Those Days":

> How poor and miserable we were,
> How seldom together!
> And yet after so long one thinks:
> In those days everything was better.[3]

I don't quite believe that in these days everything is worse, though I persist in believing that, all-in-all, the 1950's was a good time to have been a student of English. But at least a lot of things are different, and the difference should perhaps be talked about, nay even complained about, rather than smoothed away by taking large-prospected views. After all, academic-literary life could use some livening up, and there seems to me something less than heartening in the spectacle of elders smiling at and encouraging the hungry generations who are treading them down.

---

1. F. R. Leavis, *Education in the University* (Cambridge: Cambridge University Press, 1979), p. 68.

2. An example of that sort of thing paying off: at the first meeting of a large course in modern and contemporary fiction, I wrote the name of Anthony Trollope on the blackboard, and said something about how I'd been reading Trollope the past summer and how I'd rather be reading him than some of the names on the reading list. This was designed to be a provoking remark, since none of them had ever read Trollope. At the end of the term one student came up to me and asked for some suggested titles by Trollope. The following year he wrote his thesis on A.T., to my knowledge the first ever written about him at Amherst—which was judged to be of Summa quality, as indeed it was. You never know what may happen when you throw out a challenge.

3. Randall Jarrell, *The Complete Poems* (New York: Farrar, Straus & Giroux, 1969), p. 230.

The Loss of the University

Wendell Berry

The situation of literature within the university is not fundamentally different from the situation of any other discipline, which is not fundamentally different from the situation of language. The situation is that the various disciplines have ceased to speak to each other; that is, they have become too specialized, and this overspecialization, this separation, of the disciplines has been enabled and enforced by the specialization of their languages. As a result, the modern university has grown, not according to any unifying principle, like an expanding universe, but by the principle of miscellaneous accretion, like a furniture storage business.

I assume that there is a degree of specialization that is unavoidable, because concentration involves a narrowing of attention; we can only do one thing at a time. I assume further that there is a degree of specialization that is desirable, because good work depends upon sustained practice. If we want the best work to be done in teaching or writing or stonemasonry or farming, then we must arrange for that work to be done by proven masterworkers, people who are prepared for the work by long and excellent practice.

But to assume that there is a degree of specialization that is proper is at the same time to assume that there is a degree that is improper. The impropriety begins, I think, when the various kinds of workers come to be divided and cease to speak to one another. In this division they become makers of *parts* of things. This is the impropriety of industrial organization, of which Eric Gill wrote,

> Skill in making degenerates into mere dexterity, i.e. skill in doing, when the workman . . . ceases to be concerned for the thing made or . . . has no longer any responsibility for the thing made and has therefore lost the knowledge of what it is that he is making. . . . The factory hand can only know what he is *doing*. What is being made is no concern of his.[1]

Part of the problem in universities now, or part of the cause of the problem, is this loss of concern for the thing made, and back of that, I think, the loss of agreement on what the thing is that is being made. The thing being made in a university is humanity. This, given the current influence of universities, is merely inevitable. But what universities, at least the public-supported ones, are *mandated* to make, or to help make, is human beings in the *fullest* sense of those words—not just trained workers, or just knowledgeable citizens, but responsible heirs and members of human culture. If the proper work of the university is only to equip people to fulfill private ambitions, then how do we justify public support? If it is only to prepare citizens to fulfill public responsibilities, then how do we justify the teaching of arts and sciences? It appears that the common denominator has to be larger than either career preparation or preparation for citizenship. Underlying the idea of a university—the bringing together, the combining into one, of all the disciplines—is the idea that good work and good citizenship are the inevitable by-products of the making of a good, a fully developed, human being. This, as I understand it, is the definition of the name, *University*.

When the departments of a university become so specialized that they can speak neither to each other nor to the generality of the university's own students and graduates, then that university is displaced. As an institution, it no longer knows where it is, and therefore it cannot know either its responsibilities to its place or the effects of its irresponsibility. This too often is the practical meaning of "academic freedom": the teacher feels free to teach and learn, make and think, without concern for the thing made.

Language is at the heart of the problem. To profess, after all, is "to confess before"—to confess, I assume, before all who live within the neighborhood or under the influence of the confessor. But to confess before one's neighbors and clients in a language that few of them can understand is not to confess at all. The specialized professional language is thus not merely a contradiction in terms; it is a cheat and a hiding place; it may, indeed, be an ambush. At the very root of the idea of profession and professorship is the imperative to speak plainly in the common tongue.

That the common tongue should become the exclusive specialty of one department in a university is, therefore, a tragedy, and not just for the university and its worldly place; it is a tragedy for the common tongue. It means that the common tongue, so far as the university is concerned, *ceases* to be the common tongue; it becomes merely one tongue within a confusion of tongues. Our language and literature cease to be seen as occurring in the world and begin to be seen as occurring within their university department and within themselves. Literature ceases to be the commons of all speakers and readers of the common tongue, and becomes only the occasion of a deafening clatter *about* literature. Teachers and students read the great songs and stories to learn *about* them, not to learn *from* them. The *texts* are tracked as by the passing of an army of ants, but the great commons itself—the repository of our memory, our meanings and our pleasure—is almost deserted.

The specialist approach, of course, is partly justifiable—half justifiable, I would say. In both speech and literature, language does occur within itself. It echoes within itself, reverberating endlessly, like a voice echoing within a cave, and speaking in answer to its echo, and the answer again echoing. It *must* do this. Its nature, in part, is to do this.

But its nature also is to turn outward to the world, to strike its worldly objects cleanly and cease to echo—to achieve a kind of rest and silence in them. The professionalization of language and of language study makes the condition of the cave absolute and inescapable. One strives without rest in the interior clamor.

The silence in which words return to their objects and touch them and come to rest is not the silence of the plugged ear. It is the world's silence, such as occurs after the first hard freeze of autumn, when the weeks-long singing of the crickets is suddenly stopped and when, by a blessedly recurring accident, all machine noises have stopped for the moment too. It is a silence that must be prepared for and waited for. It requires a silence of one's own.

The reverberations of language within itself are finally mere noise, no better or worse than the noise of accumulated facts that grate aimlessly against each other now in think tanks and other hollow places. Facts, like words, are not things, but verbal tokens or signs of things, which finally must be carried back to the things they stand for to be verified. This carrying back is not specialist work, but an act generally human, though only properly humbled and quieted humans can do it. It is an act that at once enlarges and shapes, frees and limits us.

Beside every effort of making, which is necessarily narrow, there must be an effort of judgment, of criticism, which must be as broad as possible. That is, every made thing, made by one or another of our special arts of making, must be submitted to the question, What is the quality of this as a human artifact, as an addition to the world of made and of created things? How suitable is it to the needs of human and natural neighborhoods?

It must, of course, sooner or later be submitted as well to the special question, How good is this poem or this farm or this hospital *as such*? For it to have a human value it obviously must be well made; it must meet the specialized, technical criteria; it must be *good* as such. But the question of its quality as such is not interesting—in the long run it is probably not askable—unless we ask it under the rule of the more general question. If we are disposed to judge apart from the larger question, if we judge, as well as make, as specialists, then a good forger has as valid a claim to our respect as a good artist.

These *two* problems, how to make and how to judge, are the business of education. But education has tended increasingly to ignore this doubleness of its obligation. It has concerned itself more and more exclusively with the problem of how to make, narrowing the issue of judgment virtually to the terms of the made thing itself. But the made thing is not now a fully developed human being; it is a specialist, a careerist, a graduate. The product has become a part. In industrial education, the thing finally made is of no concern to the makers.

In some instances this is because the specialized "fields" have grown so complicated within themselves that the curriculum leaves no time for the broad and basic studies that would inform judgment. In other instances one feels that there is a potentially embarrassing conflict between judgment broadly informed and the specialized career for which the student is being prepared; teachers of advertising techniques, for example, could ill afford for their students to realize that they are learning the arts of lying and seduction. In all instances, this narrowing is justified by the improbable assumption that young students, before they know anything else, know what they need to learn.

If the disintegration of the university begins in its specialist ideology, it is enforced by a commercial compulsion to satisfy the customer. Since the student is now so much a free agent in determining his or her education, the department administrators and the faculty members must necessarily be preoccupied with the problem of how to keep enrollments up. Something obviously must be done to keep the classes filled; otherwise, the students will wander off to more attractive courses, or courses more directly useful to their proposed careers. Under such circumstances it is inevitable that requirements will be lightened, standards lowered, grades inflated, and instruction narrowed to the supposed requirements of some supposed career opportunity.

Dr. Johnson told Mrs. Thrale that his cousin, Cornelius Ford, "advised him to study the Principles of every thing, that a general Acquaintance with Life might be the Consequence of his Enquiries— Learn said he the leading Precognita of all things . . . grasp the Trunk hard only, and you will shake all the Branches."[2] The soundness of this advice seems to me indisputable, and the metaphor entirely apt. From the trunk it is possible to "branch out." One can begin with a trunk and develop a single branch or any number of branches. It may, on the other hand, be possible to begin with a branch and develop a trunk, but that is neither so probable nor so promising. The modern university, at any rate, more and more resembles a loose collection of lopped branches waving about randomly in the air. "Modern knowledge is departmentalized," H. J. Massingham wrote in 1943, "while the essence of culture is initiation into wholeness, so that all the divisions of knowledge are considered as the branches of one tree, the Tree of Life whose roots went deep into earth and whose top was in heaven."[3]

This Tree, for many hundreds of years, seems to have come almost naturally to mind when we sought to describe the form of knowledge. In our tradition it is at least as old as Genesis, and the form it gives us for all that we know is organic, unified, comprehensive, connective—and moral. The tree, at the beginning, was two trees: the tree of life and the tree of knowledge of good and evil. Later, in our understanding of them, the two trees seem to become one, or each seems to stand for the other—for in the world after the Fall, how can the two be separated? To know life is to know good and evil. To prepare young people for life is to prepare them to know the differences between good and evil. If we represent knowledge as a tree, we know that things that are divided are yet connected. We know that to observe the divisions and ignore the connections is to destroy the tree. The history of modern education may be the history of the loss of this image, and of its replacement by the pattern of the industrial machine, which subsists upon division—and by industrial economics ("publish or perish"), which is meaningless apart from division.

The need for broadly informed human judgment nevertheless remains, and this need requires inescapably an education that is broad and basic. In the face of this need, which is *both* private and public, "career preparation" is an improper use of public money, since "career preparation" serves merely private ends; and it is a waste of the student's time, since "career preparation" is best and most properly acquired in apprenticeships under the supervision of employers. The proper question for a school, for example, is how to speak and write *well*, not how to be a "public speaker" or a "broadcaster" or a "creative writer" or a "technical writer" or a journalist or a practitioner of "Business English." If one can speak or write *well*, then, given the need and the talent, one can make a speech or write an article or a story or a business letter. If one cannot speak or write well, then one will speak and write poorly, and the tricks of a trade will do no good and will confer no dignity.

If the standards for good work are to be upheld, they cannot be specialized, professionalized or departmented. Only common standards can be upheld—standards that are held and upheld in common by the whole community. When in a university, for instance, English composition is made the responsibility exclusively of the English department, or of the sub-department of freshman English, then the quality of the work in composition courses declines and the standards decline. This happens necessarily and for an obvious reason: if students' writing is graded according to form and quality in composition class, but according only to "content" in, say, history class, and in other classes no writing is required, then the message to the students is clear: the form and quality of their writing matters only in composition class—which is to say that it matters very little indeed. High standards of composition can be upheld only if they are upheld everywhere in the university.

The work that should, and that can, unify a University is that of deciding what a student should be taught—what studies, that is, would constitute the trunk of the tree of a person's education. Teachers are not doing "career preparation" so much as they are "preparing young people for life." That is not the result of educational doctrine; it is simply the fact of the matter. Teachers are preparing young people for life. To do this they must dispense knowledge and enlighten ignorance, just as supposed. But ignorance is not only the affliction that teaching seeks to cure; it is the condition, the predicament, in which teaching is done, for teachers do not know the life or the lives for which their students are being prepared. That gives the lie to the claims for "career preparation" and exposes their cynicism. Students may not *have* the careers for which they have been prepared. The "job market" may be overfilled. The requirements for this or that career may change. The student may change, or the world may. The teacher, preparing the student for a life necessarily unknown to them both, has no excusable choice but to help the student to "grasp the Trunk."

And yet the arguments for "career preparation" continue and grow in ambition. On August 23, 1983, for example, the Associated Press announced that "the head of the Texas school board wants to require sixth-graders to choose career 'tracks' that will point them toward jobs."[4] Thus twelve-year-old children would be "free to choose" the kind of life they wish to live. They would even be free to change "career tracks," though, according to the article, such a change would involve the penalty of a delayed graduation.

But these are free choices granted to children unprepared and unready to make them. The idea, in reality, is to *impose* adult choices on children and these "choices" mask the most vicious sort of economic determinism. This idea of education as "career track" diminishes everything it touches: education, teaching, childhood, the future. And such a thing could not be contemplated for sixth-graders, obviously, if it had not already been instituted in the undergraduate programs of colleges and universities.

To require or expect or even allow young people to choose courses of study and careers that they do not yet know anything about is not, as is claimed, a grant of freedom. It is a severe limitation upon freedom. It means, in practice, that when the student has finished school and is faced then, appropriately, with the need to choose a career, he or she is prepared to choose only *one*. At that point the student stands in need of a freedom of choice uselessly granted years before, and forfeited in that grant.

The responsibility to decide what to teach the young is an adult responsibility. In failing to accept that responsibility, the teacher's own learning and character are disemployed, and, in the industrialized education system, are easily replaced by bureaucratic and methodological procedures, "job market" specifications, and tests graded by machines.

If the university faculties have neglected the question of the internal placement of the knowledges of the arts and sciences with respect to each other and to the university as a whole, they have, it seems to me, virtually ignored the questions of the external placement of these knowledges with respect to truth and to the world. This, of course, is a dangerous question and I raise it with appropriate fear. The danger is that such questions should be *settled* by any institution whatever. These questions are the proper business of the people in the institutions, not of the institutions as such. I am arguing here against the specialist absorption in career and procedure that destroys what I take to be the indispensable interest in the question of the truth of what is taught and learned, as well as the equally indispensable interest in the fate and the use of knowledge in the world.

I would be frightened to hear that some university had suddenly taken a lively interest in the question of what is true and was in the process of answering it, perhaps by a faculty vote. But I am equally frightened by the fashionable lack of interest in the question among university teachers individually. And I am more frightened when this lack of interest, under the fashionable alias of "objectivity," is given the status of a public virtue.

Objectivity, in practice, means that one studies or teaches one's subject *as such*, without concern for its relation to other subjects or to the world—that is, without concern for its truth. If one is concerned, if one cares, about the truth or falsity of anything, one cannot be objective: one is glad if it is true and sorry if it is false; one believes it if it is judged to be true and disbelieves it if it is judged to be false. Moreover, the truth or falsity of some things cannot be objectively demonstrated. In determining the truth or falsity of some things, feeling and seeming, intuition and personal experience must be considered. And this work of judgment cannot take place at all with respect to one thing or one subject alone. The issue of truth rises out of the comparison of one thing with another, and out of the study of the relations and influences between one thing and another, and between one thing and many others.

If teachers aspire to the academic virtue of objectivity, they must, therefore, teach as if their subject has nothing to do with anything beyond itself. The teacher of literature, for example, must propose the study of poems as relics left by people who, unlike our highly favored modern selves, believed in things not subject to measurable proof. Thus religious poetry may be taught as having to do with matters once believed, but not believable. The poetry is to be learned *about*; to learn *from* it would be an embarrassing betrayal of objectivity.

213

That this is more than a matter of classroom technique is made sufficiently evident in the current to-do over the teaching of the Bible in public schools. Judge Jackson Kiser of the federal district court in Bristol, Virginia, recently ruled that it would be constitutional to teach the Bible to public-school students if the course is offered as an elective and "taught in an objective manner with no attempt made to indoctrinate the children as to either the truth or falsity of the biblical materials." James J. Kilpatrick, who discussed this ruling approvingly in one of his columns, suggested that the Bible might be taught "as Shakespeare is taught," and suggested further that this would be good because "the Bible is a rich lode of allusion, example and quotation." He warned that "The line that divides propaganda from instruction is a wavering line drawn on shifting sands." And he concluded by asserting that "Whatever else the Bible may be, the Bible is in fact literature. The trick is to teach it that way."[5]

The interesting question here is not whether young English-speakers should know the Bible—they obviously should—but whether a book that so directly offers itself to our belief or disbelief can be taught "as literature." It clearly cannot be so taught except by ignoring "whatever else [it] may be," which is a very substantial part of it. The question, then, is whether it can be adequately or usefully taught as something less than it is. The fact is that the writers of the Bible did not think that they were writing what Judge Kiser and Mr. Kilpatrick call "literature." They thought they were writing the truth, which they expected to be believed by some and disbelieved by others. It is conceivable that the Bible could be well taught by a teacher who believed that it is true, or by a teacher who believed that it is untrue, or by a teacher who believed that it is partly true. That it could be well taught by a teacher uninterested in the question of its truth is not conceivable. That a lively interest in the Bible could be maintained through several generations of teachers uninterested in the question of its truth is not conceivable.

Obviously, this issue of the Bible in the public schools cannot be resolved by federal court decisions that prescribe teaching methods. It can only be settled in terms of the question of the freedom of teachers to teach as they believe, and in terms of the relation of teachers and schools to their local communities. It may be that in this controversy we are seeing the breakdown of the public school system, which will be replaced by private schools and home instruction. In public education the community educates itself. The controversy over religion in the schools is a breakdown of public education, but it is a result of a breakdown of community. There is no remedy for this breakdown in courts of law.

My point, anyhow, is that we could not consider teaching the Bible "as literature" if we were not already teaching literature "as literature"— as if we do not care, as if it does not matter, whether or not it is true.

The causes of this are undoubtedly numerous, but prominent among the causes is a kind of shame among teachers of literature and the other "humanities," who regret that their truths are not objectively provable as are the truths of science. There is now an embarrassment about any statement that depends for confirmation upon experience or imagination or feeling or faith, and this embarrassment has produced an overwhelming impulse to treat such statements merely as artifacts or cultural relics or bits of historical evidence or things of "aesthetic value." We will study and record and analyze and criticize and appreciate. But we will not believe. We will not, in the full sense, know.

The result is a stance of "critical objectivity" that causes many teachers and historians and critics of literature to sound — not like mathematicians or chemists: their methodology does not permit that yet — but like ethologists, students of the behavior of a species that they do not belong to, in whose history and fate they have no part, their aim being, not to know anything for themselves, but to "advance knowledge." This may be said to work, after a fashion, but it is not an approach by which one may reach any great work of literature. That route is simply closed to people interested in what "they" thought "then." It is closed to people who think that "Dante's world" or "Shakespeare's world" is far removed and completely alienated from "our world." It is closed to the viewers of poetic devices, emotional effects and aesthetic values.

The great distraction behind the modern fate of literature, I think, must be Coleridge's statement that his endeavor in *Lyrical Ballads* was "to transfer from our inward nature . . . a semblance of truth sufficient to procure for these shadows of imagination that willing suspension of disbelief for the moment, which constitutes poetic faith."[6] That is a sentence full of quakes and tremors. Is our inward nature true only by semblance? What is the difference, in a work of art, between truth and "semblance of truth"? What must be the result of separating "poetic faith" from faith of any other kind, and then of making "poetic faith" dependent upon will?

The gist of the problem is in that adjective *willing*, which proposes the superiority of the believer to what is believed. The proposition, I am convinced, is simply untrue. Belief precedes will. One either believes or one does not. If one disbelieves, even unwillingly, all the will in the world cannot make one believe. Belief is involuntary, as is the Ancient Mariner's recognition of the beauty and sanctity of the water snakes:

> A spring of love gushed from my heart,
> And I blessed them unaware . . .[7]

This involuntary belief is the only approach to the great writings. One may, assuredly, not believe, and we must, of course, grant unbelievers the right to read and comment as unbelievers, for disbelief is a legitimate response, because it is a possible one. And we must be aware of the possibility that belief may be false, and of the need to awaken from false belief; "one need not step into belief as into an abyss."[8] But we must be aware also that to disbelieve is to remain, in an important sense, outside the work. When we are *in* the work, we are long past the possibility of any debate with ourselves about whether or not to be willing to believe. When we are *in* the work, we simply *know* that great Odysseus has come home, that Dante is in the presence of the celestial rose, that Cordelia, though she lies in her father's arms, is dead. And if we know these things, we are apt to know too that Mary mistook the risen Christ for the gardener—and are thus eligible to be taken lightly by objective scholars, and to be corrected by a federal judge.

We and these works meet in imagination; by imagination we know their truth. In imagination there is no specifically or exclusively "poetic faith," just as there is no faith that is specifically or exclusively religious. Belief is the same wherever it happens and its terms are invariably set by the imagination. One believes, that is, because one *sees*, not because one is informed. That is why, four hundred years after Copernicus, we still say, "The sun is rising."

When we read the ballad of Sir Patrick Spens we know that the knight and his men have drowned because "Their hats they swam aboone," not because we have confirmed the event by the study of historical documents. And if our assent is forced also by the ballad of Thomas Rhymer, far stranger than that of Sir Patrick, what are we to say? Must we go, believing, into the poem, and then return from it in disbelief because we find the story in no official record, and have read no such thing in the newspaper, and know nothing like it in our own experience? Or must we live with the poem, with our awareness of its power over us, as a piece of evidence that reality may be larger than we thought?

"Does that mean," I am asked, "that it's not possible for us to read Homer properly because we don't believe in the Greek gods?" I can only answer that I suspect that a proper reading of Homer will *result* in some manner of belief in his gods. How else explain their survival in the works of Christian writers into our own time? This survival has its apotheosis, it seems to me, in C. S. Lewis' novel, *That Hideous Strength*, at the end of which the Greek planetary deities reappear on earth as angels. Lewis wrote as a Christian who had read Homer, but he had read, obviously, as a man whose imagination was not encumbered with any such clinical apparatus as the willing suspension of disbelief. As such a reader, though he was a Christian, his reading had told him that the pagan gods retained a certain authority and commanded a certain assent. Like many of his forebears in English literary tradition, he yearned toward them. Their triumphant return, at the end of *That Hideous Strength*, as members of the heavenly hierarchy of Christianity, is startling but not unexpectable. It is a profound resolution, not only in the novel itself, but in the history of English literature. One hears the ghosts of Spenser and Milton sighing with relief.

Questions of the authenticity of imaginings invite answers, and yet may remain unanswered. For the imagination is not always subject to immediate proof or demonstration. It is often subject only to the slow and partial authentication of experience and of the survival of imagination in experience. It is subject, that is, to a practical, though not an exact, validation, and it is subject to correction. For a work of imagination to endure through time it must prove valid and it must survive correction. It is correctable by experience, by critical judgment and by further works of imagination.

To say that a work of imagination is subject to correction is, of course, to imply that there is no "world of imagination" as distinct from or opposed to "the real world." The imagination is *in* the world, is at work in it, is necessary to it, and is correctable by it. This correcting of imagination by experience is inescapable, necessary and endless, as is the correcting of experience by imagination. This is the great general work of criticism to which we all are called. It is not literary criticism any more than it is historical or agricultural or biological criticism, but it must nevertheless be a fundamental part of the work of literary criticism, as it must be of criticisms of all the other specific kinds. One of the profoundest human needs is for the truth of imagination to prove itself in every life and place of the world, and for the truth of the world's lives and places to be proved in imagination.

And that takes us as far as possible from the argument for works of imagination, human artifacts, as special cases, privileged somehow to offer themselves to the world on their own terms. It is this argument, and the consequent abandonment of the general criticism, that permitted the universities to organize themselves on the industrial principle, as if faculties and students and all that they might teach and learn are no more than parts of a machine, the purpose of which they have, in general, not bothered to define, much less to question. And, largely through the agency of the universities, this principle and this metaphor now dominate our relation to nature and to one another.

If, for the sake of its own health, a university must be interested in the question of the truth of what it teaches, then, for the sake of the world's health, it must be interested in the fate of that truth and the uses made of it in the world. It must want to know where its graduates live, where they work and what they do. Do they return home with their knowledge to enhance and protect the life of their neighborhoods? Or do they join the "upwardly mobile" professional force now exploiting and destroying local communities, both human and natural, all over the country? Has the work of the university, over the last generation, increased or

217

decreased literacy and knowledge of the classics? Has it increased or decreased the general understanding of the sciences? Has it increased or decreased pollution and soil erosion? Has it increased or decreased the ability and the willingness of public servants to tell the truth? Such questions are not, of course, precisely answerable. Questions about influence never are. But they are askable, and the asking would be a unifying and a shaping force.

---

1. Brian Keeble, ed., *A Holy Tradition of Working* (Ipswich, England: Golgonooza Press, 1983), p. 61.

2. Quoted in W. Jackson Bate, *Samuel Johnson* (New York: Harcourt Brace Jovanovich, 1977), p. 51.

3. H.J. Massingham, *The Tree of Life* (London: Chapman & Hall, 1943), pp. 200–01.

4. *The Courier-Journal* (Louisville, Ky., August 13, 1983), p. A3.

5. "Plan to teach the Bible as literature may wind up in the Supreme Court," *The Courier-Journal* (Louisville, Ky., September 15, 1983), p. A11.

6. *Biographia Literaria*, XIV.

7. Lines 284–85.

8. Harry Mason, in a letter.

V. Responses

Reply to Frank Lentricchia's "On Behalf of Theory"

William E. Cain

Frank Lentricchia deals cogently with certain aspects of my essay, and his comments have helped me to focus my thinking more clearly on the work that the literary theorist should perform. At the same time, however, his commentary tends to move away from me and veer toward a different set of antagonists— Walter Michaels and others ("Cain may be among them") who stand steadfastly "against theory." Though I am sometimes suspicious of "theory," as I will try to explain, I am not "against" it. My position, one that favors theory as a crucial literary and social practice, is closer to Lentricchia's than he suggests.

Walter Benn Michaels and Steven Knapp's tract, "Against Theory" (*Critical Inquiry*, Summer 1982), intrigues me, but I neither endorse their argument nor share the consternation that it has triggered among theorists. Michaels and Knapp conclude by urging that "the theoretical enterprise" should "come to an end," and this has, as one could have predicted, upset the theoretical community. But in their opening sentence, they define "theory" in a very specific way—as "the attempt to govern interpretations of particular texts by appealing to an account of interpretation in general." Most readers appear not to have grasped this qualification; they understand Michaels and Knapp to be attacking all theoretical

reflection and self-scrutiny, and they have therefore denounced "Against Theory" for seeming to sponsor any and every method and, even worse, for comforting "close readers" who uphold the traditional canon and hate to fuss about theory. Because of a frequent and unfortunate slippage of terms in their essay, Michaels and Knapp have, to be sure, encouraged this overheated response. By the third paragraph of their essay, they are employing the phrase "all critical theory," which intimates that their target is not the particular one that they announced earlier.

I admire Michaels and Knapp, but I do not wish to get embroiled in their debate with the troubled spokesmen for theory. I do not define "theory" as these two writers do, and hence I feel unthreatened by their argument. From my point of view, theory is something much more flexible, strategic, and provisional. I take it to entail, first, the critique of established practice and the beliefs and values (usually concealed) that justify this practice, and second, the inspection of new theories and forms of practice that get proposed as substitutes for what has formerly been in place. Theory exposes errors in what has been done in the past, highlights mistakes and unexamined assumptions in what is being done in the present, and remains skeptical, if also hopeful, about alternatives for the future. For me, then, theory

221

has an analytical, critical, and at times polemical force; it does not seek to fashion a grand system for "interpretation in general," one that somehow could transcend history and appraise practice from "the outside." In positive terms, theory as I define it does aim to affect interpretation, exposing, for example, the limits of the traditional canon, disputing the distinction between literary and nonliterary texts, and identifying other groups of texts that critics should examine and that students should study. Theory aims to criticize and reorient practice, not prescribe it once and for all or dictate what in some final, authoritative sense "interpretation" should be. Lentricchia, I suspect, would assent to much, maybe all, of this. Like him, I believe that theory should be historical, should slant its investigations towards culture and society, and should always seek to be *more* than purely "literary" theory.

As my original essay and this reply indicate, I grow suspicious of theory when it divorces itself from practice, when its rigors and difficulties acquire a kind of privilege and fail to connect with anything else. On the one hand, I concur with Lentricchia's remark that theoretical "meditation often requires its own discursive space." But I then want to resist the inclination—as does Lentricchia, I think—to post boundaries around this "space" and transform it into a special "field" where theorists address each other—and sometimes, it seems, meditate upon themselves—in clannish and self-congratulatory terms. Here, I think, we are talking not about a necessary "discursive space," but an area (or arena) for a coterie, one whose emblem—if I can cite an extreme case—might be Harold Bloom's recent review of two of his own books (*Yale Review*, Autumn 1982).

True, theorists often do require their "own discursive space," but this does not exempt them from having to relate their inquiries to concrete practices in research and, even more perhaps, in pedagogy. Some may balk at my emphasis on pedagogical reform and contend that this concern is futile or misguided. In my judgment, however, truly serious academic labor—the kind that strives to effect political differences—must incorporate pedagogy, theory, and research: it must be an integrated enterprise in which different demands and problems check, balance, and influence the direction of work. I did not of course mean to give the impression in my essay—for which Lentricchia rebukes me—that "real political work" in the college or university occurs *only* on the level of the department meeting. It is indeed important, as he maintains, to conduct and carry on "the long, long debate" about the function of theory and criticism in our individual acts of writing, teaching, and lecturing at conferences. But I would not want to distinguish as cleanly as Lentricchia does between this undertaking and the specific departmental, disciplinary, and administrative discussions and choices that involve courses, curricula, and appointments.

Let me give one example, which I hope will not prove trivial or tedious. As recently as two years ago, the English department curriculum at Wellesley College—a women's college and my home institution—did not include a single regular course on feminist criticism and women's writing. From time to time, someone had offered a seminar on Jane Austen or other women novelists, but none of these foregrounded feminist issues or showed special interest in the astonishingly rich range of scholarship—literary, historical, cultural, and social—by and about women. Women's college or not, most of my colleagues judged that "feminism" was an ideological approach that ministered to nonliterary concerns. After several defeats and false starts, several of us managed to win approval for an upper-level course, offered every year, on feminist literature and criticism. This may not seem like much of a victory, and admittedly it is rather late in coming to a college devoted to women's education. But this course has already proven to be extraordinary successful; it has taught students what it means to be a feminist critic and, in addition, it has made them expect (and insist) that their other courses also demonstrate an awareness of feminist issues. A course like this one has clear "political" implications within the department and college, and it influences the ways in which students reflect and act upon the politics — often an anti-feminist politics — of their culture and society. And such a course is now part of the curriculum because we debated, discussed, and argued about theory, practice, and policy at the "department" level that Lentricchia seems to disparage. It is fine to say that we should, each of us, write and teach and speak at conferences, but there are many other opportunities to be seized, opportunities within the daily academic workplace, where we can inaugurate political change. In his reply to my essay, and in *Criticism and Social Change*,* Lentricchia affirms that "our potentially most powerful work as university humanists must be carried out in what we do, what we are trained for." I agree, but define "what we do" more inclusively than he does.

---

*Chicago and London: University of Chicago Press, 1983, p. 7.

Historical Realities

Timothy Bahti

To read E. D. Hirsch, Jr., appealing for the study of literature to move "back to history" is not to receive a surprise. For a quarter-century now—since "Objective Interpretation" (1960) and then *Validity in Interpretation* (1967)—Hirsch has been one of the most persistent advocates in the Anglo-American tradition for the strict historical understanding of literature's meaning: here, "primary, historical interpretation," the attempt "to recover its past meaning." A literary text's *meaning*, as distinguished from its various secondary *significances*, can only be what its author intended—what he here calls a past speech act understood as an historical event— and this intention and meaning can be determined by historically based research and interpretation—by study of the author's biography and oeuvre, the conventions and genres of his time, and the larger historical expanse of literary conventions and genres.

Hirsch's view of literary interpretation is well known. It is known to be a minority position within the mainstream tradition of modern cultural and historical hermeneutics. Within this tradition, from Schleiermacher and Dilthey to Heidegger, Gadamer and Ricoeur, the majority position has argued from more expansive, even open-ended senses of interpretation: for interpretation as shared or "blended" subjective experience, or as openness toward possible meanings within a shared temporal predicament. Hirsch's defense of a minority argument for a solid core of historically determinable meaning has held out against the current of this modern tradition of theories of interpretation. It is, then, not his well-known call "back to history" which surprises one, so much as his couching of that appeal here, in the context of a symposium on the academization of literary criticism, as one for "the newest and most valuable kind of literary work for our students (and our culture) at the present time."

The appeal for novelty and value conjoined with that for a return to history place Hirsch in a different kind of company. I am thinking of recent calls within the American university for new historical studies of literature and culture, which appear to come as a response to or an outgrowth of what is journalistically called "literary theory"—be these calls for a "history as rupture" (Frank Lentricchia), a new and non-totalizing Marxist "History" (Fredric Jameson), or a "new historicism" (Wesley Morris), or the more shrill calls for historically based scholarship made recently by Frederick Crews or Walter Jackson Bate. The fact that some or even many of these appeals are made by those who would be sympathetic both to current trends in "literary theory" and to progressive or "leftist" political causes suggests once again that a politicized "left-right" spectrum is no more useful as an image of this issue of a return to history than it has been as an image of the "literary theoretical" debate. With the return to history, the ends of a spectrum rejoin as what they perhaps always were—a circle, a return *of* history.

But why should a *return* be promoted as new and valuable? Here Hirsch's formulations suggest a revealing if paradoxical answer. First, "for simplicity," Hirsch characterizes one "party" as "the Ancients," who stand for teaching "the old authors in the old, historical ways," another "party" as "the Moderns," who would teach "the old authors in new ways." Then he enlists "the undergraduates" on the side of "the Ancients," claiming that most undergraduate university students he knows and teaches want "primary interpretation." I think this is a misjudgment—at least it doesn't square with my experience—but I doubt that a statistical or otherwise quantitative analysis would decide anything here. By this point in Hirsch's characterization of the academy the older school of professors—"the Ancients"—and the youngest participants in their professional activity—their undergraduate students—have the so-called "Moderns" squeezed between them. Hirsch's argument continues as follows: an "interest conflict" obtains between older professors and younger students on the one hand, "modern secondary interpreters" on the other; the former stand for the institutional interest of teaching, of passing down received knowledge and values, the latter for "the institutional advantages of secondary interpretation in the sphere of professorial publication."

This squeeze, and the weighted, two-against-one character of the struggle, is not particularly shocking, certainly not to anyone running the gauntlet of the pretenure professorial life. One's senior colleagues call on the junior professor to publish, and, by definition, any new publication will have to declare itself "new," not redundant of "old" scholarship or criticism. But then one stands ready to perish on the sword of novelty, guilty of the sin of having ignored or even betrayed the institutional injunction to teach the young students the "old" and "true" "primary meanings."

The novelty and value of Hirsch's return to history, then, might ironically lie in its explicit danger, in the fact that, this time, it is presented as a double-cross: the younger, "modern" faculty try to live and earn their keep by the "old" professional standard of scholarly publication which served the older, "ancient" faculty well, and then they are told that all they are doing is "new" stuff, and that the "ancients" alone are protecting the undergraduates. Measured by Hirsch's calculus of group interest at any rate, this logic would give the tenured faculty a justification for denying membership to the younger "moderns," who are vastly supernumerary (therefore easy to fire and rehire) and who just import that "new" theory anyway.

But here I think Hirsch's characterization of the professorial structure and context may yield a more serious (and, on my part, less paranoid) insight into the academic situation he describes. For he himself has explicit reservations about what he calls "the law of interpretation," which has yielded what he identifies as "the institutional need for limitless publication." Hirsch thinks that "primary interpretation" appears to reach a threshold, whereafter a generation of "moderns" seeks to fulfill the institutional imperative to publish by moving on to "secondary creative interpretation." But he also thinks, somewhat confusingly, that the first threshold is illusory, that good primary interpretation—historical study—remains to be done and may be felt as "what is really new—that is, what is unlike ourselves," while secondary interpretation is by now "old hat."

Hirsch's analysis reveals the turn-on-the-heel performed by the "ancient" line— we were old, you were new, now you're old hat, and we are you (i.e., new)—but I think he misexplains the reasons for this logically suspect operation. If one believes in history as real, then the historical realities ought to count. The "law of interpretation" neither began some thirty years ago, nor is it correctly associated with the advent of New Criticism. Hirsch professes to consider "the humanities as historical studies" but he neglects the longer history behind the problem posed by "the law of interpretation." The humanities as historical studies have been such within the university for 150 or, at most, 200 years, first in Germany, then in the Anglo-American world and elsewhere. Governed by the historicist desire, in Hirsch's reformulation (wedding Arnold and Ranke), "to know the best that is said and thought in the world, as it was said and as it was thought," the historically-constituted study of the humanities necessarily interpreted its documents with historically determinable meaning in mind as its scholarly and cultural value. It is when, after decades of increasing positivism and specialization, historical studies of historical meaning become a kind of *formalism* of "primary interpretation," that they can be felt as "mere novelty": just as historical events can be characterized as one damned thing after another, so can each "new" primary interpretation be seen as the ever-the-same. New Criticism did not attempt to determine primary meaning in a historical sense, certainly not in the senses of authorial intention or contemporary historical reference; it tried to determine meaning in a more expansive *textual* sense, in a way that would be linked to the materiality of the text but seemingly freed from the historicity or temporal position of author and interpreter. The New Critics' example of interpretation linked above all to the text, and not to the authorial or historical past, had a salutary and almost liberating effect upon the kinds of interpretation that followed them, even if questions of the temporal status or context of interpretation have reemerged in our day as a compelling matter for academic literary studies.

And so what Hirsch is talking about with regard to the last thirty years or so ought not to be called "the law of interpretation," but rather the law of textual (or discursive) reinterpretation. Elsewhere, Hirsch has argued eloquently—and, I think, persuasively—that literacy skills (he identifies writing, reading and vocabulary, but basic critical and interpretive skills are

implied as well) cannot be successfully taught in the absence of a cultural context, which context always includes the texts of a core or canonical curriculum ("Cultural Literacy," *The American Scholar* 52:2, [Spring 1983]). It would behoove him to think the same way about historical literacy. It is the exercise of the sheer formal skill of historical interpretation (including the historical study of literature: one more monograph on the sonnet sequence between 1590 and 1600) that led to the pursuit of primary interpretation for primary interpretation's sake, within both a historical and a cultural vacuum— a formalism of history. It would appear that textual reinterpretations, from the Russian Formalists (an honorable name here) and the New Critics to what is today loosely called "literary theory," offer the best evidence of attempts at readdressing and perhaps even reconstituting cultural contexts for literary study, including the context of cultural *critique*, as opposed to what Hegel would have called the mere "pigeonholing" of so-called historical "facts" or information along the thin roost of a historical-chronological time line.

Hirsch's call "back to history" is really a call back to culturally relevant, because culturally contextualized, scholarship and criticism. But this is what I would have thought the best "secondary creative interpretation," from the first exegetes of Homer to Nietzsche and the present, had always already been doing. That Hirsch would buttress his appeal with what he calls "the long view of intellectual history" is in reality simply shortsighted. I have indicated above that he undermeasures the long life of the law of interpretation in our historically oriented studies of the humanities. He is similarly shortsighted here—"the complacent fallacy of thinking that latest is always best"—when he considers "primary interpretation" to be essentially historical interpretation. The first textual interpreters of Homer's epics asked how the canonical texts could be critically understood within the fifth century B.C.'s contexts of new physical, verbal, ethical, and theological codes or assumptions. Interpretation has primarily done the same thing ever since, and the fact that some seventy percent of recent literary scholarship has been devoted to some ten percent of the canonical authors is nothing new either: just look at medieval and renaissance writings on Virgil and Ovid for a rough analogue of a culture's concentration of its interpretive labors around a select group of authors.

That primary interpretation, which I consider to have been the reassessment and rewriting of textual meanings in the light of contemporary contexts of significance, became narrowed to "primary interpretation" in Hirsch's sense of an account of what the author meant at his time is a recent and, one hopes, short-lived historical phenomenon: it sacrifices present relevance on the altar of past reference, and the long view of intellectual history will show that it is dated from roughly the mid-1800's to the mid-1900's. This is when, as Hirsch acknowledges, the ancients became what they really are, the moderns, and to judge a whole tradition and discipline – that of literary criticism, scholarship and "theory" – by this new and brief standard of historically determinable meaning would be as silly as to judge, say, the whole tradition and discipline of philosophy by the passing standard of eighteenth-century British empiricism – that is, by the standard of empirically verifiable (or determinable) explanations of the experience of reality.

Hirsch's appeal for a return to history is, I think, the expression of an earnest desire for a return to culturally significant and relevant contextual studies of literature and other "historical" documents. This means that the real antagonists in the academy of literary criticism today are not "primary historical interpretation" and "secondary creative interpretation"; rather, they are historical interpretation with only a boring and brittle chronology of "history" behind it, and textual reinterpretation with at least the potential for enlivening and enriching the contexts within which literature's significance can be understood and appreciated. Hirsch's strict dichotomy of "meaning" and "significance" gives way, under the pressure of his own argument here, to a new distinction between meaning that is significant –

meaningful – because of its cultural context, and meaning that is insignificant – meaningless – in the absence of such a context. This desire for cultural context and significance is unlikely to be satisfied by more of Hirsch's "primary interpretation," unless it be that sort of historical reinterpretation of primary texts and authors which might enable us to shed facile assumptions about the history of literary interpretations, assumptions which our culture has unfortunately allowed to come down to us under the guise of "historical knowledge." Thomas M. Greene's *The Light in Troy*, for example, admirably undertakes this task in demonstrating that "the discovery of the past" is not some relatively uniform development that occurs during "the Renaissance," or anything that could be simply called "historical study," but rather that the modern interpretive relation to the literary past is set in a complex matrix of present contexts and interests as well as past sources of authority and inspiration.

Whether the similar-sounding calls for a "return to history" made by others in literary studies today are as earnest and tough-minded in their cultural criticism as Hirsch's would be the topic for a much longer disquisition. But one suspects that the structure of their argumentation would be similar to his: the "new" is to be a return to the "old," the "old" thereby is made new. This circle of historical argument is perhaps most tellingly revealed in Hirsch's mistranslation of the passage from *Faust*: "What you call the spirit of the times – why, that's really your own spirit, in which the times reflect themselves." What is reflected back is not "your own spirit" (Hirsch's misinterpretation, perhaps a primary one), not the interpreter engaged in some navel-gazing creativity, but "the times," and in their plurality and flow they seem to form a circle around the quasi-virtual center of a pier glass, which is the interpreter's gaze. The new turns toward the old, "to keep alive in the present the meanings of the past," and the old turns into the new, "the newest and most valuable kind of literary work for our students (and our culture) at the present time," and this temporal circularity would be the reflection of time within the labor of "historical" interpretation and misinterpretation. Any understanding of time as history issues from this circle of interpretation between a text at once detached from and reattached to a present moment of interpretation. It is in the context of ever-present interpretations that all meaning and value will be critically determined for anything worthy of the name of "culture," and this is both very old and always renewed.

Short Response to Timothy Bahti

E. D. Hirsch, Jr.

A couple of factual points:

1. Timothy Bahti is wrong to propose that the norm of the author's intention is a minority norm in the tradition of hermeneutics. Bahti says: "Within this tradition, from Schleiermacher and Dilthey to Heidegger, Gadamer, and Ricoeur, the majority position has argued from more expansive, even open-ended senses of interpretation." On the contrary, intentionalism characterizes almost all writers on the subject up to Heidegger, and it remains the position held by most nontheorists of the present day. Gadamer spends many preliminary pages of *Truth and Method* (pp. 153–235 of the English translation) attacking the intentionalism of Schleiermacher, Dilthey, Chladenius, Savigny, Boeckh, Steinthal, Ranke, Droysen. What does Bahti think Gadamer is up to in clearing the decks this way, and in claiming that Heidegger's theory is a radical departure? But why bring up this matter of majority and minority views? Surely it's just a hidden appeal to authority, and no argument at all. To be part of the larger crowd does not determine the truth of one's views. The rhetorical appeal is invalid in another way, if it turns out that one doesn't even belong to the larger crowd.

2. Bahti is not on safe ground when he calls my translation of the passage from *Faust* a "misinterpretation." The passage is:

Die Zeiten der Vergangenheit
Sind uns ein Buch mit sieben Siegeln.
Was Ihr den Geist der Zeiten heisst,
Das ist im Grund der Herren eigner Geist,
In dem die Zeiten sich bespiegeln.

In my essay I rendered it as: "The times of the past are to us a book that is sealed with seven seals. What you call the spirit of the past—why that's your own spirit reflecting back at you." Bahti apparently wants to interpret it as, for instance, Carlyle MacIntyre does:

The past is a book of seven seals, and what
you call the spirit of the times, in the end,
is merely the spirit of those gentlemen
in whom the times are mirrored.

Whatever that means! And, where in this is the force of *eigner*?—surely an important clue to the intended meaning. It seems far more likely that *der Herren* refers directly to *Ihr*, the second-person familiar plural. This association of *Ihr* and *Herr* is a firm signal of an ironic tone, as when Mephistopheles says:

Wozu der Lärm? was steht dem Herrn zu Diesten?
(What's all this noise about? The gentleman
wishes service?)

And Mephistopheles continues after Faust's reply:

Ich salutiere den gelehrten Herrn!
(I salute the learned gentleman.)

Faust, no less ironic, replies in the same *Ihr—Herr* vein:

> Bei euch, ihr Herrn, kann man das Wesen
> Gewönlich aus dem Namen lesen.

> (With types like you—you gentlemen—one can
>   usually read the essence from the name.)

For all the problems with translating in rhyme, Bayard Taylor at least renders the ironic, skeptical sense:

> What you the Spirit of the Ages call
> Is nothing but the spirit of you all,
> Wherein the Ages are reflected.

But against all this, let me suppose that Bahti is right about my interpretation of the passage from *Faust*. From a theoretical standpoint, what in heaven's name does he think he is doing, when he speaks so unqualifiedly of my "misinterpretation"? I am willing to concede whatever point he wishes about interpreting *Faust* if he will stick to his slip about "misinterpretation," a word which rigorously implies intentionalist norms and assumptions.

Gadamer himself is not immune from this kind of slip, so powerfully does intentionalism infuse our sense of written or spoken discourse. That is especially the case when our theoretical guard is down, and we are talking about something we care about. In 1966, in a letter to Emilio Betti, Gadamer wrote that my criticism of his views entailed a misinterpretation of them. Betti and I took pleasure in the irony. Much of my theoretical work has defended the right of Gadamer, Bahti and anyone else to use the term "misinterpretation." But, to use it with cogency, they will have to give up their theories. The word "misinterpretation," despite protests to the contrary, is a thoroughly intentionalist word.

3. Professor Bahti says that the narrowing of interpretation to a study of what an author meant in his own time is a "short-lived historical phenomenon: it sacrifices present relevance on the altar of past reference." This simplification so trivializes historical interpretation that it amounts to a factual mistake. To intentionalists and anti-intentionalists alike, present relevance alone counts. The issue between them is: *which* meaning shall be made presently relevant? Shall it be what the author meant, or shall it be what the critic (re-authoring the text) meant? The point of my essay was that the author's (historical) meaning is usually more relevant than the (equally historical) meaning of the critic. Present relevance can vary for each reader on each occasion; rarely will present relevance be the same for reader and critic—and all the more rarely in view of the nonpresentness of academic publication.

As far as relevance goes, the issue mainly concerns how we shall teach. Except insofar as academic criticism impinges on teaching, it is irrelevant to the larger culture. The various schools of critical re-authorship which Professor Bahti praises are "relevant" only to the small group among literature professors and graduate students who are preoccupied with publication. Even within this small group, the re-authoring methods of criticism are "relevant" only on the occasion of professional publication. When these critics are existentially engaged in reading or writing, as with Bahti on *Faust* and Gadamer on himself, they become historical intentionalists like everyone else.

Short Reply to E.D. Hirsch, Jr.

Timothy Bahti

I'm not sure what Hirsch thinks he's doing in invoking the veracity of the historical account of hermeneutics in *Truth and Method* (a work whose argument he distrusts), but I do know that the Schleiermacher texts edited after Gadamer's book, the manifest Hegelianism of Ranke's "doctrine of ideas" and the nonintentionalist model of "shared" meaning in Droysen and Dilthey would all dispute Hirsch's claim for an intentionalist tradition. We'd have to look at each text in its specifics, but I acknowledge his wish to have the greater numbers on his side. I also know that I don't have to address the intentionalist argument (I may not know or care what Goethe thought), just be a thorough and grammatical exegete, to know that Hirsch's initial interpretation of the *Faust* passage failed to account for the words "in which the times" (*in dem die Zeiten*)—a point he concedes by adopting Bayard Taylor's translation. "Whatever that means!" remains precisely the unanswered question.

But the main disagreement between us resurfaces in his third remark. Hirsch's essay, like much of his work, privileged historical intentions as the foundation for interpretations with present relevance: a foundational move that seemed to oppose and even exclude the co-presence of determining cultural contexts. But this move was then followed by a confusing modulation between the sufficient primacy of "primary interpretation" and the necessary conditions of "the present time" and its cultural context ("present relevance alone counts"). Which way will he have it, and which way should it really be? As Richard Rorty (in "Texts and Lumps," forthcoming from *New Literary History*) and others have shown, one doesn't need the notion of a "right interpretation" to ground claims for useful and relevant understandings. Furthermore, why should Hirsch spend several pages castigating the impact of "modern" literary theorists and interpreters in the academy, then turn around and claim they're irrelevant except to some small group? As Paul de Man wrote, "When it becomes fashionable to dismiss fashion, clearly something interesting is going on, and what is being discarded as *mere* fashion must also be more insistent, and more threatening, than its frivolity and transcience would seem to indicate."* Hirsch first decries the "moderns," then derides them as old hat and largely irrelevant, and this anxiety signals a threat—the threat, I would suggest, that our present academic literary culture is showing some signs that it's becoming dis-

---

*Paul de Man, Introduction to Hans Robert Jauss, *Toward an Aesthetic of Reception*, trans. T. Bahti (Minneapolis: University of Minnesota Press, 1982), p. xx.

satisfied with an intentionalist model of cultural history and historical interpretation. This is not something that arguments alone decide, but rather that interests and circumstances determine—and that analyses can address. University presses, professional and editorial offices, foundation fellowships and grants, academic appointments, and graduate and undergraduate curricula (including their theories and practice of pedagogy) all testify to the interest and importance—the present relevance—of contemporary theories and reinterpretations. Yes, Virginia, there is literary theory *à la mode*, and it's even served in our classrooms.

Contributors

Reginald Gibbons has published two books of poems and other works. His new volume of poems, *Saints*, will be published in 1986. He has been editor of *TriQuarterly* since 1981. ★ ★ ★ **Wallace Douglas,** emeritus professor of English at Northwestern University, is the author of *Wordsworth: The Construction of a Personality* (Kent State, 1968) and numerous articles in the fields of literary criticism, composition theory and English education. He is currently at work on a sequel to his essay in the present volume. ★ ★ ★ **Gerald Graff,** professor of English at Northwestern University and director of Northwestern University Press, is the author of *Literature Against Itself* (University of Chicago Press, 1979) and has recently completed a book on the history of professional literary studies from which his essay in this volume is adapted.

William E. Cain teaches English at Wellesley College. His recent publications include *The Crisis in Criticism: Theory, Literature, and Reform in English Studies* (Johns Hopkins, 1984). ★ ★ ★ Author most recently of *Criticism and Social Change* (University of Chicago Press, 1983), **Frank Lentricchia** teaches English at Duke University. He is currently general editor of the Wisconsin Project on American Writers. ★ ★ ★ **Sandra M. Gilbert** is coauthor, with Susan Gubar, of *The Madwoman in the Attic: The Woman Writer and the Nineteenth-Century Literary Imagination* (Yale University Press, 1979) and coeditor, again with Gubar, of the recently-published *Norton Anthology of Literature by Women: The Tradition in English*. In the fall of 1985, she will join the English department at Princeton University.

Gene H. Bell-Villada is associate professor of romance languages at Williams College. His articles and reviews on literature and politics have appeared in many journals including the *New Republic, Commonweal, Monthly Review, In These Times* and the *Nation*. ★ ★ ★ Professor of English at Queens College, **Morris Dickstein** is the author of *Keats and His Poetry* (University of Chicago Press, 1971) and *Gates of Eden: Ameri-*

can *Culture in the Sixties* (Basic Books, 1977). ★ ★ ★ **Mark Krupnick** is the editor of *Displacement: Derrida and After* (Indiana University Press, 1983). He is at present completing a study of Lionel Trilling as cultural critic. ★ ★ ★ Professor of English at Vanderbilt, **Donald Davie** is a well-known poet and critic. His latest publication is *Collected Poems, 1970–83* (Notre Dame University Press, 1984). ★ ★ ★ **Patrick Colm Hogan** is assistant professor of English at the University of Kentucky. His articles on psychoanalytic, philosophical and literary topics have appeared in English-, French-, German- and Slovene-language periodicals.

E. D. Hirsch, Jr., has published several books, including *Validity in Interpretation* (University of Chicago Press, 1967) and *The Philosophy of Composition* (University of Chicago Press, 1978). He is professor of English at the University of Virginia. ★ ★ ★ **William H. Pritchard** is Henry Clay Folger Professor of English at Amherst College and, most recently, author of *Frost: A Literary Life Reconsidered* (Oxford University Press, 1984). ★ ★ ★ **Wendell Berry** is the author of a book of essays, *Standing By Words* (North Point Press, 1983). North Point has also just published his *Collected Poems* and a revised edition of his first novel, *Nathan Coulter*. ★ ★ ★ **Timothy Bahti** teaches comparative literature at Northwestern University. He has published essays on English romanticism and modern criticism. He is finishing a book on *Allegories of History: Literary Historiography After Hegel*. ★ ★ ★ **Gini Kondziolka** is the design director of *TriQuarterly*. With her husband, she runs the Kondziolka and Takatsuki design studio in Chicago.

*"Warning! You will not be able to put this book down
—even though it may be putting you down!"*
David V Erdman, SUNY Stony Brook

Hershel Parker, *Flawed Texts and Verbal Icons: Literary Authority in American Fiction*

A sharply original contribution to editorial theory and recent critical disputes over questions of intention, meaning and interpretation. Parker argues that readers often need to know how a text came into being— how it may have been changed by editors or even botched by a revising author—in order to determine what it means. Failing to understand this principle, interpreters of classic American novels—by Crane, James, Twain, Fitzgerald, Mailer, etc.— have made unified "verbal icons" out of texts so radically flawed as to be uninterpretable. Written with clarity, wit and polemical vigor, *Flawed Texts and Verbal Icons* provocatively challenges all the current schools of literary theory. $19.95

"An important and comprehensively subversive book. Parker's intensive investigations of the perilous and sometimes disastrous textual histories of American novels—many of them victimized by their own authors—provide the basis for a tough-minded and zestfully combative attack on major aspects of modern editorial theory and practice and on current critical assumptions about the 'authorless text.'"
Michael Millgate, *University of Toronto*

"Flawed Texts and Verbal Icons *is wonderfully written and absolutely captivating. It should certainly stir things up."*
Stanley Fish, *Johns Hopkins University*

"Flawed Texts and Verbal Icons *is a passionate, unsparing, brilliant and witty book. Above all, it is an important book—a principled manifesto whose implications are revolutionary… for the entire field of literary study."*
Frederick Crews, *University of California at Berkeley*

Northwestern University Press
1735 Benson Avenue
Evanston, IL 60201
312-491-5313

TriQuarterly

Twentieth Anniversary Issue

SUBSCRIBE TO *TRIQUARTERLY* now and receive *TQ 20*, a very special anthology of the best from *TriQuarterly*'s first twenty years. *TQ 20* will contain almost 700 pages of distinguished fiction, poetry, essays and graphics, and will be sent to subscribers at no extra cost as part of their regular subscription.* Containing the work of such writers as Saul Bellow, James T. Farrell, Vladimir Nabokov, William Goyen, Raymond Carver, William H. Gass, Joyce Carol Oates, Lorraine Hansberry, Roland Barthes, Gabriel García Márquez and over seventy others, the issue is without question the most significant in *TriQuarterly*'s history—and one of the most important "little" magazine releases of the last twenty years. Reserve your copy now by subscribing!

*The newsstand price of *TQ 20* will be $12.95.

RSVP

Yes, I wish to reserve a copy of *TQ 20*. Please enter my subscription order for:

☐ 1 year ($16)*   ☐ 2 years ($28)*   ☐ life ($100)
*Foreign add $4/year
☐ I enclose $_____   ☐ Please bill me
☐ Charge my VISA/MasterCard # _____

Signature_____   Exp. date _____
Name _____
Address _____
City _____ State _____ Zip_____

Northwestern University   1735 Benson Avenue   Evanston, IL 60201

TriQuarterly